MW01630219

LEONARDO, MICHELANGELO, AND THE ART OF THE FIGURE

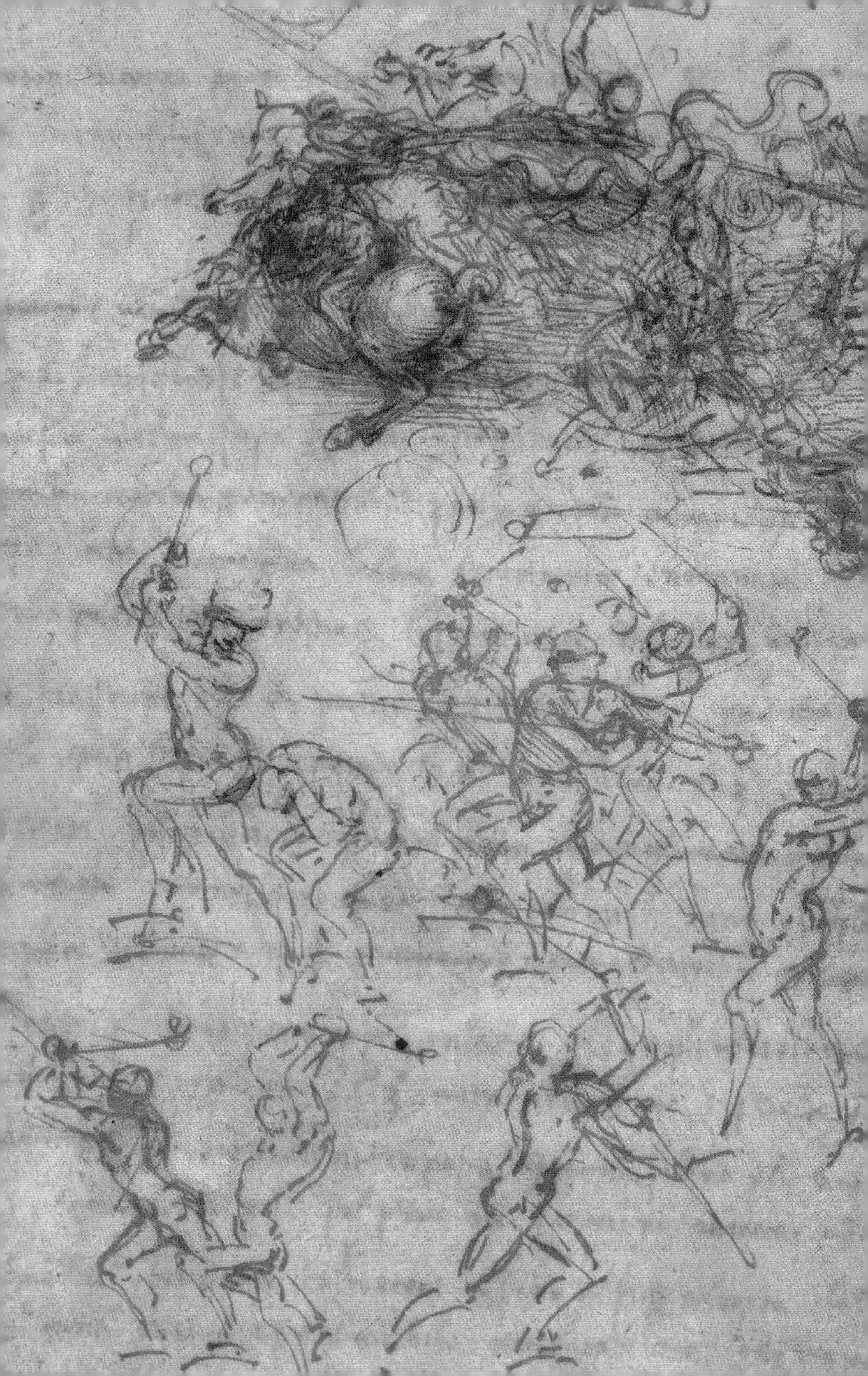

LEONARDO, MICHELANGELO, AND THE ART OF THE FIGURE

MICHAEL W. COLE

YALE UNIVERSITY PRESS
NEW HAVEN AND LONDON

Copyright © 2014 by Michael W. Cole

Designed by Gillian Malpass

Printed in China

Library of Congress Cataloging-in-Publication Data
Cole, Michael Wayne, 1969–
Leonardo, Michelangelo, and the art of the figure / Michael W. Cole.
pages cm
Includes bibliographical references and index.
ISBN 978-0-300-20820-7 (cl : alk. paper)
1. Figure painting–Italy. 2. Painting, Italian–16th century. 3. Human beings in art.
4. Leonardo, da Vinci, 1452–1519. Battle of Anghiari.
5. Leonardo, da Vinci, 1452–1519–Criticism and interpretation.
6. Michelangelo Buonarroti, 1475–1564. Battle of Cascina.
7. Michelangelo Buonarroti, 1475–1564–Criticism and interpretation. I. Title.
ND1293.I8C65 2014
757.0945–dc23
2014012688

A catalogue record for this book is available from
The British Library

Frontispiece   Leonardo, studies for the *Battle of Anghiari* (detail of fig. 70)

To Madeleine

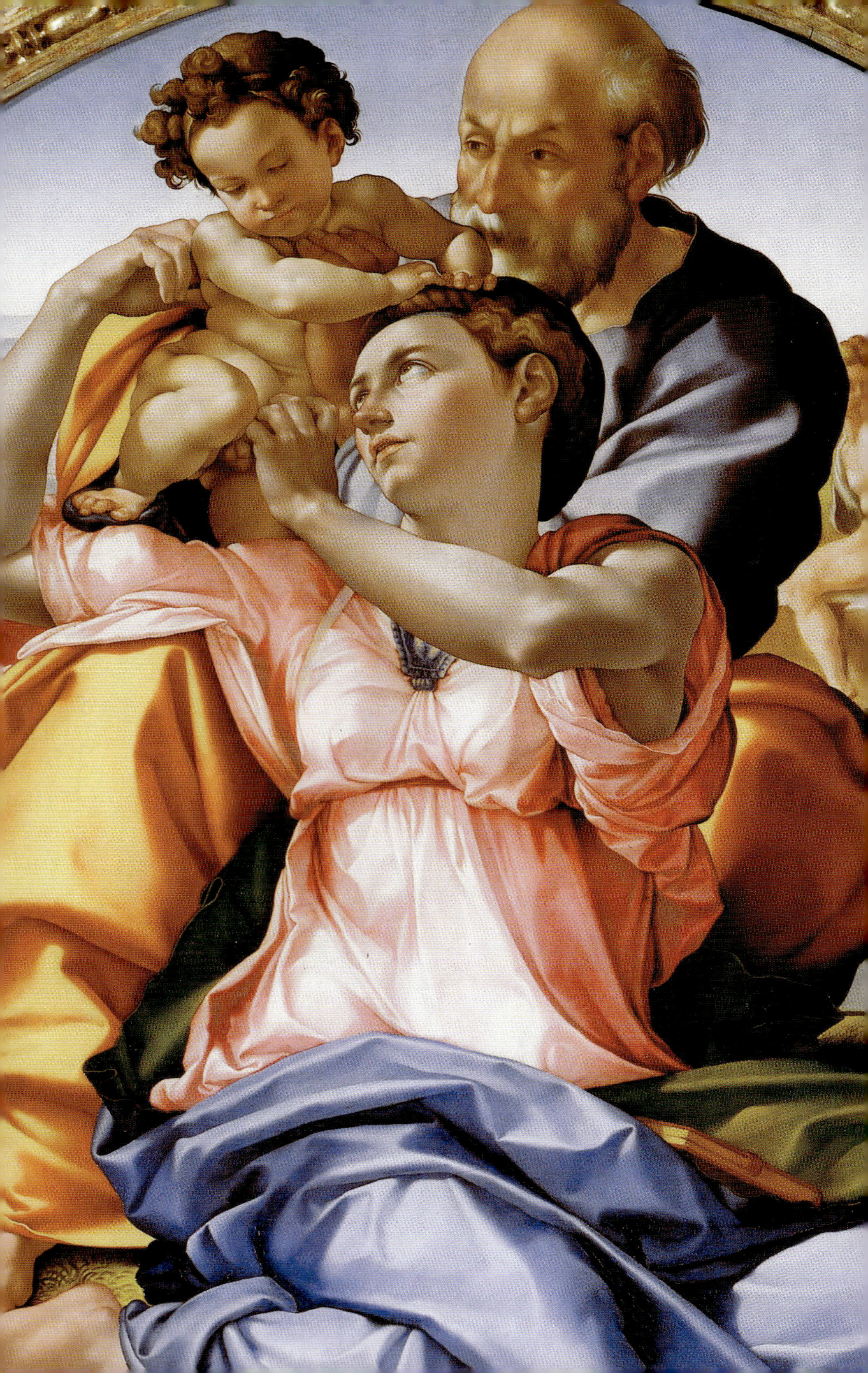

CONTENTS

facing page　Michelangelo, Doni Tondo (detail of fig. 21)

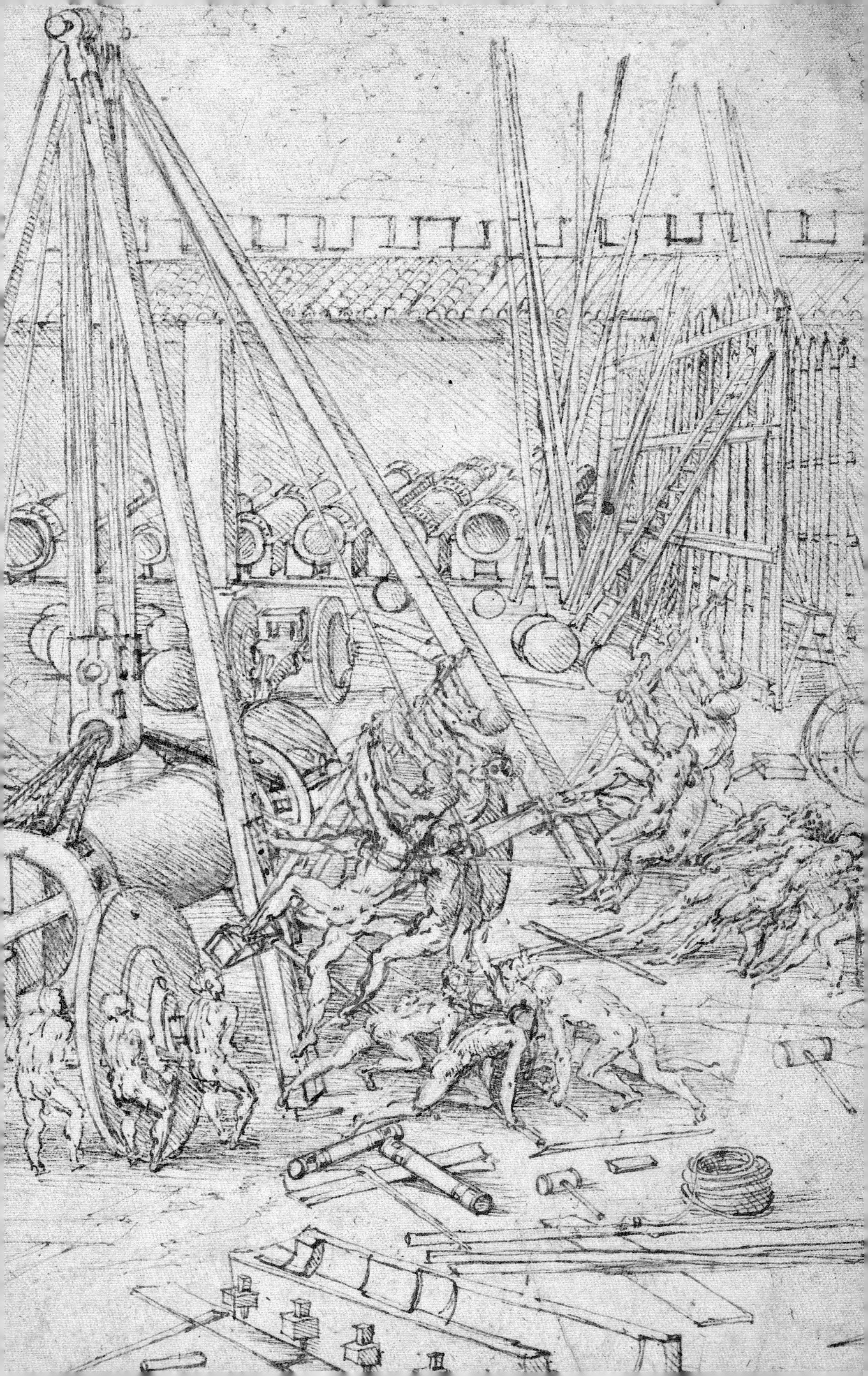

PREFACE

Historians of Italian Renaissance art like origin stories. When we write or talk about our period, we pause at those moments when art began to employ new or newly recovered visual idioms: perspective, for example, or the grotesque, or the architectural orders, or landscape. But what, then, should we say about the human figure, the single most continuous feature of Italian Renaissance art?

Perhaps we do not need to say anything at all: the very ubiquity of the figure in Renaissance art demonstrates its banality, its unworthiness of a separate history. Yet this is not the way contemporaries saw things. When the Portuguese painter and writer Francisco de Holanda had the Michelangelo character in one of his dialogues assert that in Flanders, "they paint stuffs and masonry, the green grass of the fields, the shadow of trees and rivers and bridges," he was reminding us of the things Michelangelo did *not* paint.[1] Renaissance artists and viewers alike knew that making paintings of figures rather than of other things was a choice, and a deliberate one. Today, we can see even more clearly than the cosmopolitan Holanda could that the figure set Italian Renaissance art dramatically apart from many contemporary world traditions.[2]

facing page Leonardo, *Cannon Foundry* (detail of fig. 58)

But perhaps what needs to be said about the Renaissance figure has already been said, often and well: some of the foundational literature in the field, after all, centers on the new attention that artists gave to the overwhelmingly figural sculpture of antiquity and to human anatomy. Stepping back, though, such interests may well begin to look more like symptoms than causes. We could not conclude that drawing after sarcophagi or assembling ancient marbles into garden collections in any way produced a new art of the figure or made the figure more important as a pictorial element. Artists studied the ancient past to improve their approach to what they were already doing, that is, portraying human forms. Statues that came out of the ground, moreover, were likely to be restored in ways that made over the past in the image of the present rather than the opposite. As for anatomy, it is true that in the late sixteenth century, Michelangelo's art was treated as though it largely represented an anatomy lesson, and this was used both to justify and to condemn Michelangelo's relentless focus on the figure.[3] Large parts of this book, moreover, will be in tune with those recent histories of anatomy that emphasize violence and spectacle no less than knowledge and investigation.[4] Still, it is worth remembering that Renaissance visualizations of human anatomy were themselves already figural: the entire canon of early modern anatomical illustration belongs to the same art of the figure as painting and sculpture. The makers of anatomical images, particularly in the later Renaissance, often modeled their work on paintings and sculptures, and we should expect them to have shared more than to have driven the preoccupations of the other figural arts.

Of course, the rendering and the meaning of the figure could change. Many historians of Renaissance art, for example, now regard the spiraliing *figura serpentinata* as a motif that first appeared in painting around 1500, thereafter becoming a widespread ideal. The emergence of arresting new artistic models – the unearthing of the *Laocoön* in 1506, for example, or the unveiling of the Sistine Chapel ceiling in 1512 – sometimes looks to have rooted a new aesthetic. And well before all of this, Leon Battista Alberti's *De pictura* (1435) may seem to have offered a new notion of figuration. While a deep medieval theological tradition characterized the "figure" as a non-mimetic sign, a mysterious other that required reflection on the virtuality of all appearances and on the ultimately inscrutable nature of the divine, Alberti and the painters who followed his precepts turned that medieval proposition on its head, presenting the figure as an aspect, a resemblance, a configuration of the visible world.[5]

Certain moments, in other words, must indeed count as touchstones in the history of the Renaissance figure. Yet we would still be hard-pressed to say that an account of such moments concerns any real origins. The motif of the *figura serpentinata* appeared in painting at least eighty years before any writer records that he had recognized it as such. Can we really, then, locate the beginning of this thing that had no name? As Aby Warburg memorably remarked more than a century ago, the discovery of the *Laocoön* did not really inaugurate a new style. "It was a revelation of something that Italians had long sought – and therefore found – in the art of the ancient world."[6] Furthermore, however alien Alberti's book on painting might seem with respect to medieval paradigms, the preoccupation with the human figure as a pictorial subject hardly began in 1435. In these and other instances, what appears to be a beginning, a watershed, is at most an adjustment, a shift of frame or emphasis, with regard to what came before. This book is guided by a sense that certain moments do matter more than others, that the Renaissance had its crucial artistic events, but it suggests that we should watch not for starting points but for the moments that define conflicts.

Today, our view of the Renaissance figure is profoundly shaped by recent histories of the body, of gender, and of sexuality. It will escape no one's notice that the paintings that are the focus of this book – paintings that contemporaries regarded as epochal works – were paintings of men, by men, and for the most part for men. Nor is it irrelevant that the two artists in my title were both attracted to other men. What makes the preoccupations of Leonardo da Vinci or of Michelangelo compelling for us today may or may not be a matter of identification. Either way, though, there is a distinction to be made between representation and its instruments, the subjects of pictures and their vehicles. To use an obviously limited analogy, the fact that a sentence in a Romance language contains only masculine nouns does not necessarily tell us much about that sentence's meaning.[7] The broadest topics of this book – the uneasy subordination of the figure to the narrative expectations of Renaissance art, the basic technical and stylistic decisions that Leonardo and Michelangelo presented for later artists and their patrons (male and female alike) – are topics as much for the history of science, religion, and magic as for other historical fields.

My sense is that the rich literature of the last thirty years or so has made it easier for us to see how paintings adhere to or reinforce social constructs – conventions of beauty, say, or norms of masculinity and femininity, or principles of good comportment. We remain less well equipped to talk in historical terms about pictorial language that does not simply give onto culture practices. Put another way, we remain less attuned to the artifice as opposed to the transparency of painting, the elements from which a picture is built as opposed to the everyday world that paintings represented. Yet the best Renaissance artists – like the best artists in any time or place – reflected carefully on their means.

The chapters that follow pursue three broad arguments: that in Central Italy by around 1500, figuration had come to be understood as a register of force, to the extent that force had become a primary subject of what we now call "High Renaissance" art; that two especially consequential but by no means eccentric formulations of this idea of the figure were to be found in the painting of Leonardo and Michelangelo; and that the differences between Leonardo's and Michelangelo's conception of the figure came into particularly sharp focus when the two were working simultaneously on a pair of battle pictures for the City Hall of Florence. A further argument is that the centrality of the "forced" figure to Leonardo and especially to Michelangelo, and the influence of this on the artists who followed them, became a major concern to church writers in and after the 1560s. The Counter-Reformation texts that we often read for their instructions regarding the way that devout artists should paint in fact give us a powerful early historical account of Renaissance art as such.

Artists in the late fifteenth century and writers in the late sixteenth sought to define what it meant to paint with figures, what it meant, that is, both to take the figure as the basic element of painting and to use the figure as part of something larger. The positions that artists and viewers adopted on these matters had implications for far-reaching parallel discussions: what was the nature of invention? What was an artist? By the time of Leonardo and Michelangelo, to render a figure in one way rather than another was to accept certain pictorial premises, and to invite a certain kind of response.

The book takes the confrontation between Leonardo and Michelangelo in 1503–5 as its central event. It aims to consider together two projected paintings – *The Battle of Anghiari* and *The Battle of Cascina* – that have largely been treated in isolation from one another.[8] Still, it is not a monograph: rather, it uses the two battle paintings as points of refraction. On the one hand, it looks at how they synthesized the concerns of a broader artistic practice that must itself be examined if we are to understand what Leonardo and Michelangelo were doing. On the other, it follows how the two battle paintings became crucial reference points for artists and viewers in the century that followed. The book's primary argument is that as the figure became the unmistakable locus of Italian Renaissance painting, Leonardo and Michelangelo's competing conceptions of the figure came to represent two nearly antithetical alternatives, and that the two battle scenes clarified the choice.

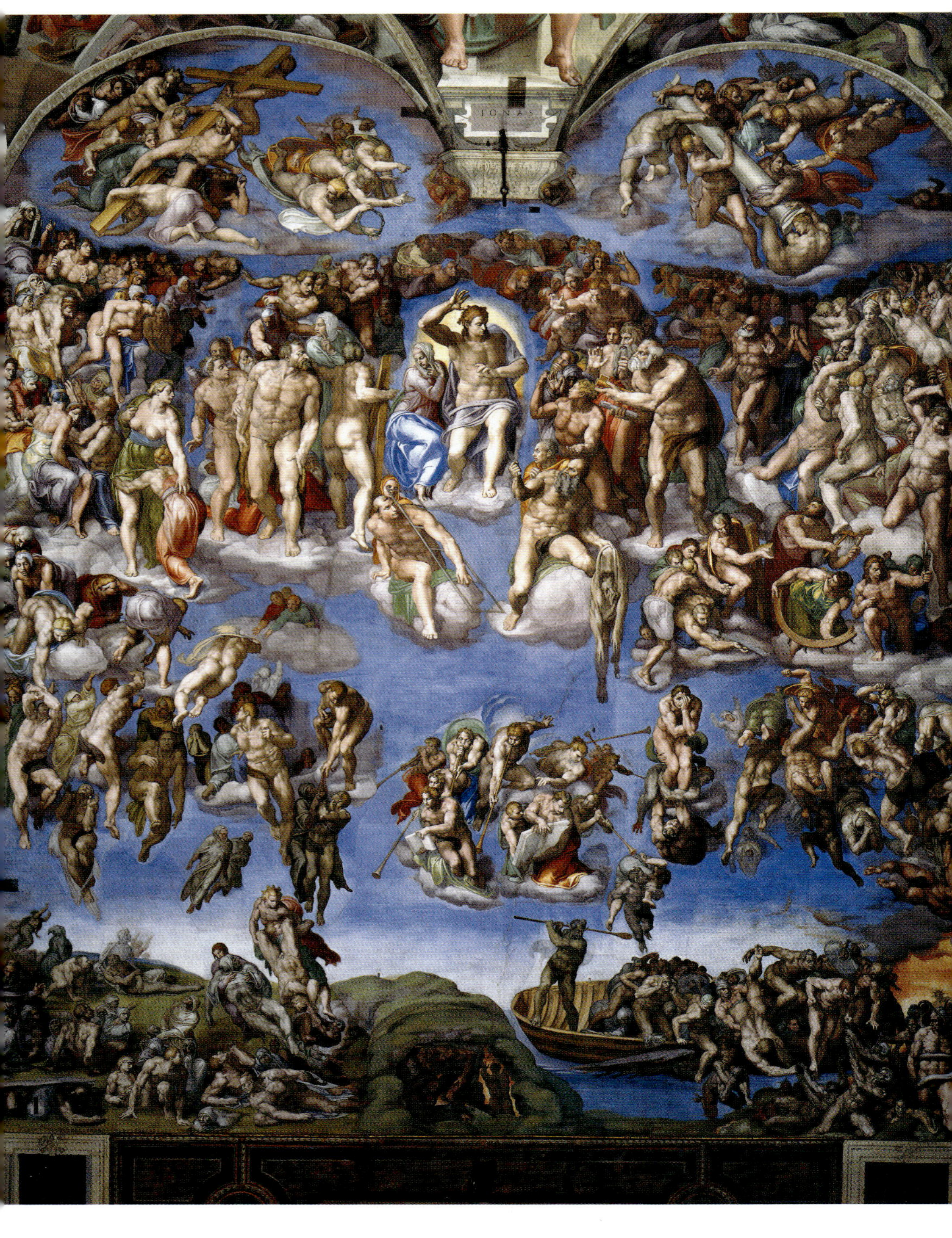
IONAS

1

THE FORCE OF ART

Describing what made the previous century of Italian art superior to all that had come before, Giorgio Vasari referred to its distinctive "force." When Leonardo da Vinci launched what Vasari took to be modernity, he did so in the first place through "the force and boldness of his drawing" but also through his new color and chiaroscuro, "whereby the moderns have given great force and relief to their figures." In the Sistine Ceiling, a work so perfect as to make it unnecessary for young painters to study anything else, Vasari admired the "forza della arte" that Michelangelo exhibited in the illusionistic treatment of the vaults. With regard to the *Last Judgment* (fig. 1) later added to the apse wall of the same space, Vasari similarly praised Michelangelo for "giving such force to the paintings."[1]

Vasari was hardly alone in seeing things this way; many early viewers report on the overwhelming effect that the new painting of the late fifteenth and sixteenth centuries had on beholders. Yet even as such remarks became common, a more skeptical audience saw in the very paintings that Vasari celebrated a different kind of force. Among the most widely read and influential was Giovanni Andrea Gilio da Fabriano, a priest whose 1564 dialogue "On the Errors of History Painters" began with a preface lamenting that the art of painting "has neither book nor rule that

1   Michelangelo Buonarroti, *Last Judgment*, fresco, Sistine Chapel, St Peter's, Vatican

could give painters the way and the order in which they ought to make every manner of figure." Because of this, he continued,

> most of these painters go dissolutely along, committing infinite errors in their histories [*historie*], as one can see clearly throughout Italy, and still more in Rome. It seems to me that for this reason, modern painters today, when they have to make some work, have as their first intent to twist the head, the arms, or the legs of their figures. Thus one says that they are forced [*sforzate*], and these labored poses [*sforzi*] are sometimes such that it would be better for them not to be there, for the painters think little about doing the subject of their story, if they consider it at all.[2]

The dialogue that followed did not neglect the variety of force that Vasari described. A character named Silvio, for example, concluded that Michelangelo had given the angels in his *Last Judgment* overwrought poses so as to show "the force of art."[3] Yet even this characterization of Michelangelo began with the image of a force that had reversed its direction, moving not out from the work and onto the beholder, but *into* the painting, overtaking the characters that should have been playing out its narrative.

Gilio's publication came on the heels of the Council of Trent, from which there had issued a short set of decrees on the principles meant to guide Catholics in image-making. Nothing in those decrees really presaged the kind of criticism that Gilio launched with his dialogue, but what he wrote strongly oriented subsequent interpretations of the new Tridentine rules. To many writers, what Gilio identified as Michelangelo's "errors" came to look paradigmatic for a whole era of painting. In Florence, Raffaello Borghini had a character in his own 1584 dialogue *Il Riposo* use Gilio's arguments to attack Pontormo's now lost frescoes of the *Deluge* and the *Last Judgment* in San Lorenzo:

> But because Giovanandrea Gilio da Fabriano has written about this at length in that dialogue of his on the errors of painters – the one about Michelangelo's *Last Judgment* – suffice it to say this small bit to show how much Pontormo strayed from the truth. As you know, he made a great mountain of hideous bodies, a vulgar thing to see, in which some

show themselves to be resuscitating, others already to be resuscitated, and others to be dead, and to lie in unseemly poses. And above this he made some giant putti with forced gestures, who play trumpets, and I think he wanted these to be recognized as angels.[4]

The *Riposo* reenacted in Florence the very controversy that had been played out two decades earlier in Rome, with Pontormo now favoring precisely the "forced" forms that Michelangelo exemplified, and his critics singling out that very thing for condemnation.[5]

In Milan, a full half-century after Gilio's publication, Archbishop Federico Borromeo could still lament how, "Some [artists] so display the bending and joining of individual parts and limbs of the body, that it seems they would sooner exhibit anatomical illustrations for the treating of wounds than incite devotion. Verily they add to those bodies of theirs such a degree of violence and tension that the body would not even be suitable for a soldier."[6] The passage appears in a chapter "On Athletic Bodies" in Borromeo's 1624 treatise *De sacra pictura*, which went on to point to the by then long-dead Michelangelo as a chief example of the problem.[7]

In Seville, the poet Francisco de Rioja wrote to the painter and theorist Francisco Pacheco, praising Pacheco's decision, when portraying the Crucifixion, to show Christ "with majesty and decorum, without contortion and discomposure, as is fitting to the sovereign grandeur of our Lord"; he characterized this as a rejection of Michelangelo's lesson.[8] Pacheco himself reported of a priest who, saying Mass one day, looked up at a 1570 figure that Maarten de Vos had made "with extreme beauty but more discomposure"; such was the power of this figure on the priest's imagination that he nearly went insane. Remembering some difficult travels he had undertaken while he was younger, the priest told Pacheco that he would rather be in a storm at sea than before such a work.[9] Yet Pacheco prefaced this anecdote by boasting that he himself, while keeping a mind to decorum, had painted a figure in imitation of the twisting Charon in Michelangelo's *Last Judgment*. He wrote that he was prepared to defend Michelangelo against "certain Italians" who criticized the painting, and he praised Michelangelo's superiority "in the grandeur and force [*grandeza y fuerza*] of the nude."[10]

All of these remarks were written with a certain prescriptive intent. Their authors all hoped to guide the contemporary practice of painting. Still, Gilio was writing in the first place about a fresco that had been completed more than twenty years earlier, and his followers, too, focused mostly on what had happened generations before. Their descriptions of art read not just as criticism but also as history: no less than Vasari, they depend on a particular conception, and they provide an early account, of what late Renaissance painting was all about. One might even conclude that the diagnosis that these texts consistently offer amounts to an early version of what twentieth-century writers, no longer with any comparably didactic goals, would come to call Mannerism. Dagobert Frey saw the most characteristic paintings of the mid-sixteenth century as those containing variously posed figures "which have no connection to the [painting's] content and which are there above all to fill a purely aesthetic function."[11] Arnold Hauser found that the mannerist nature of a work was often betrayed by "something affectedly dance-like or tortured," "an over-extension of beauty, which became too beautiful and thus unreal, of force, which became too forceful and thus acrobatic, of content, which became too full and thus meaningless, of form, which became independent and thus empty."[12] Georg Weise's "principle motifs of mannerist stylization" included "the artificial and mannered arrangement of the hands, arms, and bust," "the angling of the knee and the rotation of the body," and "the bipartite or tripartite counterposing of the attitudes and movements."[13]

These modern writers, like their sixteenth- and seventeenth-century predecessors, saw the late Renaissance as an age in which painters had come to be more interested in artfulness than in representation. Still, there was a difference. When twentieth-century art historians wrote of Mannerism, what they had in mind was primarily a style, a painterly technique that extended across the pictorial surface. What bothered viewers in the decades following the Council of Trent, by contrast, had more to do with artistic priorities. The problem they saw is neatly summed up in a remark attributed to the late sixteenth-century Dutch painter and theorist Karel van Mander: "in the *Last Judgment*, Michelangelo attended more to each figure *per se* than to the disposition of the narrative."[14]

The sense the earlier viewers shared was that a preoccupation with painted force had reoriented Renaissance painting, narrowing its focus from the composition to a smaller pictorial unit. When Borghini writes that the poses of Pontormo's angels make them unrecognizable, when Borromeo asserts that bent bodies are suited for no characters, not even soldiers, when Rioja counterposes contortion and decorum, they draw the same conclusions. These writers believed that the dynamic of painting at the end of the Renaissance was one that operated between the depicted figure and the artist who made it, rather than between that figure and its neighbors on the canvas or wall, let alone between that painted group and its beholders.

Figure and Composition

Today, few would agree that late Renaissance painting had so resolutely abandoned narrative. Michelangelo, after all, was much invested in the subjects he depicted, as we know from his own poetry and from his exchanges with Vittoria Colonna and other reformers. Still, Gilio's criticism may let us question some of the conventions that we have adopted in telling the history of Renaissance painting.

When Gilio writes that artists in his day had ceased to concern themselves with *storie*, he employs a variant of a fundamental term in Leon Battista Alberti's *De pictura* (*Della pittura; On Painting*), a text that had been written some 130 years before, but that had been published for the first time in the 1540s, and had gone through multiple editions since. In Gilio's world, Alberti's idea of painting was a newly enlivened topic of discussion, and one way of getting at the core ideas in Gilio's dialogue is to look at the way it inflected Alberti's language. Alberti himself had used the word *istoria* to refer to any painting that placed multiple figures in some kind of relationship: one of his examples is *The Three Graces*, a subject with no narrative at all. Beginning with its title, by contrast, Gilio's dialogue proposes a narrower sense for the word, describing only paintings of true occurrences — whether from the past or, like the *Last Judgment*, from the future. The change of meaning reflects a change of purpose but also a new sense of painting's recent history: Alberti was seeking to explain how paintings that adopted systems of perspective and played out in measured settings might intelligently be assembled; Gilio was lamenting that paintings had, as he saw it, become little more than collections of figures.

Both look today like writers concerned with notions of visual unity. Michael Baxandall's still fundamental book on the language of Early Renaissance painting went so far as to maintain that with his remarks on *compositio*, "Alberti was providing a concept of total interdependence of forms that was quite new, rather unclassical and, in the long run, much the most influential of the ideas in *De Pictura*."[15] The later sixteenth-century writers at whom we have been looking might well seem to illustrate this influence: when they object to the *figura sforzata*, they do so in the name of formal interdependence, pictorial coherence. In fact, the specification by Gilio and others that it was "modern" painters who had ceased to concern themselves with *storie* even allows a different possibility, that an earlier era in which painters made compositions had somehow come to an end, that painters like Michelangelo had come to work in opposition to the Albertian composition.[16]

Let us for the moment evaluate this proposal: to the extent that Michelangelo did privilege the part over the whole, was he doing something radical? Was composition really the place where his immediate predecessors had located their art? Alberti, identifying recent examples of *istorie* composed in the way his treatise recommended, might well have pointed not just to frescoes like Masaccio's but also to relief sculptures like those that Lorenzo Ghiberti was making for the Gates of Paradise. As Julius von Schlosser pointed out long ago, Ghiberti's own *Commentarii*, a text known from a manuscript written about a decade after Alberti's *Della pittura*, itself takes up cognates of Alberti's term, referring for example to the ancient Greek artist Parrhasius as one who "composed many things."[17]

Yet the differences between Ghiberti's language and what Baxandall taught us to notice in Alberti's are just as telling. What Ghiberti actually singled out for praise in Parrhasius's work were not compositions but "figures with marvelous posings," the *ignudi* which Parrhasius rendered "with most perfect art."[18] When Ghiberti wrote about his own work, similarly, he seems to have thought it was his fertility in generating figures that would most impress viewers: the *istorie* he made for the Gates of Paradise, he boasts, were "molto copiose di figure", and he sought to carry them out "with excellent and lavish compositions and with many, many figures."[19] The fifteenth-century biographer Antonio Manetti similarly suggests that it was the poses of the figures in Ghiberti's competition panel that secured him the commission for the first Baptistery doors.[20] The outsize role that Alberti has come to play in our understanding of fifteenth-century art may lead us to attribute particular significance to Ghiberti's use of the word *componimenti*, but we could just as easily do the opposite, choosing Ghiberti rather than Alberti as our witness to current priorities, and emphasizing, with him, the centrality of the figure.[21]

This would be truer to the way that fifteenth-century pictorial ideas were disseminated. One telling case is that of the so-called "Lippi and Pesellino Imitator," an otherwise anonymous Florentine who made his living copying the works of others. Today we would expect a professional copyist to occupy himself especially with the replication of compositions, sacrificing color and detail as necessary to convey the whole. But with the Lippi Imitator, the opposite was true. In his work, to quote the chief study of the artist, "the representational space is conceived in terms of the background (*campo*) and the figures (*figure*) treated as separate units with little attempt to establish a setting through spatial integration."[22] In a copy after a painting of the Madonna and Child, that pair could appear alone or with attendant figures, "these secondary figures . . . cleverly inserted into the interstitial spaces of the paintings."[23]

This, in turn, reflects the way that most artists learned their crafts. Alberti was not a professional painter, and his book had little to say about the material side of artistic practice, but it was with drawings that all artists began their training, and drawings often depended on a mentality of *dis*assembly. Apprentices would draw from modelbooks, in which individual motifs were generally isolated on the page. So were the motifs artists would have copied from the unbound drawings preserved in the painter's studio. When they moved on to studying exemplary paintings by older masters, students would draw after figures and the occasional small figure group, rarely copying complete works. This itself may be one reason that many more fifteenth-century drawings of figures than of other subjects have come down to us.

The artist's primary concern did not entirely change when, having mastered the basics of his craft, he began to make preparatory drawings for actual paintings. When Domenico Ghirlandaio, Michelangelo's teacher, composed the sinopia underdrawings for his frescoes, he at least sometimes used composite cartons: one-to-one scale designs for individual figures or small groups, which he assembled only on the wall. This occasionally resulted in figures that overlapped in inconsistent ways, as is evident, for example, in his *Pietà* for Ognissanti (fig. 2).[24] Other artists, isolating figures or their parts in a similar manner, found ways to reuse a single invention, either at the same site or across multiple commissions.[25] After the completion of the work, cartoons also helped painters to think through the examples of their predecessors. Among the rare surviving fifteenth-century cartoons are those that the Umbrian painter Giovanni di Pietro (called "Lo Spagna") made after Perugino's *Agony in the Garden*, which dismember the larger work into its component parts (fig. 3).[26]

One might object that these examples just underscore what it was that set good and bad artists apart: if Alberti aligned invention with composition and privileged those two practices, it was precisely to distinguish ambitious painting from the mere copying of the figure. But "inventive" drawings, too, show artists thinking at the elemental level. A sheet in the Albertina, presumably exploring ideas for a representation of Christ's *Flagellation* (fig. 4), has long been attributed to Ghiberti. Whether it is by him or a follower, it concerns itself with the poses of figures rather than with their interdependence. Other sheets show artists producing studies after ancient sculptures, after people they encountered, and – especially later in the century – after studio assistants (fig. 5). Drawings from life, too, could involve invention, since the master or the model had to decide on a pose; the result, though, was once again an image of the figure.

To be sure, artists composed narrative frescoes and panels with underdrawings that are now largely invisible. Some, perhaps most Quattrocento artists made compositional drawings on paper as well, though surviving

2 Domenico Ghirlandaio, *sinopia* underdrawing for the *Pietà*, Ognissanti, Florence

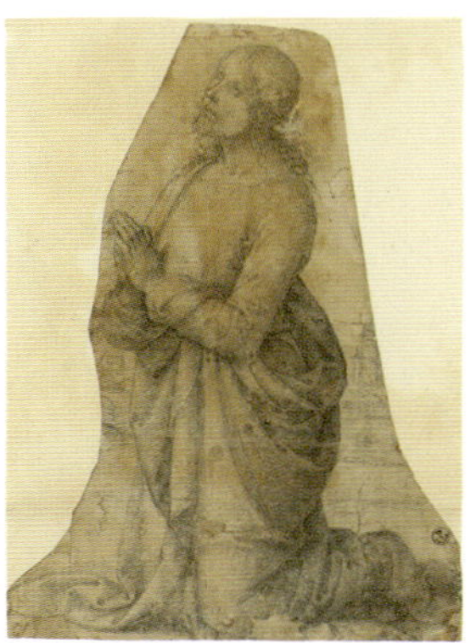

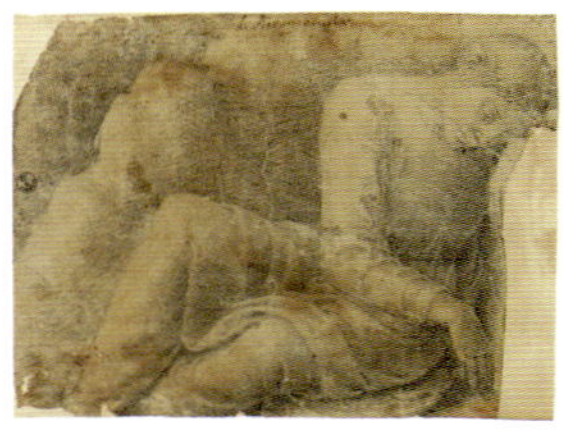
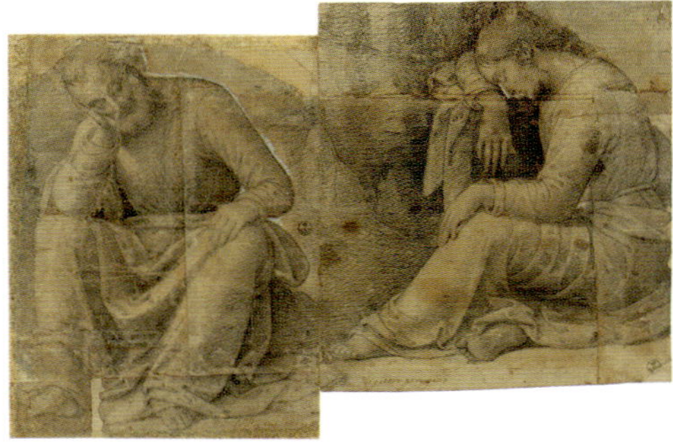

3   Giovanni de Pietro, called Lo Spagna, cartoon fragments after Perugino's
Agony in the Garden, Uffizi, Florence

examples of these, even from decades after Alberti's text, remain rare:
teachers who collected exemplary works for students to understand
through imitation evidently did not think the value of their drawings
extended beyond the moment of their initial use. Some compositional
drawings, moreover, must have been nothing more than provisional
indications of how a painter intended to fulfill a contract, a proposal he
might well abandon down the line. Ghirlandaio's painting of the
Confirmation of the Rule in Santa Trinita in Florence is typical in that it
conforms broadly but not rigorously to the surviving compositional
drawing (fig. 6); numerous figures were added, removed, or changed when
he moved to the wall. Contracts sometimes made explicit allowances for

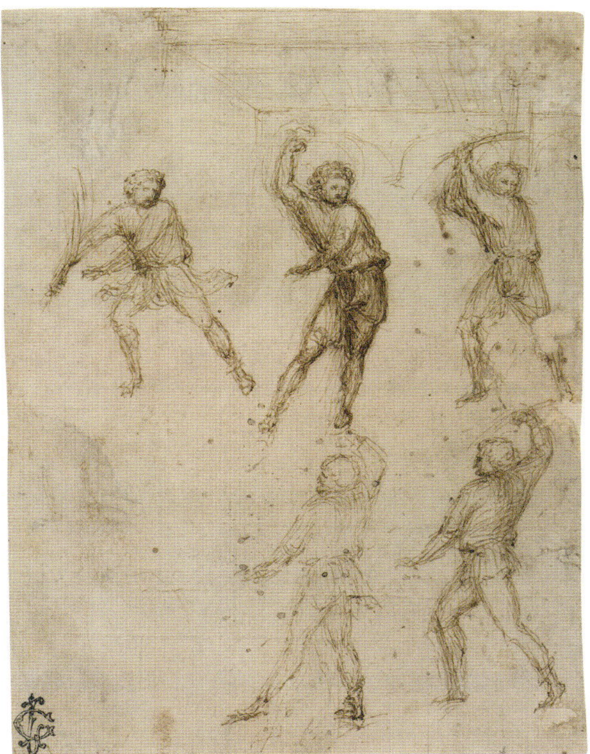 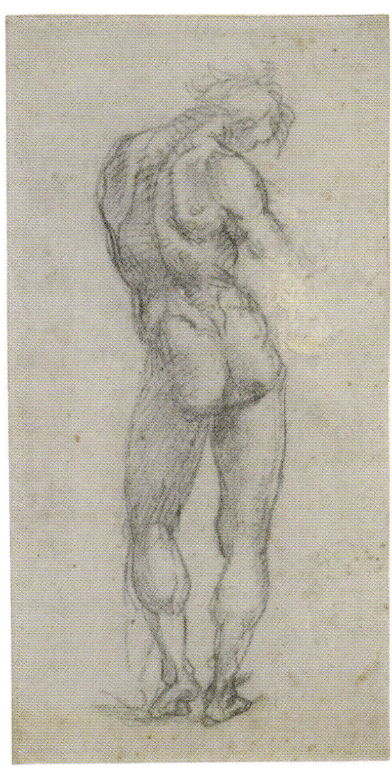

4 (*above left*)   Lorenzo Ghiberti (attr.), figure studies, pen and brown ink on paper, Albertina, Vienna

5 (*above right*)   Luca Signorelli, figure study, black chalk on paper, British Museum, London

such deviations. The agreement that Luca Signorelli signed in 1500, revising the stipulations for his painting of the San Brizio Chapel in Orvieto Cathedral, specified that he was to follow drawings he had shown his employers, "albeit with more figures if they occur to him, just not with fewer."[27] Signorelli's patrons wanted to leave open the option that the painting could be improved by the addition of new figural inventions; they regarded the figure as both a quantitative and a qualitative basis for evaluating a painting.

Alberti may have believed that a compositional "invention" could give pleasure without even being executed, but as the new availability of paper

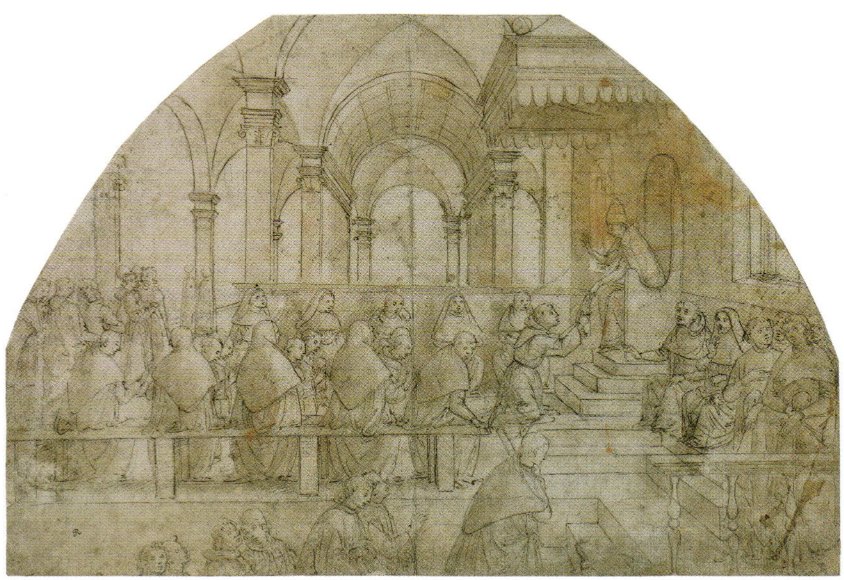

6   Ghirlandiao, *The Confirmation of the Rule*, ink and wash over black chalk on
paper, Staatliche Museen, Berlin

allowed for more disposable sketches, it was often the drawing of figures
that led to a picture's invention rather than the other way around.[28] This
is true even for Leonardo, the fifteenth-century artist who most stands out
for his use of drawing to explore relationships between individual figures
or between the figural group and the framed planar support. Leonardo's
sheets from the 1490s show him developing new exploratory functions for
the medium (fig. 7), yet even these begin with the figure, multiplying and
transforming it across the page. In a note he made from just this period,
Leonardo remarked:

> I say that first one ought to learn the limbs and their labors. Having
> mastered that, one ought to proceed by studying poses, according to the
> circumstances that befall a man. Third comes the composition of *storie*,
> the study of which will be done following the properties of random
> natural poses: pay attention to these things in the streets, in the squares,
> and in the countryside, and note them down with quick linear des-
> criptions – that is, make an "O" for the head and a straight or bent

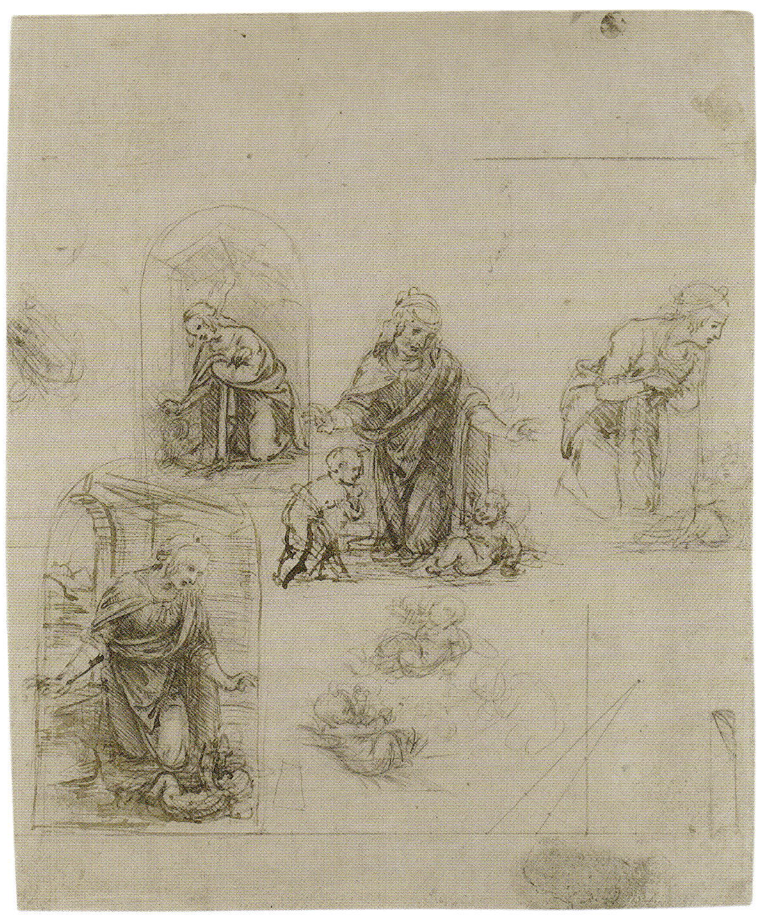

7   Leonardo da Vinci, compositional studies,
silverpoint and dark brown ink on pink prepared paper,
Metropolitan Museum of Art, New York

line for an arm, and proceed in the same way with the legs and the chest. When you have returned home, work those records up into a finished form.

The student adhering to these guidelines would think only about composition after mastering the individual human form. And composition itself amounted on these guidelines merely to the deployment of a repertory of poses captured from life. Leonardo's discussion continues:

> It will be objected that to become a practitioner and actually carry out works, it is better that the first period of study be devoted to copying various compositions made by various masters on paper or on walls; in this way, one quickly learns proper techniques and good habits. To this, I respond that such techniques would be good if they were based on good compositions by learned masters, but that since such masters are so rare that few can be found, it is much better to turn to nature . . .[29]

Composition, Leonardo now suggests, was one field in which his predecessors were particularly weak. For this reason, students should not even trouble themselves with the arrangements that earlier artists had left. The young artist should instead observe the behavior of individuals in the street.

Leonardo vs. Michelangelo

Counter-Reformation critics who worried that artists had come to place the figure before the story laid much of the blame for this at Michelangelo's feet. They used Michelangelo's work to typify a recent shared pictorial practice, even as they characterized that work as a shameless departure from a more accommodating and devout earlier manner. The same writers had views of Leonardo, too, which differ in emphasis but not entirely in substance from those found in the writings of Leonardo himself. Leonardo, no less than Michelangelo, could exemplify an approach to painting that centered on the human figure. Yet perhaps for this very reason, when late sixteenth-century writers sought to question Michelangelo's particular figural art, Leonardo offered them a foil.

Leonardo turns up as a character in the fourth *Ragionamento* of Gian Paolo Lomazzo's *Libro dei Sogni* (1563), written the year that the Council of Trent concluded. It is in the mouth of this Leonardo that Lomazzo places the charges that would become standard Counter-Reformation criticisms of Michelangelo. Do you know what the rabble and the prince would have said, Lomazzo's Leonardo asks, if I were to have made my *Last Supper* in the way I should have? "They would have said that my apostles, together with Christ, look like so many criminals, escaped from the galleys, just as they still say about Michelangelo's own stupefying *Last Judgment*."[30] Asked by Lomazzo's other characters to elaborate, "Leonardo" goes on to report that Michelangelo was accused of assembling a crew of porters or comic actors, of showing all of his characters "jumping about," of filling the painting with indecencies. The shared perception was that Michelangelo did not paint characters but, rather, variations on an anonymous, undifferentiated moving figure. "It was only a few months or years ago," Lomazzo's Leonardo concludes, "that Pope Paul IV, called 'the Theatine,' wanted to tear the whole thing down, saying that it wasn't appropriate, in Saint Peter's, to have such knavish apparitions, and to show limbs with such histrionic movements."[31]

The fiction here is complex: "Leonardo" at once recounts in delighted detail the many insults he had "heard" about Michelangelo's painting and distances himself from those views. He holds Michelangelo up as the example he "should have" followed while also making clear that he restrained himself, painting in a way that both his patron and the broader public found more acceptable. The suggestion is that Leonardo already foresaw the kind of charges that Gilio was formulating in the 1560s – that, as one of the cleric's characters lamented, the Sistine *Last Judgment* was filled with "*sforzi*, moresques, and bagatelles, which you admire only because Michelangelo did them."[32] Lomazzo implies that Leonardo's painting knowingly followed Counter-Reformation principles even before they were formulated.

Roughly two decades after Lomazzo, the painter Giovan Battista Armenini penned a similar conceit:

Not a few people [who have seen Michelangelo's *Last Judgment*] say that he had several works of wax, made with his own hand, and that he twisted their members in his way, first dipping their joints in warm water to resoften them, a process I leave to anyone who wishes to try for himself. I am also well aware that Leonardo da Vinci, seeing [Michelangelo's painting] and perhaps learning of Michelangelo's procedure – at least according to what I heard from one of his students in Milan – hastened to say that this was the only thing that displeased him in

Michelangelo's work, that too often Michelangelo used few figures and that he seemed to see the same muscles in the figure of a youth and of an old man, and that the same was true of the contours.[33]

Leonardo could not, of course, have seen Michelangelo's *Last Judgment*, which was painted long after the older artist's death. While it is possible that Armenini simply confused the ceiling and the altar wall of the chapel, the fact that Lomazzo had made the same "mistake," having Leonardo anachronistically comment on the same painting, suggests that Armenini's fiction was a knowing one.[34] So why did two painters, writing decades apart in different cities, attribute to Leonardo such similar thoughts?

Certainly Lomazzo and Armenini both follow common rhetorical practices of the day, arguing from counter-examples: when Lodovico Dolce criticized Michelangelo's obsessively figural (and excessively masculine) painting, he did so by comparing Raphael's and then Titian's wider range of subject matter.[35] Both may also have been picking up on rumors of Michelangelo's and Leonardo's mutual dislike: a writer in the late 1530s and early 1540s who has come to be known as the Anonimo Magliabecchiano had Michelangelo publically insult Leonardo for his failed attempt at monumental sculpture – "you made a design for a horse so as to cast it in bronze, but then you couldn't cast it and to your shame you abandoned it" – and Vasari wrote of the enormous disdain ("sdegno grandissimo") that the two artists had for one another.[36] Lomazzo, at least, suggested that he regarded Leonardo as a muralist who offered a particularly strong contrast to Michelangelo: the *Last Supper* carefully individualized each Apostle at Christ's side, assigning them dramatic but not histrionic poses. And, though the two writers may not have known it, the exchanges they imagined did also capture something like the real words Leonardo seems to have penned in the 1510s, after seeing Michelangelo's Sistine Ceiling: "O anatomical painter, beware, lest in the attempt to make your nudes display all their emotions by a too strong indication of bones, sinews, and muscles, you become a wooden painter."[37]

In the early sixteenth century, Leonardo had announced himself to be an antithesis to Michelangelo. By the last decades of the century, however, Leonardo's opposition had become a lens for seeing a different but related conflict over images that had Michelangelo's *Last Judgment*, not the paintings Leonardo in fact knew, as its first touchstone. Already in their time, but more clearly in retrospect, the paintings of Leonardo and Michelangelo could be read as mutual critiques, Leonardo faulting Michelangelo for the mysteriously motivated actions of his figures, Michelangelo, Leonardo for sacrificing a focus on the figure in favor of something else. The second and third chapters of this book will take up each of these matters in turn. We should be aware from the outset, though, of the degree to which Leonardo/Michelangelo was – and is here – an antithesis of convenience, designed to bring out differences in the ways artists worked. As the book will also show, Leonardo and Michelangelo had much in common. Each gives us a perspective on what it might mean to make the figure the central topic for painting. And each was preoccupied with painted force.

Anghiari and Cascina

With all of this in mind, the single occasion on which Michelangelo and Leonardo worked together – or rather, worked in direct competition – invites particular attention. The circumstances were these:

In 1494, in conjunction with a reform of the Republican government that had been established after the exile of the Medici, a new meeting space was constructed in Florence's old City Hall. Its function was to house a Great Council of citizens, its decoration to feature patriotic paintings and sculptures by the city's leading artists. After the completion of a basic architectural framework, however, the project lapsed. Only in 1502, with the election of Piero Soderini as Florence's de facto political leader for life did it get under way again. By October 1503, Soderini had commissioned Leonardo to paint a 1440 battle between the Florentine and Milanese armies that had taken place at Anghiari, a small town near the Florentine possession of Arezzo; in 1504, Soderini commissioned Michelangelo to paint a 1364 battle between Florence and Pisa at Cascina, a site along the Arno, the river that connected those two cities.[38]

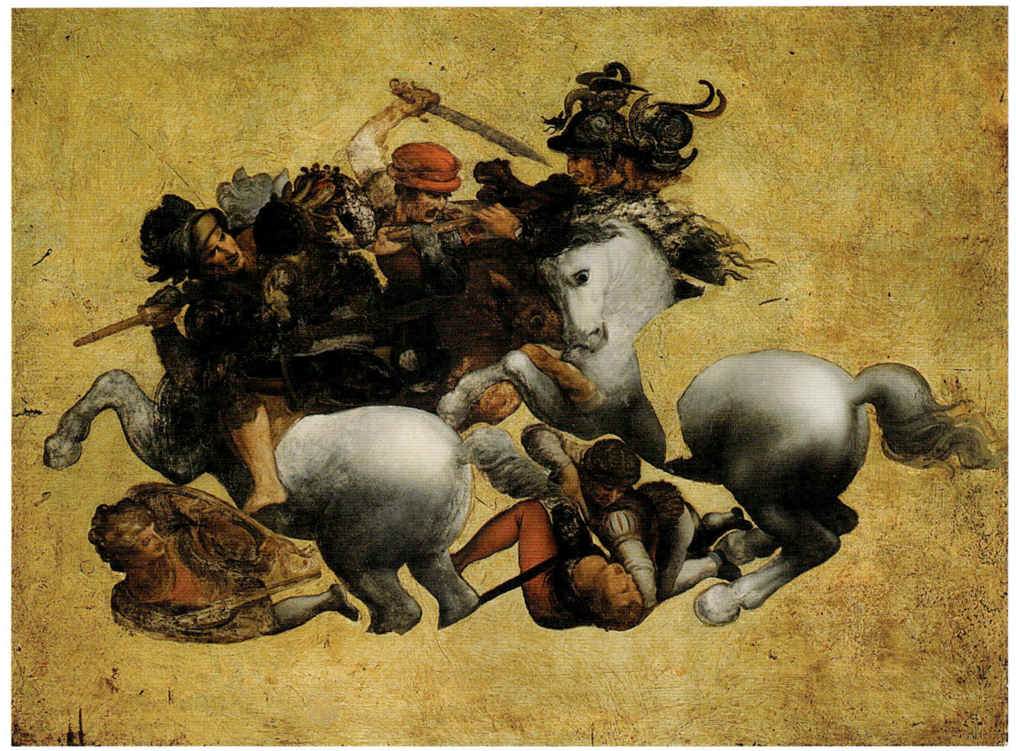

8   Anonymous sixteenth-century copy after Leonardo's *Battle of Anghiari* (the "Tavola Doria"),
oil on panel, private collection

The expectations that Soderini held for his artists have been the subject of long debate. Among the various texts that described the events at Anghiari, the most important should have been Leonardo Dati's *Trophaeum Anglaricum*; Agostino Vespucci provided an Italian translation and summary of this for Leonardo, which survives, along with a list of the names of the most important soldiers involved.[39] The text suggests that the painting was to include recognizable portraits, including, presumably, one of Giampaolo Orsini, the commander of the Florentines; Ludovico Trevisan and Michelotto Attendolo Sforza, leaders in the Papal and Venetian alliance that Florence had joined; and Niccolò Piccinino, the *condottiere* who led the Milanese enemy. Dati, however, provides no description of the central

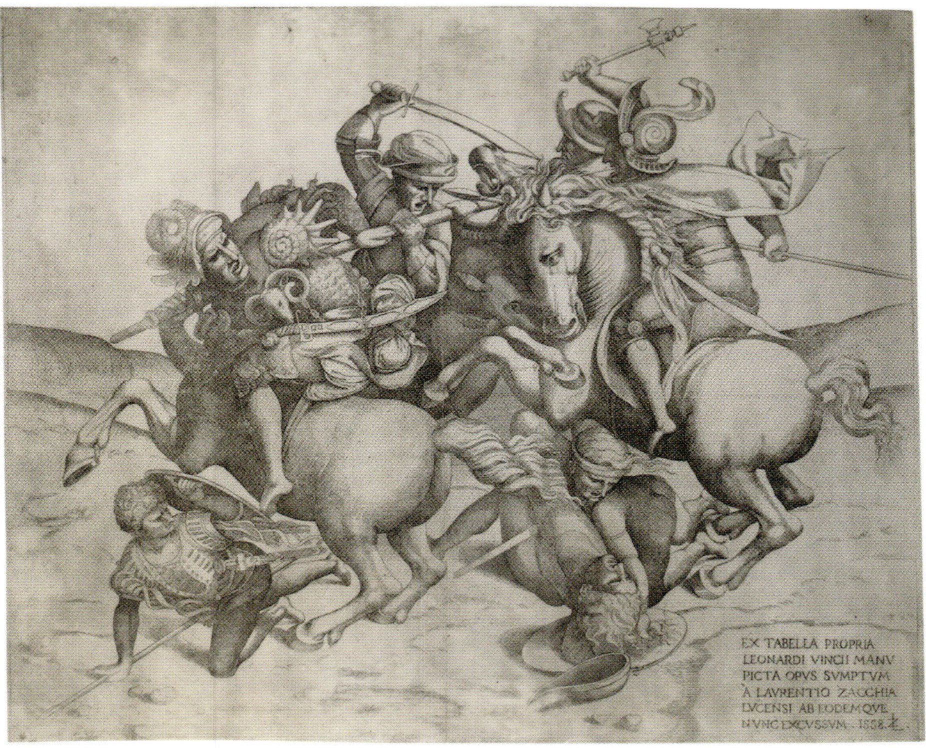

9   Lorenzo Zacchia, engraving after Leonardo's *Battle of Anghiari*

scene that copies after Leonardo show him actually to have depicted (figs. 8 and 9), and the only writer to recall anything like this portrayed event, Neri di Gino Capponi, does not link actions to names: "Our captain rushed forward from the other side with circa four hundred war horses; he went to conquer the Standard of the enemy, and having taken it, the enemies were destroyed."[40] In recent years, a consensus has gradually emerged that in Leonardo's painting, the Florentines are on the right and the Milanese on the left. The central soldier with raised sword is probably Piccinino; for both this figure and for the one at the extreme right, riding the horse we see in profile, Leonardo prepared independent head studies (figs. 10 and 11), indicating his interest in giving them recognizable

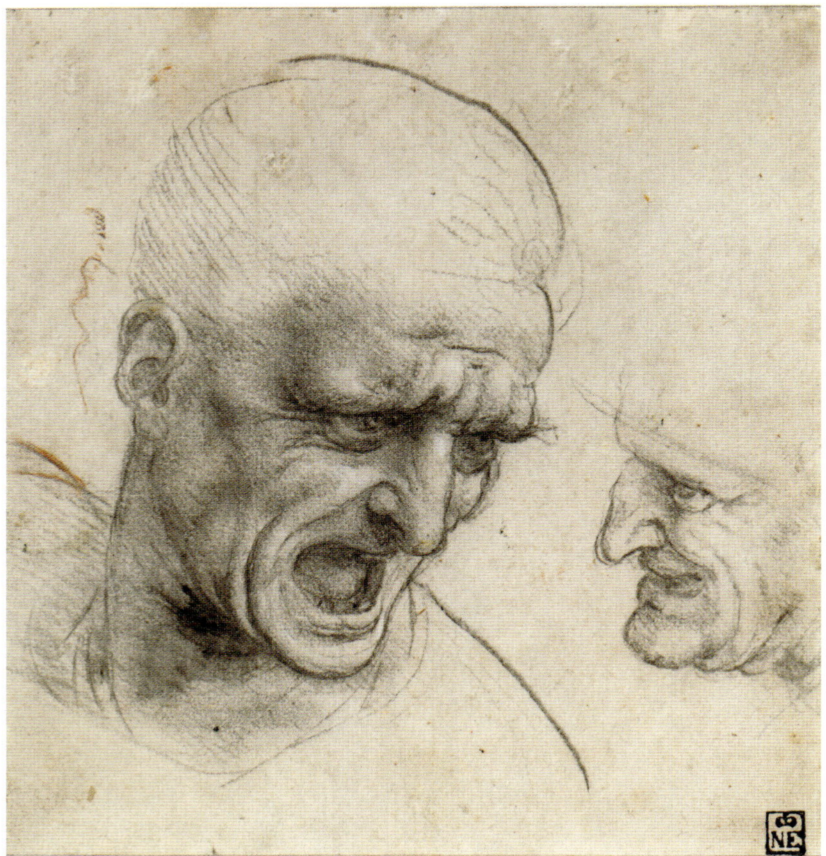

10   Leonardo da Vinci, *Head of a Warrior*, black chalk on paper,
Szépmûvészeti Múzeum, Budapest

features.[41] Few recent specialists are willing to go much further than this, however, in connecting the painting to a concrete historical episode or to the recorded actions of specific individuals, or to speculate on how the surviving copies relate to the larger mural that Leonardo was planning.[42]

With regard to the Cascina project, it had long been thought that Michelangelo had been asked to base his picture on the account of the battle in Filippo Villani's late fourteenth-century *Cronica*. According to this, the Florentine troops had collapsed from heat and exhaustion at the side

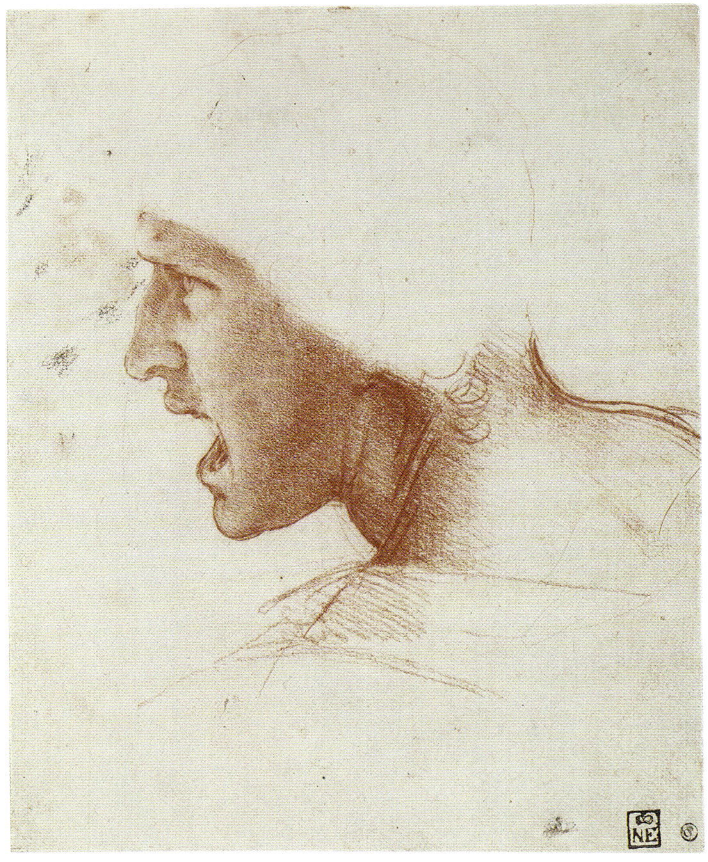

11   Leonardo da Vinci, *Head of a Warrior*, red chalk on pink prepared
paper, Szépmûvészeti Múzeum, Budapest

of the river. Some had disarmed to bathe, and their aging commander,
Galeotto Malatesta, had taken to bed with a fever. Fearing an impending
Pisan attack, Manno Donati and Bonifacio Lupi sounded an alarm,
restoring order in the camp and allowing the Florentines to withstand a
subsequent Pisan assault. More recently, Michelangelo's design has been
linked to a different available source with a quite different narrative. According to Leonardo Bruni's *History of the Florentine People*, which had been
translated from Latin into Italian in 1473, the Pisans had tormented the

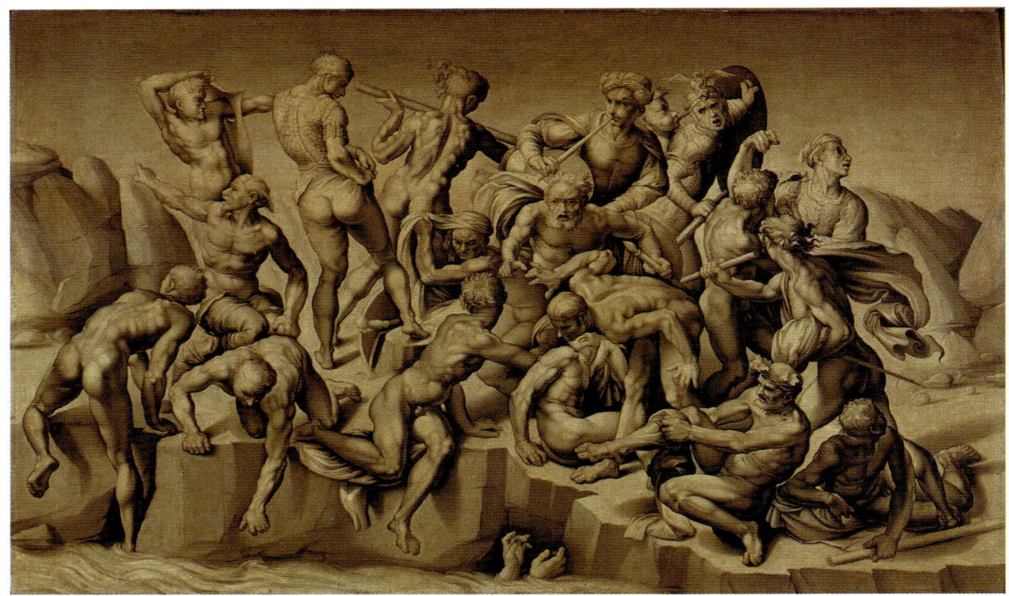

12   Aristotile da Sangallo, after Michelangelo, *Battle of Cascina*, oil on panel,
Holkham Hall, Norfolk, U.K.

Florentine camp for days by sending soldiers to its outskirts to make a noise; as soon as the Florentines pulled themselves together, these soldiers would retreat. Later, the Pisans attacked in silence, after stealthily approaching the camp. If Michelangelo followed Bruni's account, it would mean that the cartoon he was preparing for his fresco showed not a false alarm or a preparation for battle, but the troops' surprise at the beginning of the actual fight. In the end, though, the most informative surviving visual record of the work allows little basis for such a distinction (fig. 12).[43] In Michelangelo's design, like Leonardo's, it should be possible to assign historical names to one or two characters, but the scene as a whole re-imagines the action it portrays; it does not simply illustrate a known text.[44]

Leonardo and Michelangelo were almost certainly expected not only to look at historical sources but also to accommodate their paintings to the functions of the room. One of these was to display captured standards, including those from Anghiari.[45] Another was to host council meetings, with Soderini, whose title was Gonfaloniere ("standard-bearer") of the Republic, presiding. It seems likely that standards would have featured prominently in all the room's decorations: the "Cristo Salvatore" that Andrea Sansovino was commissioned to carve in June of 1502 would – if it followed the conventional iconography of the Resurrection – have held a banner. In the altarpiece that Fra Bartolomeo began to paint (fig. 13), Saint Victor, at right, holds a large banner as well. Fra Bartolomeo's painting, to follow Vasari, included "all the protectors of the city of Florence, and the saints on whose feast days the city has had its victories," and it was on the feast day of Saint Victor that the Florentines had won the Battle of Cascina.[46] The standard was a crucial motif in Leonardo's painting, and a character in the center background of Michelangelo's design – which the artist isolated for independent study (fig. 14) – appears to be raising a standard as well. One of the things that makes a comparison of the two designs revealing is that the artists built them from the same basic elements.

At the time of the commission, Soderini's decision to assign the two murals to Leonardo and Michelangelo probably seemed daring. Leonardo had not done a large-scale painting in years; the previous one he had attempted, the *Last Supper* in the church of S. Maria delle Grazie in Milan, may already have been coming off the wall, executed as it was in an experimental oil medium rather than in fresco. The twenty-nine-year-old Michelangelo, for his part, had trained in the workshop of the Domenico Ghirlandaio, but he had never before painted an independent mural. Yet even if Soderini avoided safe commissions in favor of something less predictable, he would also have had good reasons to turn to this pair.

Two years before receiving his own commission, Leonardo had attained the remarkable distinction of being the first artist publicly to exhibit a drawing – a large cartoon depicting the Madonna and Child with Saint Anne, which Florentines thronged to see in the church of the SS. Annunziata. It was the first mature example of his *sfumato* effects to be seen in Florence, and a drawing by Michelangelo now in Oxford suggests that he studied it with particular attention.[47] The phenomenon of the exhibition, moreover, is the most immediate precedent for the broad

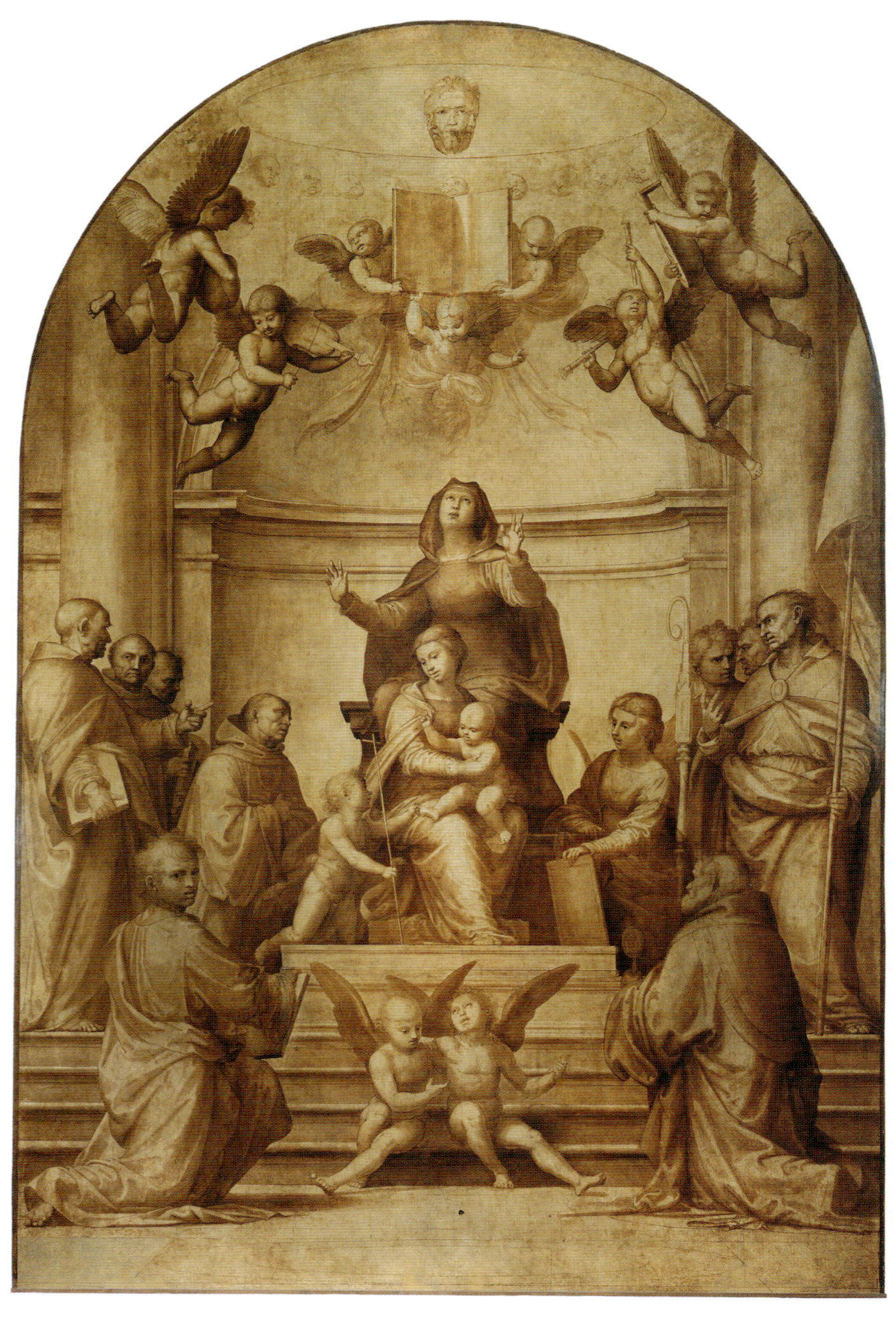

13   Fra Bartolomeo, unfinished altarpiece for the Great Council Hall,
oil on panel, Museo di San Marco, Florence

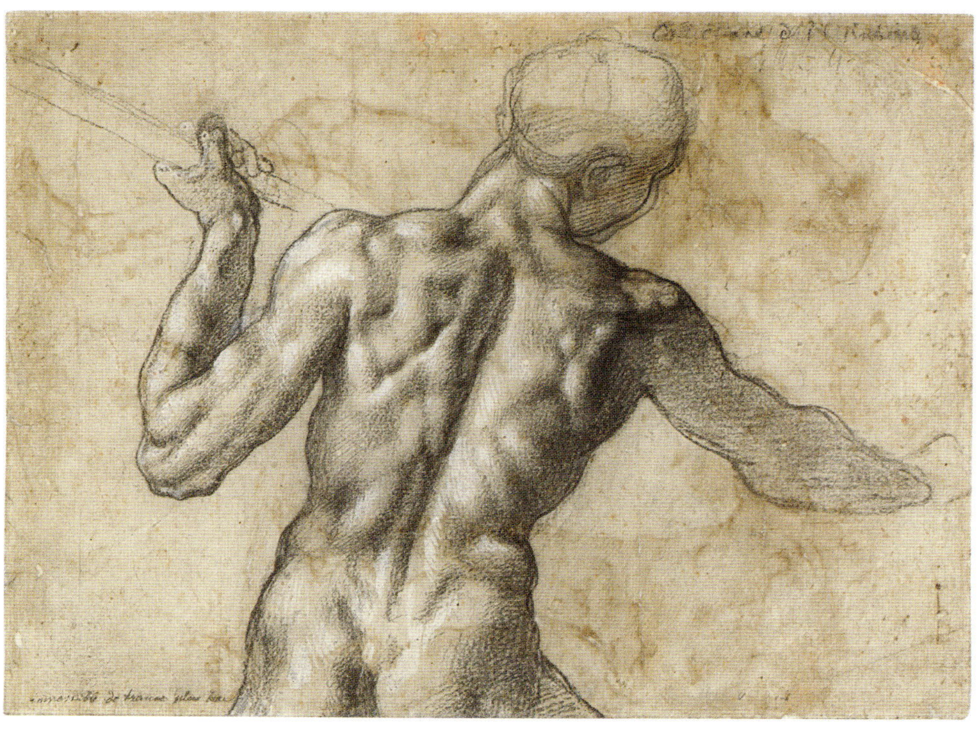

14   Michelangelo, figure study for the *Battle of Cascina*,
black chalk with white heightening on paper, Albertina, Vienna

response that Michelangelo's *Cascina* cartoon, another publicly exhibited drawing, would garner. Also relevant is the fact that in the ten months preceding his commission, Leonardo had worked for the warlord Cesare Borgia. He had probably witnessed real combat and he may have received the commission while at the siege of Pisa – one of the cities whose defeat the murals were supposed to celebrate. Soderini would have known that Leonardo, perhaps more than any living artist, was an expert in things military. The last painting that Leonardo had actually made in Florence, the unfinished *Adoration* now in the Uffizi, included fighting soldiers in the background (fig. 15).

Michelangelo could claim no comparable experience, even if he later helped Florence redesign its fortifications. Yet he, too, would have looked like an artist particularly prepared to undertake a grand patriotic subject:

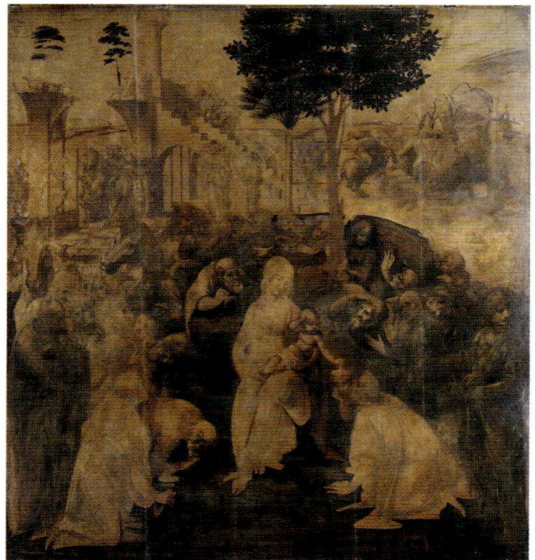 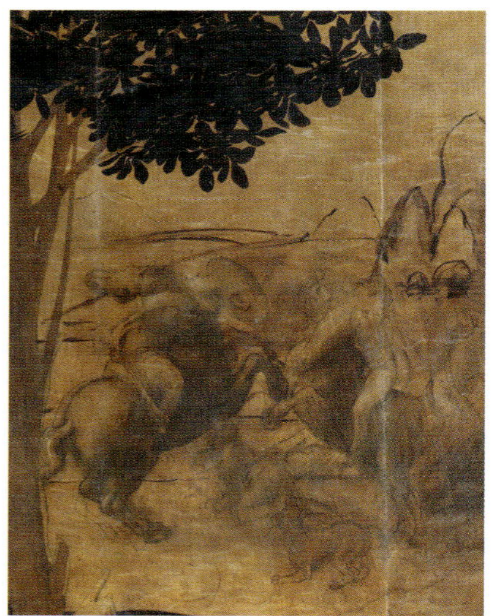

15a and 15b   Leonardo, *Adoration of the Magi*, oil on panel, Uffizi, Florence

his colossal, fierce *David*, originally meant for Florence Cathedral, had been set up instead before the Palazzo dei Priori (fig. 16), the very building that housed the room where Soderini wished him to paint.[48] The fact that the marble treated a theme familiar from predecessors including Donatello and Verrocchio made it clear how different Michelangelo's vision for art was, especially in his rendering of the body: not a soft ephebe or a wiry adolescent but a physical marvel, a previously unseen fusion of beauty and strength. Although Michelangelo's projected mural was intended to include a skirmish with horses, the choice to center on the Arno episode must have been made in the knowledge that it would let him paint bathers – nude figures, similar to the *David* in type and well over life size.[49]

Both Leonardo and Michelangelo, in 1504, would have seemed to be making art for a new century, consciously distancing themselves from the ways of the past. Modern writers have characterized both designs as radical departures from the traditional battle painting in particular.[50] Novelty must even have been something the patron encouraged, commissioning projects meant to celebrate a new government and a reborn state. In the end, though, neither painter completed his task. In March 1505, Michelangelo

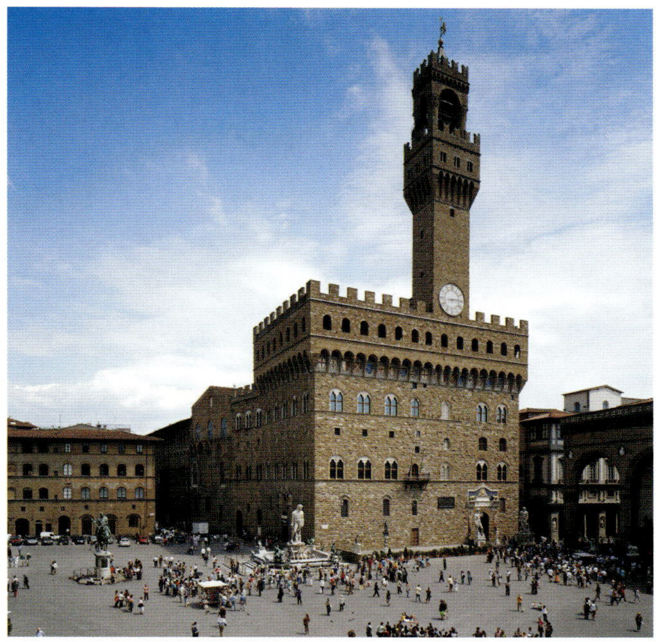

16 Palazzo dei Priori, Florence

was summoned to Rome, where he would receive from Julius II the commission for the pope's tomb. Although he returned to Florence the following month, it is unclear whether he continued with the cartoon; certainly he had broken off work on it completely by the summer of 1506.[51] Leonardo may have started painting in the summer of 1505, using oil rather than true fresco in order to maximize the atmospheric effects – there were stories of him lighting a fire at the base of the wall in an attempt to get the binder to dry more quickly.[52] In May 1506, he was given a three-month leave to visit Milan – whose defeat he was supposed to be celebrating in his fresco – and he, like Michelangelo, never returned to the project. The sources appear to suggest that Michelangelo's cartoon could, with permission, be visited in the Council Hall from 1507, though it had been removed from there by 1516 at the latest.[53] Whatever drawing or painting of Leonardo's remained was demolished or obscured by Vasari when he supervised a remodeling of the room in the 1560s.

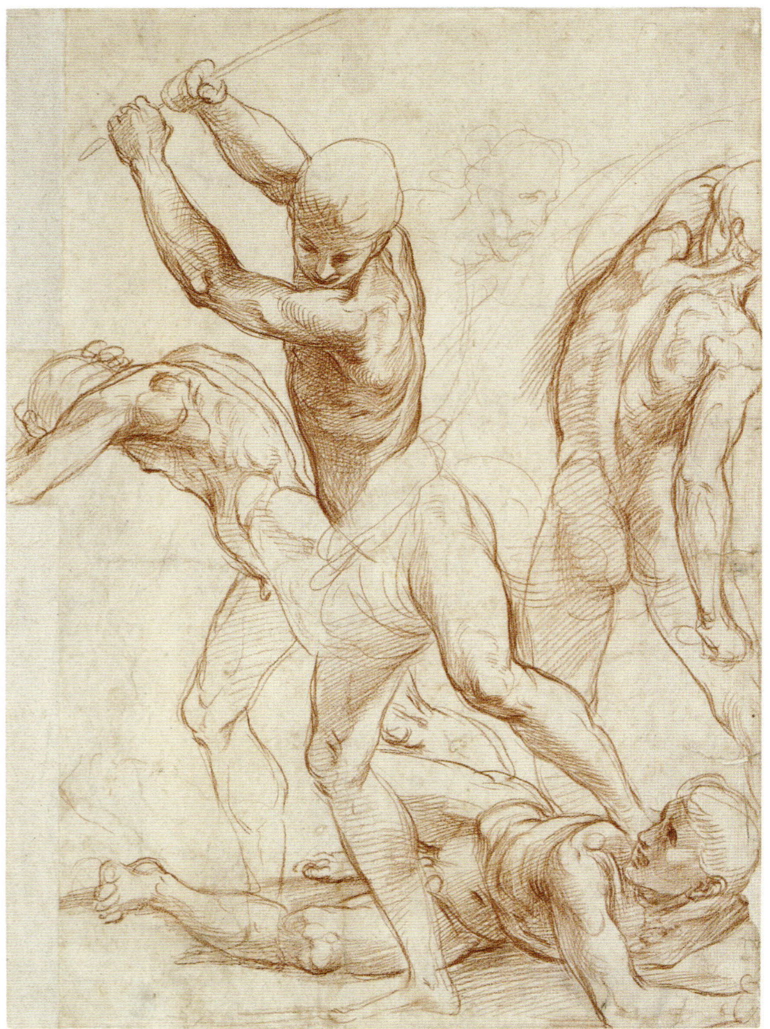

17   Raphael, *Fighting Men*, red chalk over stylus on paper,
Ashmolean Museum, Oxford

Perhaps because of their very invisibility, the two artists' designs acquired a kind of mythic status. Kenneth Clark went so far as to say that they represented "the turning point of the Renaissance," Paola Barocchi that they "created a new taste." Michelangelo's greatest modern biographer, John Addington Symonds, was no fan of Michelangelo's cartoon but he nevertheless imagined that it had an "extraordinary effect, as of something superhuman." "I cannot refrain from thinking," he continued, "that the Cartoon for the Battle of Pisa, taken up by [Michelangelo] as a field for the display of his ability, must by its very brilliancy have accelerated the ruin of Italian art."[54] While it may seem exaggerated to regard the design of one or two paintings as such a momentous artistic event, period voices support these remarkable assertions.[55] Giorgio Vasari and Benvenuto Cellini both referred to Michelangelo's cartoon as a "school."[56] Vasari went so far as to assert that all who studied it, whether natives of Florence or visitors, eventually became famous. To prove the point, he took the trouble of listing them: "Among those who studied the cartoon were Aristotile da San Gallo . . . Ridolfo Ghirlandajo, Raphael Sanzio of Urbino, Francesco Grannaci, Baccio Bandinelli, Alonzo Berughetta, Andrea del Sarto, Franciabigio, Jacopo Sansovino, Rosso, Maturino, Tribolo, Jacopo Pontormo, and Perino del Vaga, and all these became excellent Florentine masters."[57]

By mid-century, the Great Council Hall projects looked like a generational compass point. Raphael allegedly came to Florence for no other reason than that foreign painters had been extolling Leonardo's *Anghiari* and Michelangelo's *Cascina*.[58] He drew after both Leonardo's and Michelangelo's cartoons, then made his own battling nudes in 1507–8 (fig. 17), shortly before moving from Florence to Rome. Later, when a Florentine was pope, Raphael's shop would execute monumental battle scenes in the Vatican. In the same period, the engravings made after Michelangelo's cartoon would be the first mass-produced reproductions of a design for a painting. In the decades after that, most of the artists whom Vasari mentioned would paint works that referred to or even cited one or both of the Council Hall projects. Vasari did this himself, when working for the second Duke of Florence in the 1560s: whatever the shortcomings of his frescoes, he must have understood himself to be carrying through a cycle of the sort that Leonardo and Michelangelo never managed. By the end of the century, the Italian battle painting would be broadly recognized as the chief site for the reinvention of the figure.

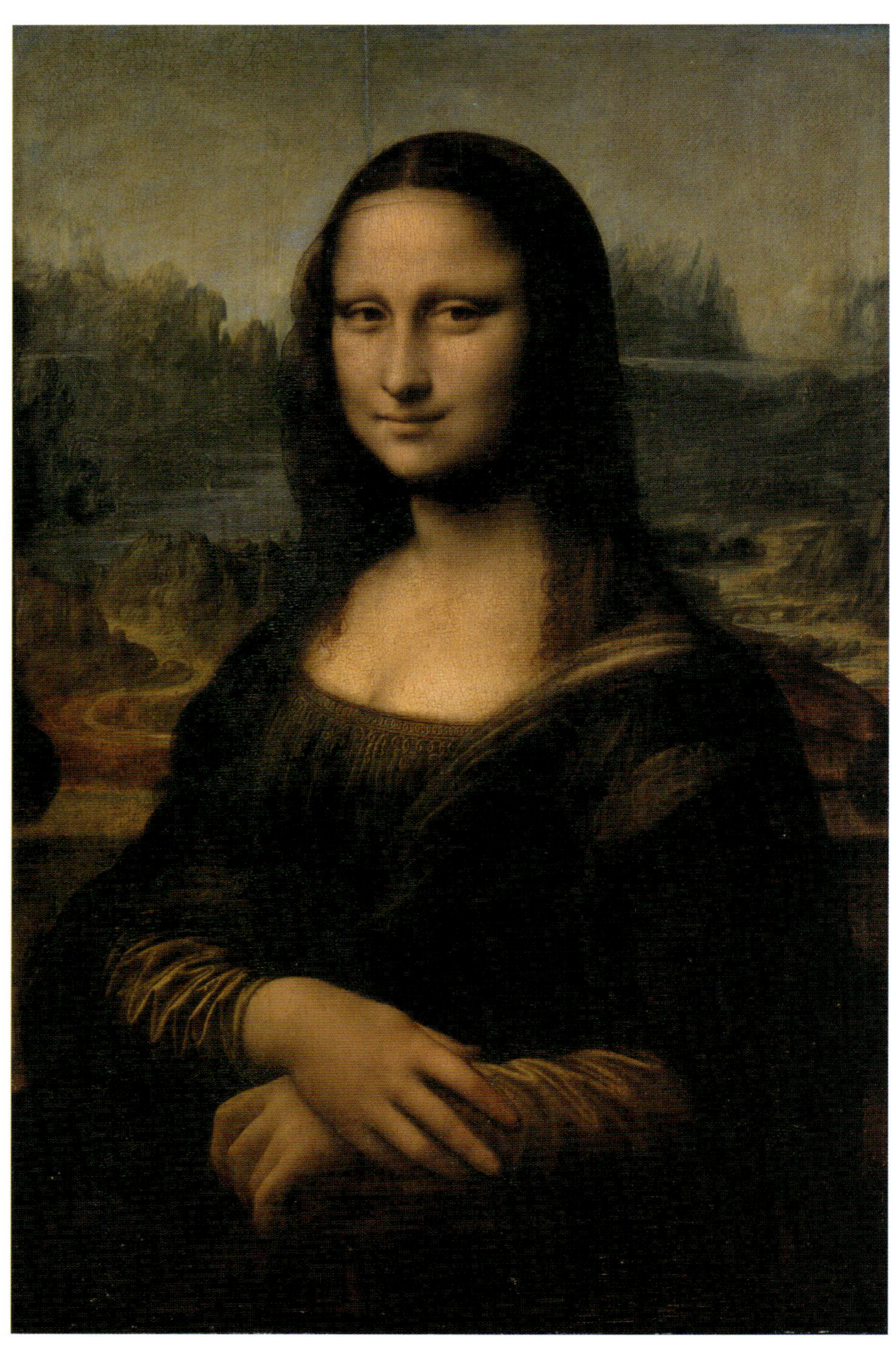

18   Leonardo da Vinci, *Mona Lisa*, oil on panel, Louvre, Paris

2

CIRCUMSCRIPTION

Against Sfumato

Leonardo never completed his painting of the Battle of Anghiari, and what he did paint was almost certainly later destroyed. We can infer a certain amount, nevertheless, about how the mural would likely have looked. The narrative would have unfolded in an open landscape, similar to the environment Leonardo had just been painting in the background of the *Mona Lisa* (fig. 18); Agostino Vespucci, the same official who provided Leonardo with a source text for the Anghiari painting, even suggested that the *Mona Lisa* established the expectations for the mural.[1] The setting would have allowed for strong atmospheric effects of the sort about which Leonardo had been writing; the oil binder in which he was reportedly attempting to work would have been particularly well suited to the almost liquid air of the deeper spaces.[2] Preliminary drawings for a group of riders (figs. 19 and 20) emphasize not only the wind that makes the banners flutter but also the clouds of dust kicked up by the horses. This recalls the imagined "Way of Representing a Battle" that Leonardo had penned in the early 1490s:

> First you must represent the smoke of artillery mingling in the air with the dust tossed up by the movement of horses and the combatants.

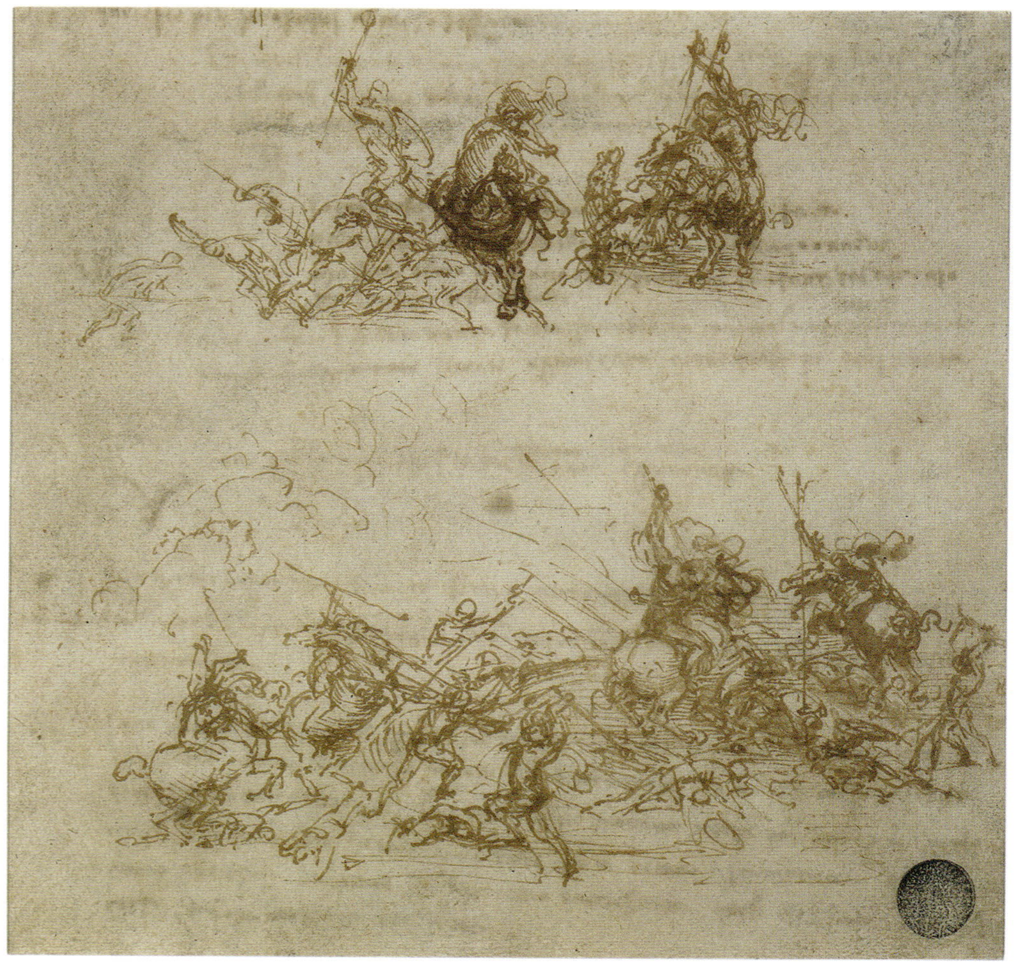

19   Leonardo, battle scenes, pen and brown ink with wash over stylus on paper,
Accademia, Venice

. . . The higher the smoke mixed with the dust-laden air rises towards a certain level, the more it will look like a dark cloud; and at the top the smoke is visible rather than the dust; the smoke will assume a bluish tinge and the dust will tend to its color. . . . The more the combatants are in this turmoil the less will they be seen, and the less contrast will there be in their lights and shadows. . . . And if you introduce horses

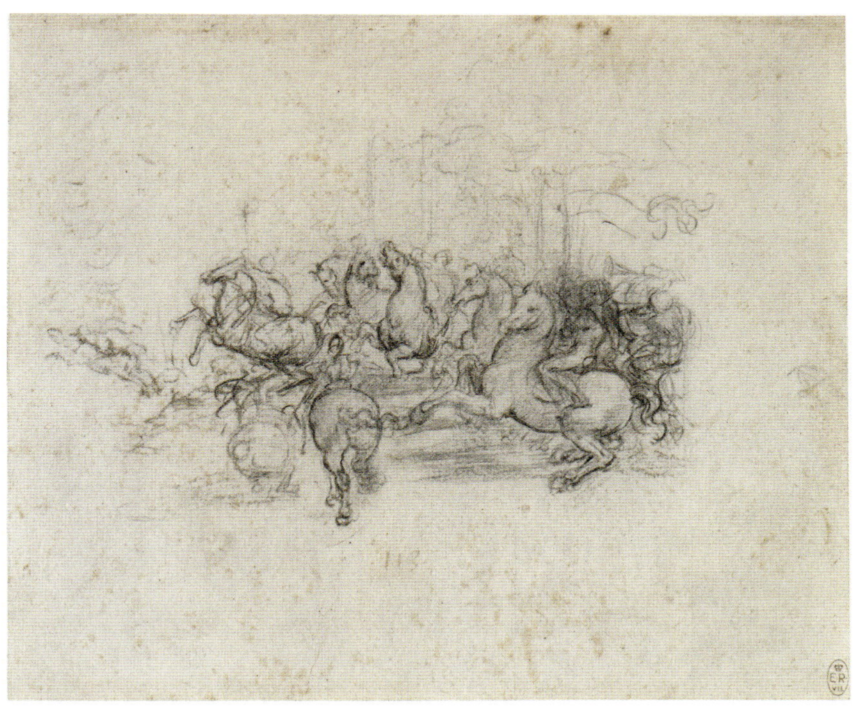

20   Leonardo, group of horsemen with standards, black chalk,
Royal Library, Windsor

galloping outside the crowd, make the little clouds of dust distant from
each other in proportion to the strides made by the horses . . . The balls
from the guns must have a train of smoke following their flight. . . .
You would see some of the victors leaving the fight and issuing from
the crowd, rubbing their eyes and cheeks with both hands to clean them
of the dirt made by their watering eyes smarting from the dust and
smoke.[3]

As these excerpts show, the appeal of the battle subject to Leonardo lay
to a large extent in what could happen *around* the figures, in the air. The
Windsor drawing's overlaid lines, along with the strong shadows and the
soft blur of the rubbed chalk medium, all add to an impression of optical
haze, indistinctness.

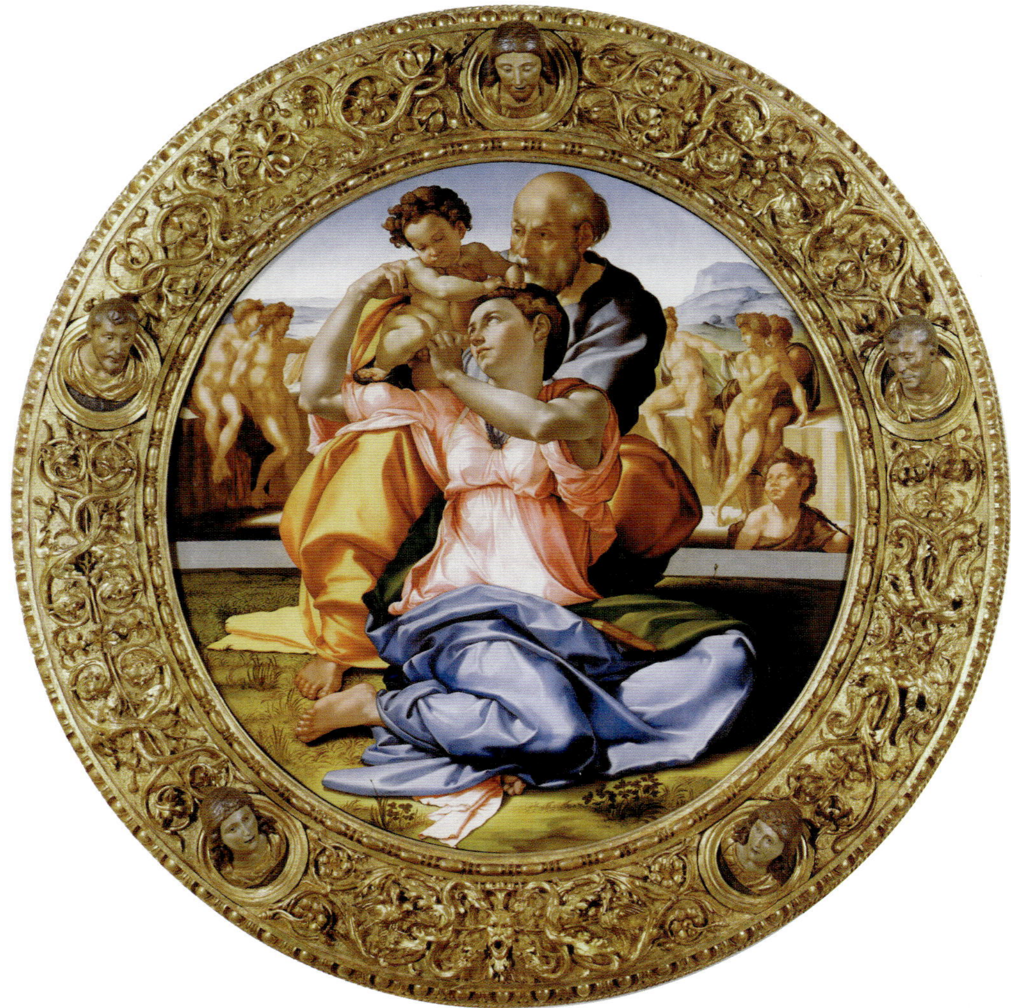

21   Michelangelo, Doni Tondo, oil and tempera on panel, Uffizi, Florence

The evidence we have for what Michelangelo would have painted is equally indirect. Still, the Doni Tondo (fig. 21), undertaken at roughly the same time, gives a sense of Michelangelo's current style.[4] Ever since the rediscovery of its original frame at the beginning of the twentieth century, the painting has generally been thought to have been commissioned shortly after the wool merchant Angelo Doni's marriage to Maddalena Strozzi in late 1503 or early 1504. More than one writer has, in trying to describe it, reached to the language of sports; here is an instance where modern viewers have agreed with Borromeo in placing Michelangelo's forced figures under the heading "Athletic Bodies."[5] Still, at the time he painted it, Michelangelo's intertwining of the Holy Family into a complex figural group would have looked like nothing so much as a response to Leonardo, as would the fact that Michelangelo drew a study for the work in red chalk, the medium that Leonardo had recently introduced to Florence.[6] This dialogic aspect of the painting, its evocation of Leonardo, only draws more attention to what Michelangelo did differently. In Michelangelo's picture, every form has a hard, continuous outline. The landscape seems to double the setting of the Cascina, disposing its figures along a riverbank, except that here there is no water to be seen, as though Michelangelo sought to insist on the absence of any medium that could allow an atmospheric filter. John Addington Symonds's distaste for the painting is illuminating: "In technical execution the Doni Madonna is faithful to old Florentine usage, but lifeless and unsympathetic. We are disagreeably reminded by every portion of the surface that Lionardo's subtle play of tones and modulated shades, those *sfumature*, as Italians call them, which transfer the mystic charm of nature to the canvas, were as yet unknown to the great draughtsman."[7] It is difficult to believe that the Cascina mural that Michelangelo was to paint, at the same time, in direct competition with Leonardo, would have exhibited this difference any less.

Symonds drew his conclusions about the Doni Tondo in the years before the rediscovery of its frame; when he wrote, it was still possible to believe that Michelangelo had painted the panel at the very beginning of the century, before Leonardo's return to Florence. No one today would conclude that Michelangelo approached the Doni as he did because Leonardo's *sfumature* were as yet unknown to him, and Vasari wrote even in 1550 that some of the figures in the *Cascina* cartoon were *sfumate*. Vasari may not be an entirely reliable witness here; he had probably never seen the cartoon himself, and the copyists certainly give no indication of any *sfumato*. Perhaps Vasari was thinking not of the cartoon but of the drawings

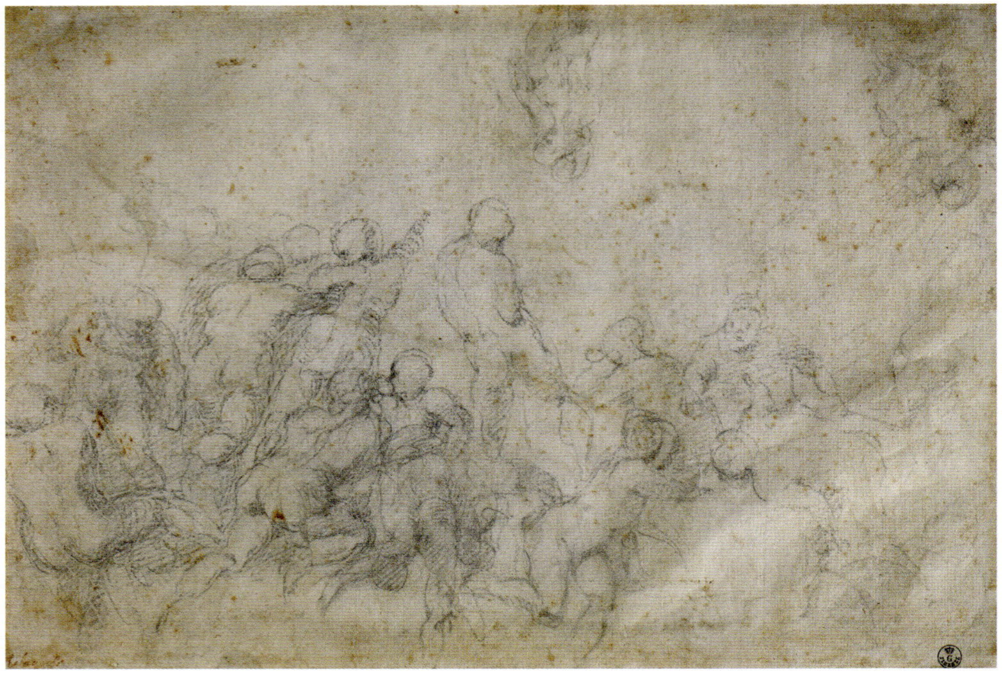

22   Michelangelo, study for the *Battle of Cascina*, black chalk over stylus on paper, Uffizi, Florence

that led up to it (fig. 22): these were among Michelangelo's first works in chalk. Or perhaps the cartoon's figures were less sharply defined than we imagine, and the copyists amplified the harder stylistic qualities that most set Michelangelo apart. The collective evidence, in any case, suggests that Michelangelo had in fact studied Leonardo's atmospheric effects, then rejected them in favor of strong contour. The Doni Tondo and the Cascina project both established that *sfumato* and contour were choices, and that it was possible to favor the latter – indeed, this would become a rallying point for Michelangelo's Florentine followers. Contour was central to the way that Cellini and Vasari later wrote about the arts, and the late sixteenth-century painter and writer Alessandro Allori formulated a theory of *disegno* based explicitly on Michelangelo's manner of delineating the contours of the nude figure.[8]

As painters, Vasari and Allori tend to be regarded today as lesser academic imitators of Michelangelo. Yet there is good reason to think that Allori was perfectly correct in maintaining that contour was of central importance to Michelangelo. The residual, shared belief that contour was a commitment, one with prominent opposition, should sharpen our sense of what the debate inherent in Michelangelo's and Leonardo's murals was about. It was traditional, particularly before the cleaning of the Sistine Chapel ceiling, to describe Michelangelo's approach to painting as "sculptural."[9] That no longer seems quite right, however, especially if we are trying to get at its difference from Leonardo's manner: Leonardo's *chiaroscuro*, after all, has itself long been regarded as a means of creating "relief." What we can say is that Michelangelo's approach to the *Battle of Cascina* was polemical. Leonardo had been working on his project for months by the time that Michelangelo received his own commission. Michelangelo looked at the *sfumatura* that Leonardo's admirers later regarded as one of his most important contributions to the practice of painting and produced its near pictorial opposite. Why? What were the stakes here?

Nine Ways of Looking at an Outline

The sixteenth-century Florentine painter Agnolo Bronzino, whose paintings show him to have taken Michelangelo's opposition to *sfumatura* completely to heart, put things this way: "all that pertains to art are the lines that circumscribe a body, which are on the surface."[10] Like Leonardo himself, Bronzino recognized that the contours he used were just things of paint; they were not found in nature. A painter might depict a person whom he had or once had had before his eyes, but the contours he drew around his painted forms were not themselves part of the thing depicted.

If contours were artificial, if they were forms that a painter willfully imposed on the colored surface – and, after Leonardo, did so knowing that there was another option – what was their purpose? Michelangelo would presumably have begun to think about that question while training in the studio of Domenico Ghirlandaio in the 1480s. While it is difficult to go as far as Symonds and conclude that Michelangelo's device was "faithful to old Florentine usage," we might well ask how a painter who came of age in late Quattrocento Florence could have understood a contour line's function and meaning.

I   EDGE

In giving emphasis to contour lines, some Quattrocento artists may have been imitating the ancient Greek painter Parrhasius. Pliny, whose *Natural History* had been published for the first time in 1469 and had appeared in Italian translations already in 1473 and 1481, wrote that all ancient artists regarded Parrhasius as the supreme painter of contours, adding that contour was, in painting, "the very highest point of skill": "making the bodies' extremities, knowing how to bring a painting to an end, this is something that is rarely brought to perfection in art." Pliny's celebration of the device may have informed a view like Bronzino's, that contour could be identified with art *per se*. It also allowed that contour could be admired almost in the abstract – that the contour amounted to what William Hogarth would eventually call "the line of beauty." Yet Pliny's discussion of Parrhasius went on to indicate that contour lines had a further purpose: the form that the 1481 Italian text referred to as the *externa linea* had to turn around itself ("debba circundare se medesima") and in so doing had to "promise something more, to show the very thing that it hides."[11]

On the Plinian account, in other words, contour was not really a line at all but rather a narrow plane, wide enough to block the sight of something behind it. In its curves, it overlapped itself, effecting a kind of elision.[12] A simple illustration of the principle would be the line that surrounds the halo over Christ in Ghirlandaio's *Calling of the Apostles* in the Sistine Chapel (fig. 23). We see an oval but we understand a circle; to follow Pliny, we notice that the side of the halo appears shorter than the top, and from that we infer that the visible portions of the contour line partially block our view of the immediately adjacent portions of the line that stand farther back in space. The example of the halo introduces a principle that bears on any contour that represents a foreshortened form,

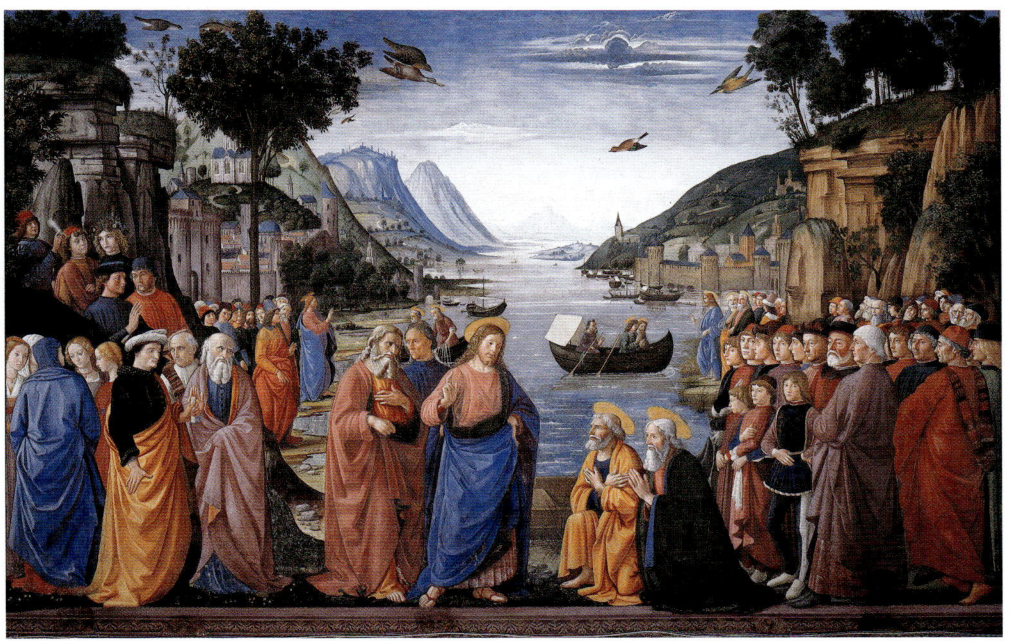

23   Domenico Ghirlandaio, *Calling of the Apostles*, fresco,
Sistine Chapel, Vatican

a recession in space – in the Ghirlandaio *Calling of the Apostles*, the lower
edge of Christ's right sleeve, the inside of his right foot, the drapery above
his left foot.

2   INTERSECTION

In the paintings of Pliny's Parrhasius, contour distorts an implied shape so
as to generate an effect of dimensionality. We might imagine such a reading
of the device to have been particularly compelling in the century we
associate with the rise of linear perspective, and in fact Alberti's *De statua*
(1462) offered a close paraphrase of the idea, demonstrating its availability
even before the publication of the *Natural History*.[13] Alberti concluded this
passage by remarking that the observation of outlines "is more a matter
for the painter than the sculptor," so it is not surprising that the topic also

comes up in *De pictura*. In that text, though, he arrived at a rather different way of rationalizing the depicted edge.

When explicating the practice of perspective, Alberti described the picture surface as a transparent plane, behind which the painting's contents were implicitly positioned. The painting is constructed so as to correspond to an optical phenomenon: its objects are shown as though rays have reached out from the eye to apprehend them or rays they project have conveyed their appearance to the eye, in both cases passing through the picture plane; the painting's surface thus corresponds to a section taken through the pyramid or cone formed by the visual rays. For their part, the rays that pass from eye to object, through the transparent picture plane, differ in kind, strength, and capacity. One variety is what Alberti's Latin text terms "extrinsecos radios," his Italian "razzi estremi." The slightly more elaborate Italian version of the pertinent passage reads: "Some of these rays, reaching the edge of the surface [of the visible object], measure all of its dimensions. For this reason – because they crash into the final and extreme parts of the surface – they are called 'extreme' or if you like 'extrinsic.'"[14] Alberti's extrinsic rays are measuring tools. The painter's contours represent the information those tools provide.

That artists could in fact work in ways that map on to this scenario is suggested by such paintings as Ghirlandaio's portrait of Giovanna Torna-buoni in the Museo Thyssen-Bornemisza (fig. 24). There is no question that the painter took some care with his perspectival construction here: infrared reflectography and x-radiography reveal the orthogonals and other lines that the painter incised into the gesso to guide him.[15] He also painted a brown frame around the entire composition, as though to establish the borders of a transparent surface behind which the woman sits. To describe the painting in Albertian terms, Ghirlandaio gives us a surface with an image upon it, and that image comprises the points through which visual rays passed in their extension between Giovanna's face and the viewer's eye. The contour line tracks the points of contact of the extrinsic rays whose function it was just to provide dimensions.

Alberti follows his brief remark about extrinsic rays with a comment on what he calls "median rays" ("razzi mediani" or "medios radios"): their

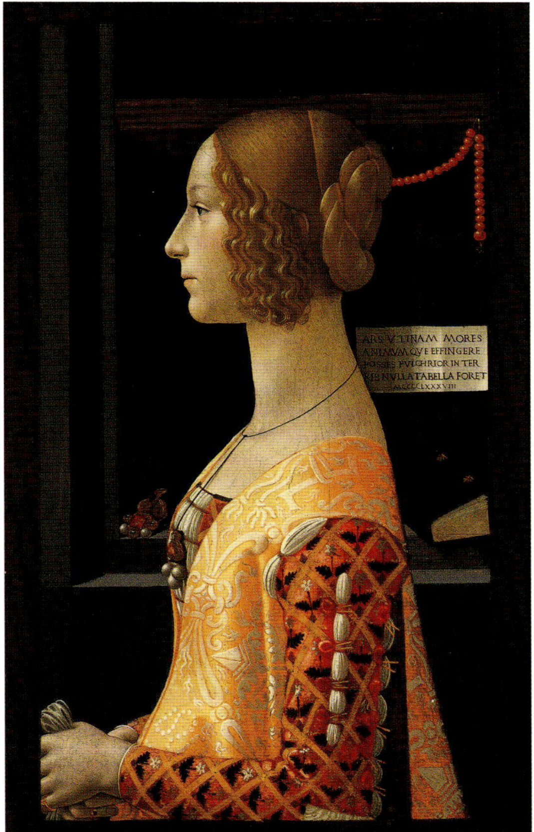

24   Ghirlandaio, *Giovanna degli Albizzi Tornabuoni*,
mixed technique on panel,
Museo Thyssen-Bornemisza, Madrid

job was to transport light and color. The implication is that extrinsic rays are colorless, which is suggestive in connection with the neutral brown tone that Ghirlandaio used to outline the face and hands of his sitter, along with the lower part of her bodice, her sleeves, and her pearls. Alberti's idea is that we would not perceive these lines if we actually saw a woman through a pane of glass, even though it is a theory of vision that rationalizes their presence in the painting. The lines are not material, as Pliny's contours were, but mathematical.[16]

3   SILHOUETTE

Alberti's extrinsic rays intersected a transparent plane, and the painted contour represented the conjunction of their points. But this is not the only way that Quattrocento painters and viewers could think about projection: shadow allowed another. Here Pliny is once again relevant, for he attributed the origin of sculpture to the daughter of the Greek clay modeler Dibutades (Butades): "having been overtaken by love for a young man who wanted to travel to another land, she made the shadow of his person appear on the wall with a lamp, then circumscribed this with lines." Her father then modeled the form in clay.[17] The episode became a popular subject for painting only in the eighteenth century, but several versions of the story would have been known to Alberti in the 1430s, and it helps to explain the shadow that the man projects on the rear wall in Filippo Lippi's *Woman at a Casement* of about 1440 (fig. 25).[18] Paintings like Lippi's, showing beautiful young women, were typically commissioned by men, and in recent decades it has become common to understand all of them as records of the beauty that men perceived, the love or desire that the men who commissioned those paintings felt. Yet the Lippi example shows that painters, their patrons, and viewers might have been just as interested in female subjectivity. To take the connection to the Butades myth seriously is to cast Lippi's woman in the role of the modeler's daughter and the man as her departing or departed lover. The fact that he is smaller than she is – he seems to be slightly behind her, positioned in a way that she cannot really see him – only makes him seem more like a memory.

If, however, this portrait alludes to a story about the origin of portraiture, that story would bear not only on the depicted man but also on the woman. Lippi's lady, too, is now a thing of the past: in fact, all portraits are "memories of faces." One question that arises with regard to Ghirlandaio's *Giovanna Tornabuoni* is why, a decade after Leonardo had introduced the three-quarter format for painted portraits, Ghirlandaio or his patron still preferred to see a profile. The Butades myth may have aligned the image more strongly with an act of remembrance, giving the contour line in this case an associative as much as a perceptual significance.

★ ★ ★

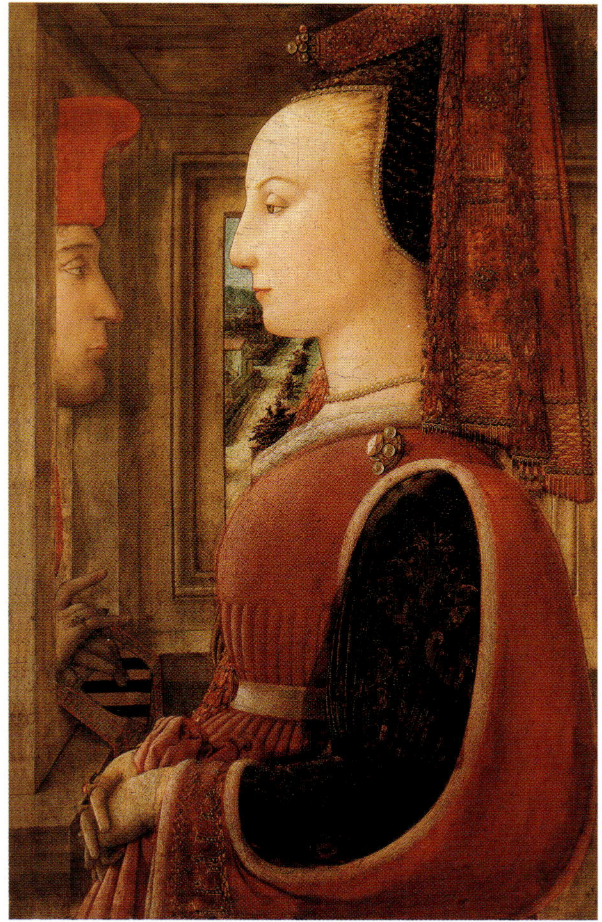

25   Filippo Lippi, *Woman at a Casement*, tempera on panel,
Metropolitan Museum of Art, New York

4   ENCLOSURE

During the iconoclast controversy of the eighth century, opponents of
images drew what they considered to be a fundamental distinction
between the *graphe*, the inscription, and the *perigraphe*, the circumscription
– between lines that allow mimetic representation and an enclosure that
"imprisons" a form. Especially where the image of Christ was concerned,
iconoclasts regarded the very idea of circumscription as a kind of

blasphemy, a false limitation of God's infinity.[19] The counter-position was formulated powerfully by the Patriarch Nikephoros:

> While in circumscription [Christ] is of necessity present, in what is painted nothing is present . . . for while a man is certainly painted in his icon, he is not circumscribed in it, as it is not the place proper to circumscription. . . . Moreover, painting presents the corporeal form of the one depicted, impressing its outline [*schema*] and its shape [*morphen*] and its resemblance [*emphereian*]. Whereas circumscription, having nothing in common with these three modes of which we have spoken, delimits boundaries.

One thing that emerges from this debate is that destroyers and defenders of images shared an understanding of circumscription, regarding it as a kind of containment in place, an encirclement of the volume a person occupies in the world. Where iconoclasts and iconodules differed was in the way they saw the painted body and the line that surrounds it; those who would allow for a painting of Christ simply insisted that the *perigraphe* (circumscription) and the *schema* (outline) were categorically different, that one did not implicate the other.[20]

Byzantine icons were well known in Italy from the late Middle Ages on, and it is not to be excluded that the influx of artists after the Ottoman invasion of Constantinople in 1453 resulted in a movement of ideas about earlier Byzantine painting as well.[21] Still, the sketchy evidence we have suggests that where Byzantine conceptions of outline were translated, they were usually purged of their theological stakes. Alberti writes in *Della pittura* that "seeing something, we say that that thing occupies a place," and that the painter's circumscription describes that space: this sounds very much like the old iconoclast's premise, only secularized.[22]

When describing how it was that Giotto and his followers overthrew the Byzantine manner, Vasari wrote that they "swept away the outlines that wholly enclosed the figures."[23] Yet, without the worry that painters would try to contain God on a piece of wood, it became possible to embrace the idea of the contour as a kind of enclosure. This is implicit in Alberti's remark about contour describing a place, and explicit in the quite different way that late sixteenth- and seventeenth-century viewers characterized Michelangelo's contours. The Dutch painter and biographer Karel van Mander wrote that Michelangelo's paintings were "full of the structure of muscles but enclosed by a beautiful, generous outline."[24] Pacheco, similarly, admired the "entereza" of Michelangelo's contours: "having seen the beautiful and perfect profiles [*perfiles . . . enteros*] of Michelangelo, you will know how to select from nature what is best and to reject what is . . . graceless."[25] The remark returns us to the notion already conveyed by Pliny, that contour lines could be part of a painting's appeal, but it also attributes to that line a new effect: the contour line closes off a body from what surrounds it, declaring that body to be a coherent individual object of contemplation. This happened regularly in icons, whenever a gold ground created a formless zone around the form of

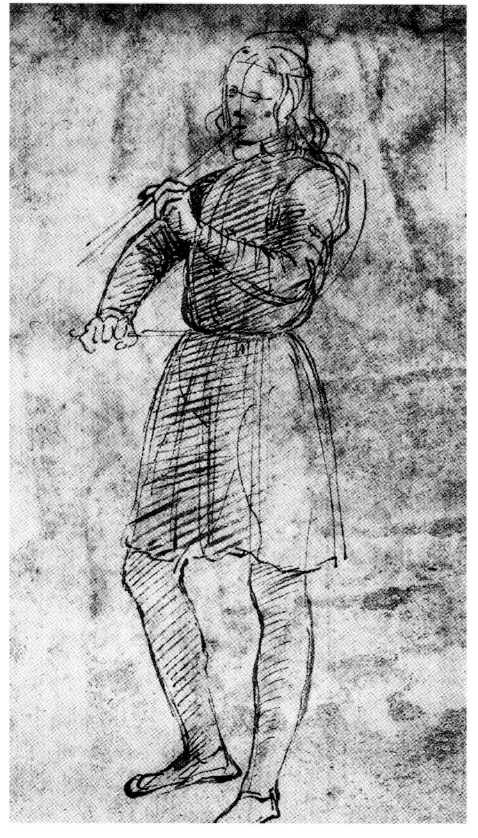

26   Ghirlandio, *Standing Youth Playing a Flute*, pen and brown ink and wash on cream-colored paper, Uffizi, Florence

Christ or a saint. It was also a normal function of contours in Quattrocento drawings. In Ghirlandaio's study on the verso of Uffizi 292 E (fig. 26), to take an almost random example, there is no sense that the boy is playing his pipe for someone, or for that matter that he has any company at all. The drawn figure does not belong to any space, though its painted double was placed into one, the background of the *Marriage of the Virgin* in Santa Maria Novella.[26]

Like many painters, Ghirlandaio would lift figures out of a larger composition for individual study; conversely, he would build compositions

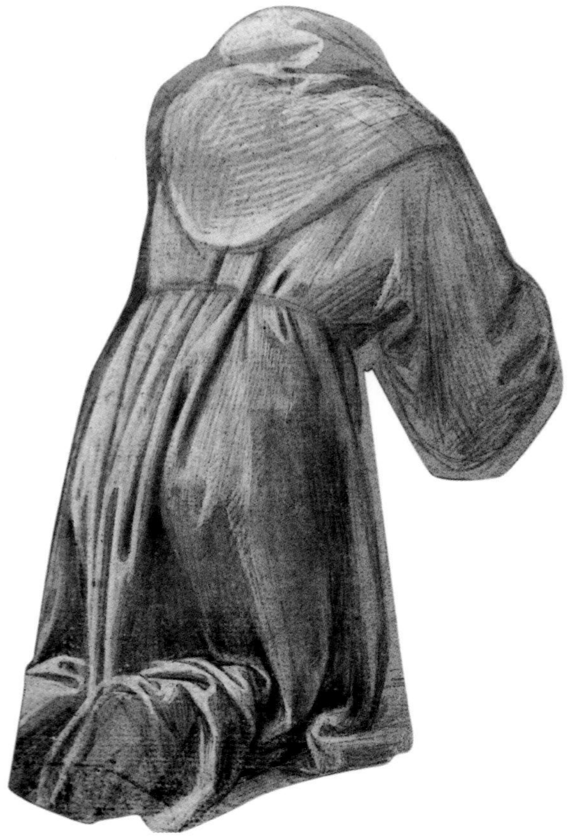

27   Ghirlandaio, *St. Francis*, metalpoint and white heightening on
prepared grey paper, Collection of John and Alice Steiner, New York

from individually studied figures. In such a process, the contour line
represented the cut of the object from an environment, a cut that was
sometimes literalized by collectors who trimmed drawn figures along their
contours (fig. 27).[27]

5   TRACE

In the drawn silhouette of Butades, the contour followed an earlier form;
it recorded the fugitive shadow for posterity. Other practices, too,
contributed to the sense that the contour was a kind of vestige.

Tracing, for example, was a common method of transferring finished designs to the wall or panel: the artist would lay his sheet over the surface to be painted, then incise the outlines of his forms with a stylus or pounce them with charcoal dust.[28] Tracing was also a basic student exercise. Cennino Cennini's *Libro dell'arte* (ca. 1400) advises the young apprentice to study older masters by using translucent paper. "In order to take the contours correctly" from another drawing or panel painting or fresco, the apprentice was to place this paper over the "figure or true design" he wished to study, attaching the sheet in the corners with wax. With the paper in place, the student would then follow what Cennini called the "contorni elle stremità" of his model; removing the paper, he could subsequently add highlights and relief as it pleased him.[29] Such practices survived from the Middle Ages; they would have been especially well suited to the outline drawings that constituted the medieval pattern book, but they were still common into the late fifteenth century and beyond.[30] Just knowing that young artists commonly transcribed outlines from a predecessor before working up interior forms, moreover, may affect the way we see a wider range of drawings.

Among Ghirlandaio's most discussed sheets is one now in Darmstadt, showing two girls (fig. 28). It is possible that this derived from another drawing (fig. 29), made in the Filippo Lippi workshop, for or after Lippi's own fresco of the *Feast of Herod* in Prato Cathedral. The connection, if correct, would shed light on artistic pedagogy in the period: the Darmstadt drawing illustrates the distinctive cross-hatching technique that Ghirlandaio developed and taught to his apprentices; it may be that he had come into the possession of some drawings that Lippi or Lippi's students had made and then used these for teaching purposes, or even that Ghirlandaio himself had been apprenticed with Lippi and later used the materials he had retained from those years to instruct his own *garzoni*.[31]

Currently, nevertheless, there is no scholarly consensus about any of this. No solid documentary evidence tells us where Ghirlandaio trained, and we cannot say with any certainty whether he drew the Darmstadt figures directly after Lippi's fresco or after another drawing. Even if the two drawings are completely independent, however, their comparison is revealing. In the case of the drawing that may come from the Lippi

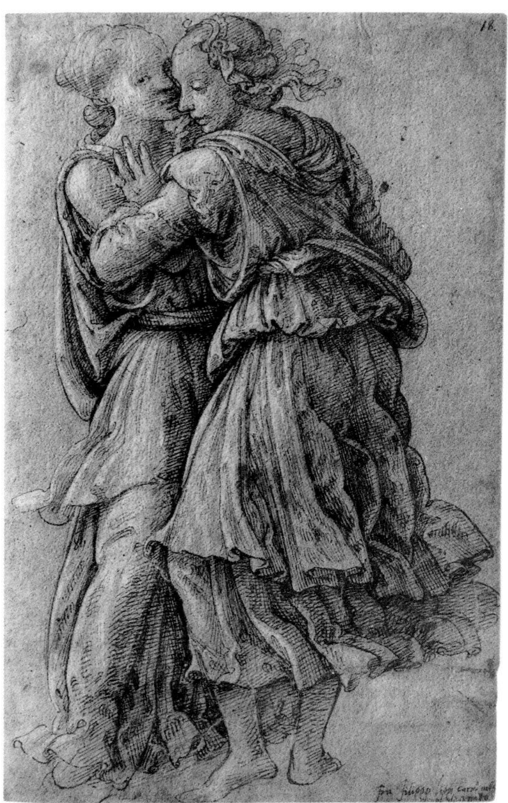

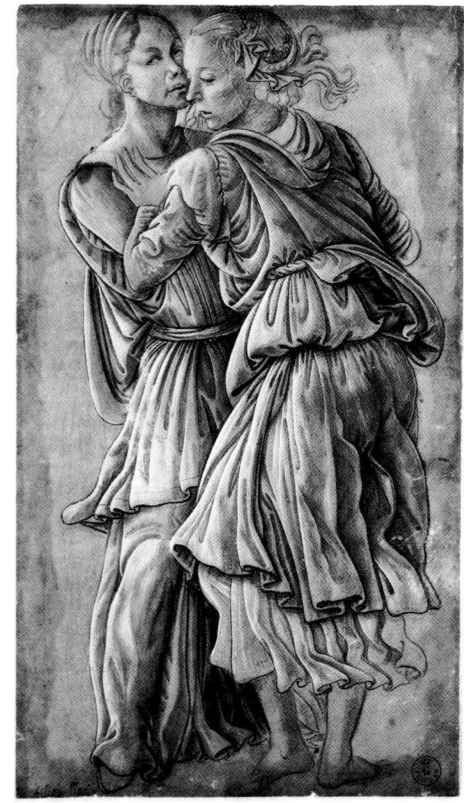

28 (*above left*)   Ghirlandiao, *Two Girls*, pen and brown ink with white heightening on blue paper, Hessisches Landesmuseum, Darmstadt

29 (*above right*)   Workshop of Filippo Lippi, *Two Girls*, silverpoint with white heightening on prepared paper, Uffizi, Florence

workshop, silverpoint lines define folds that are no longer visible in the painting itself; added white heightening and wash then build relief. Ghirlandaio's sheet, by contrast, shows nothing of these liquid additions or of the fresco's color modeling, returning instead to the outline. His cross-hatching, no less than paint or wash, establishes interior forms, but with entirely different means. Neither of the drawings was made on what Cennini called "carta lucida" – neither was literally traced from anything

– but they reveal a similar procedural and conceptual division. Together, they show that it was the outline more than anything that survived from generation to generation, like a soul that could be reembodied time and again.

6 ARREST

Drawing practices occasionally make contour into a visual echo of something that came before – a repetition from a preliminary design, a quotation from an earlier work. But drawing was always also the medium that most readily invited experimentation. Drawing had long enabled artists to move through ideas that were meant to disappear, and the falling price of paper in the late fifteenth century allowed artists a new freedom, even a new wastefulness.

Where drawing involved sketching, contour could amount to a decision, however provisional. Cennini, in explaining how one draws on parchment, describes an *ordine* – conventionally translated as "process" but literally an "order" – whereby the artist would begin by sketching with a stylus on a surface brushed with bone dust. He continues: "If, after you have drawn with the stylus, you want to better clarify the design, fix it with ink in its contours and in the necessary places."[32] Elsewhere in the treatise, Cennini advises the artist to sketch underdrawings on panels in charcoal before establishing their contours with ink.[33]

The procedure of the arrest reverses that of the trace. In the drawings after Lippi just considered, the contour anchored the freer sketching, the filling in of forms, that followed. In more inventive drawings, by contrast, contour is what brings the process of sketching to a (momentary) end. Cennini's chapters suggest that this gesture of conclusion might be announced by a change of materials, and we can find examples of this throughout the period: when Ghirlandaio produced the compositional study now in Berlin (see fig. 6) for his frescoed lunette in the Sassetti Chapel in Florence, he tested one possible arrangement of the elements in a light black chalk sketch, then established more determined contours in ink. Yet the arrest of a design through contour did not require a shift in medium. In his exploratory pen drawings, Ghirlandaio would often work out the poses of his figures with sketchy, discontinuous strokes. Only after the volumes of the body were clear in his head would he surround them with drapery, rendered with longer, more confident lines.[34]

7   DURATION

When Cennini writes of "fixing" a contour, he imagines the artist mapping a path that was initially unknown. A substantial group of late Quattrocento drawings, however, records the profiles of stable forms, available for long observation. Some, like Pollaiuolo's drawing of a nude youth in Bayonne

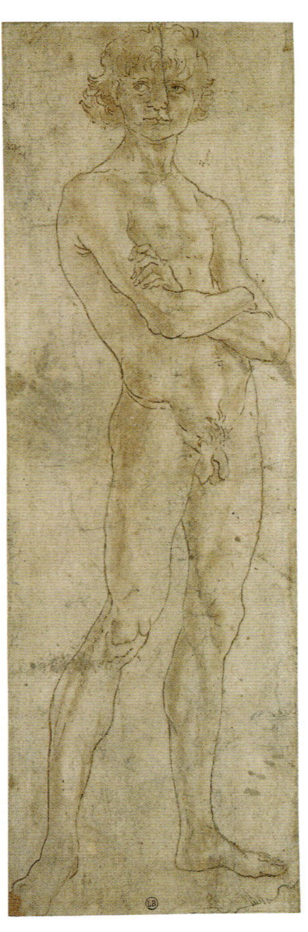

(fig. 30), seem based on posed studio assistants. Others, like Ghirlandaio's various drapery studies, were produced after dolls or arranged textiles. If the line is confident here, it is not just because it follows the course of an earlier one, done in a safer medium, although some artists did change tools in the midst of a life study exercise. A sheet by Pollaiuolo in the Louvre (fig. 31) has been called a "sculptural drawing" because it shows its author viewing a model three-dimensionally, "as though sketching the form on three faces of a block of marble before carving." In fact, Pollaiuolo never worked marble, so it is unlikely that this is what the artist had in mind. What's more, another fifteenth-century artist later copied this drawing's contours: as the copy demonstrates, a drawing showing three views did not need to come from, or work toward, a three-dimensional object.[35] Where the comparison to sculpture – or better, to the statue – may be maintained across both drawings is in their stasis. Vasari would later encourage the young painter to draw after sculptures, plaster casts, and clay models because "these objects, being motionless and insensate and steady,

30 (*above*)   Antonio del Pollaiuolo, *Nude Youth*, brown ink and wash over black chalk or charcoal on paper, Musée Bonnat, Bayonne

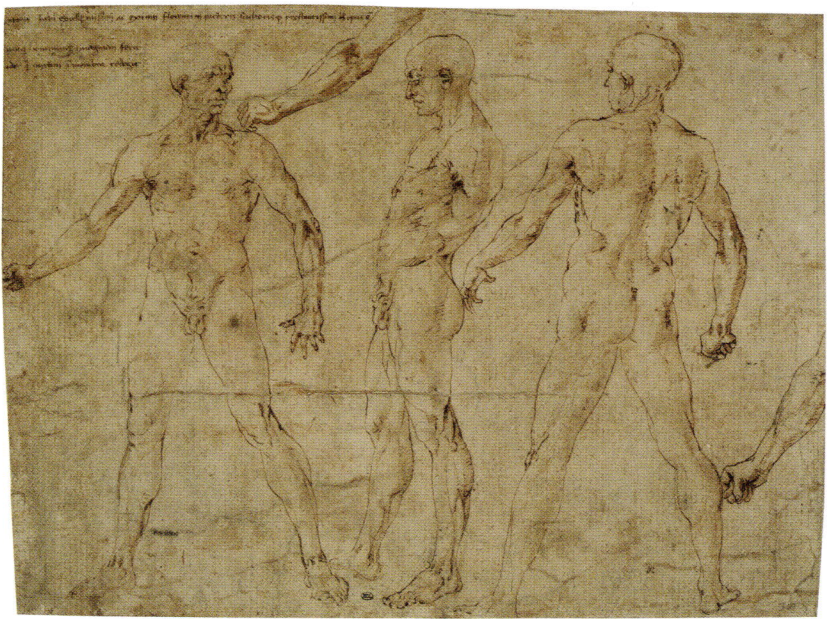

31   Antonio del Pollaiuolo, figure studies, pen and dark brown ink
with light wash on paper, Louvre, Paris

facilitate the draftsman, which does not happen with living things that
move."[36] Pollaiolo and his copyist could each have worked slowly, looking
up at his subject then down at his sheet as much as necessary. The
steadiness of the line reflects the stillness of the drawing's contents, the
motionless depicted thing.

8   BOUNDARY

The figures in the Pollaiuolo drawing look sculptural in part because they
seem to show multiple views of a single, readjusted model, in part because
the drawn contours themselves look impermeable. Each figure is abutted
by a neighboring hand that does not appear to be able to cross its line.
Yet, further reflection on just what it is that we are seeing here may change
our impression of the effect. The disposition of the figures, and especially

their placement next to the two fragmentary arms, contradicts any sense of bodies occupying a shared space. If the contours are inviolable, this is not because they are hard surfaces but because they are uncrossable borders.

Such a conception of contours – as features of the plane rather than as evocations of a third dimension – was essential to painters. When making gold-ground panels, for example, the artist would score essential contours into the surface. Cennini devotes an entire short chapter to explaining "How you should indicate the outlines of the figures when you are going to make a gold ground": the artist, he writes there, should first sketch his drawing on the prepared panel, then use a needle to "engrave the outlines of the figure which come against the background that you are going to cover with gold."[37] A later chapter clarifies that such incisions formed a kind of moat around the region where the adhesive bole was to be applied: the point was to ensure that the gold would not run into the area that was to be painted; any gold that passed the line would have to be scraped away, or the paint would not adhere.[38] The technique, though old, was still in use in the Ghirlandaio workshop. Incisions at the edges of the gilding are easily visible both in the *Virgin and Child* in Washington (fig. 32) and the gilded *Coronation of the Virgin* (1486) in Narni.[39]

By the time the painter of a gold-gound panel first picked up his brush, the broadest elements of his design would already have been outlined. This was just the beginning, though. A painter like Ghirlandaio still worked largely in tempera. Typically, he would take up only a single hue at a time, from a palette on which the various tones of that hue had been arranged from dark to light. Even in panels like the San Giusto altarpiece (fig. 33), which did not involve extensive gilding, Ghirlandaio would have looked at what he was making as a patterned surface, with the contour establishing the territory to be covered by a given palette; only after the artist had completed work with one color would he move on to the next.[40] In the San Giusto painting, a dark red line separates the sleeve of the Virgin's right forearm from the adjacent green field that represents the inside of her cloak. Further down and to the left, a dark yellow line demarcates the yellow of Saint Michael's boot. The purpose of such contours was to

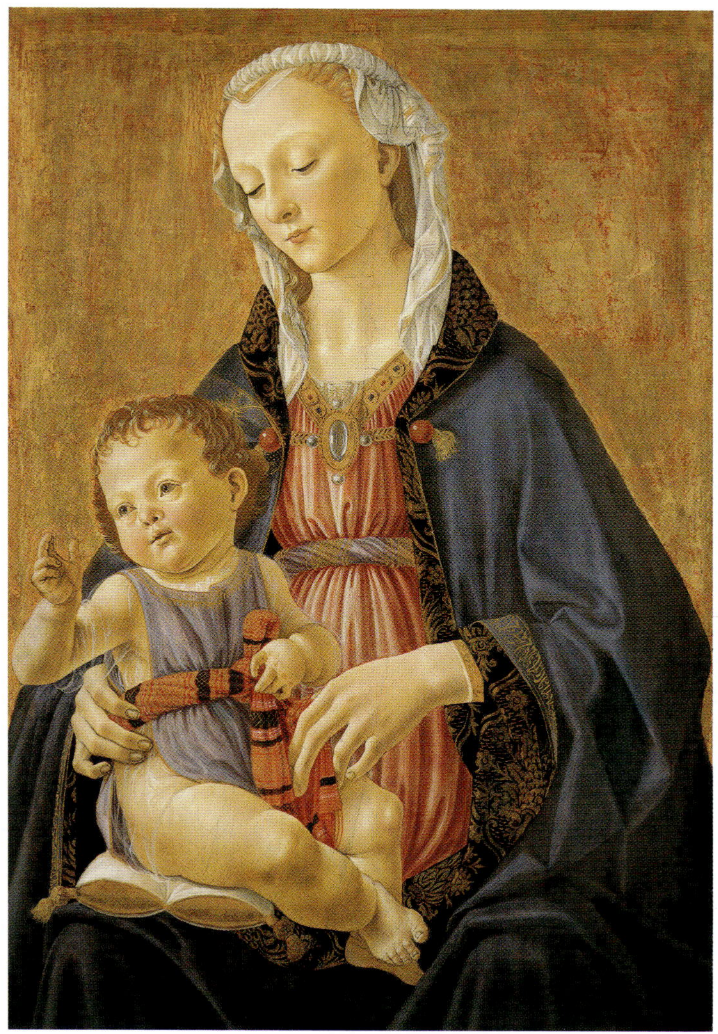

32   Ghirlandaio, *Virgin and Child*, tempera and gilding on panel
transferred to hardboard, National Gallery of Art, Washington

establish an area to be "filled in" with modeling. If these contours can still
be read as edges, they are edges not of three-dimensional forms but of flat
tonal planes; the contours generate an effect akin to the marquetry images
that Ghirlandaio also designed.[41] These contours eliminate depth.

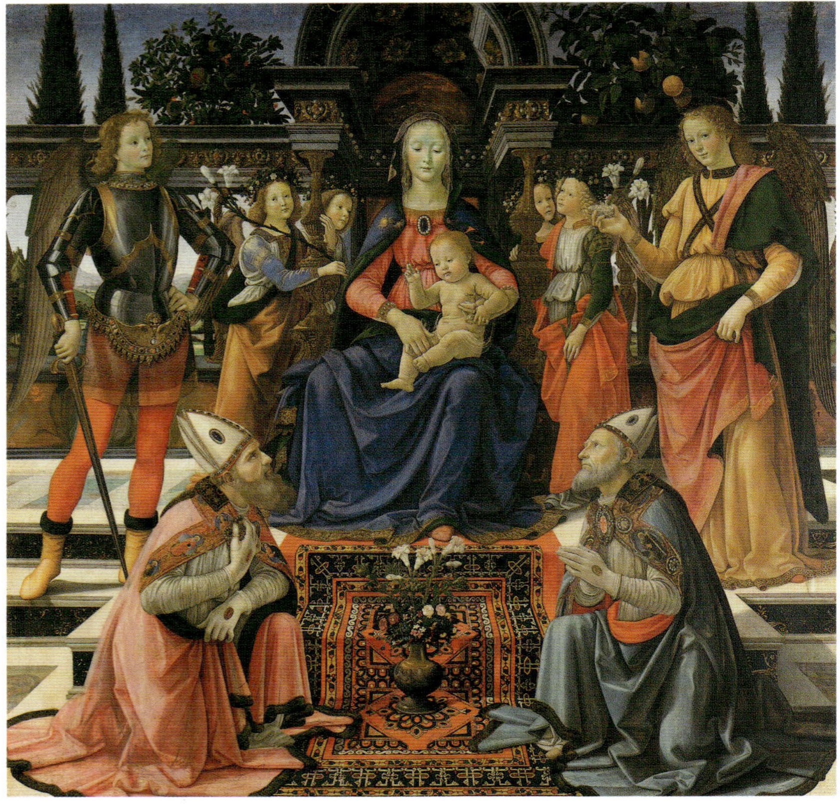

33   Ghirlandaio, San Giusto altarpiece, tempera and gilding on panel,
Uffizi, Florence

9   INTERVAL

Along the edges of figures in late fifteenth-century frescoes, we find other
physical borders. Fresco painters, too, needed to delimit zones in
preparation for gilding, as Cennini indicates when discussing the depiction
of haloes in chapter 101 of the *Libro*. But frescoes bear additional lines
from the discontinuous processes by which they had to be carried out.
Whereas panel painters could work with a single color on multiple zones
of the prepared surface, allowing the image to emerge mosaic-like over
time, frescoists had to move steadily across and down the wall, determining
in advance just how much wet plaster to add at the beginning of each

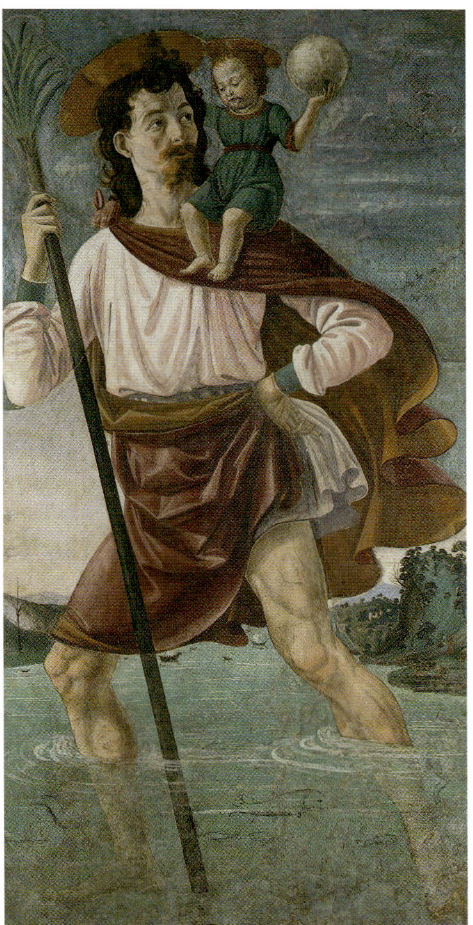

34   Ghirlandaio, *St. Christopher*, detached fresco,
Metropolitan Museum of Art, New York

day. Often it made sense to draw the line along a figure, both because each figure required one or two days' work and because the edges of figures, with their simply colored draperies, provided natural divisions of the picture surface. Once a day's work was complete, the painter or one of his assistants would physically cut away the excess plaster, following the path of the painting itself, so that new plaster could be added there the next day. In a fresco like Ghirlandaio's *Saint Christopher* (fig. 34), the figure's lower right arm and outer left thigh each have a double contour, painted and incised.[42] At these points, the edges of the figure mark units of time.

★   ★   ★

This no doubt incomplete list of possibilities moves between registers: some contours are depictions, others point to the practicalities of painting as such. An edge can generate the illusion of depth; a boundary can keep us on the surface. What is more, it is not at all clear which register would most have attracted the Quattrocento eye. In *Della pittura*, immediately after invoking Parrhasius's innovations, Alberti wrote that "circumscription is nothing other than the drawing of the edge, and where this is done with too apparent a line, it will not look like the limit of a [depicted] surface but rather like a crack [in the painting itself]."[43] Alberti worried that a motif on which painters relied to establish a three-dimensional illusion could also be the very thing that undermined it. At a more banal level, he suggested that it was not always easy to determine whether one was seeing a painted line or a break in the paint.

A more positive formulation of the same point would be that the different registers, or qualities, of the painted contour were not mutually exclusive.[44] Nor should we expect painters to have made contours as illustrations of any particular theory. A painter could draw a contour to establish a three-dimensional form, reinforce it because he found the line as such to be particularly beautiful, follow this with an incision so as to lay gold beyond its border, then paint a line of color beside that groove so as to clarify the field to be filled. The viewer, dwelling on a figure's edge, might admire the painter's ability to generate volumes out of a spaceless reflection, even while appreciating the way that the gold and the intense tempera hues framed the line, making the contour no less than the larger illusion a display of the painter's skill.

Whatever their appearance, though, contours divided the painting rather than unifying it. And in doing this, they tended especially to make the figure, more than composition, the unit of art. When Pliny writes of Parrhasius, his topic is what Parrhasius did with "the extremities of bodies" (*le extremita de corpi*). The shadow that Butades's daughter outlines is of a person. Cennini's instructions for tracing focus on the "figure or true design" that the apprentice wishes to study, just as his chapter on gilding comprises instructions for "how you should indicate the outlines of the figures." It may not be surprising, then, that when Leonardo used the term *figura*, it sometimes seems to be nothing other than a synonym for "contour."[45]

Sfumatura as Polemic

To see the roles of contour in Quattrocento painting – an armature of practice, a condition of depiction, an inheritance from a treasured past, a symbol – is to change our sense of what Leonardo was up against.

Leonardo seems to have had a distaste for the "entereza" that viewers admired in Michelangelo. In the Codex Atlanticus, he wrote that the painter should "not regard the members of the figures in narratives as many do, when, making their figures whole [*per fare le figure intere*], they ruin their compositions."[46] The use of *sfumatura* was one way in which Leonardo avoided this alleged fault.

Much good writing in recent years has sought to describe just what Leonardo's *sfumato* represented, or meant. One classic study characterized it essentially as an art that hides art, driven by the belief that "the trace of the artist's 'hand' in the work was an index of his failure to accomplish the goals of naturalism."[47] *Sfumato* was "a technique designed to leave no traces," the replication of an effect that nature itself created. The more recent literature has paid closer attention to Leonardo's writings on the nature of seeing, one scholar emphasizing the artist's fascination with the swimming of forms seen at a distance, another Leonardo's conception of the blurring of forms seen in movement by a moving eye.[48]

What these accounts have in common is an idea of what *sfumato* oriented itself against – contour.[49] Some passages in Leonardo's notebooks reflect on the inability of the eye to see contours in nature. Others seem to concern perception not in space but in time. All of this aligns with ideas that Renaissance writers from Alberti to Bronzino were also articulating. Still, to pair *sfumato* with vision and contour with artifice distorts a more complicated reality. After all, it would be possible to "naturalize" contour, taking the contour to register the fact that the things we encounter do have surfaces and edges; objects do not simply merge into the world around them.[50] Conversely, *sfumato* paintings can be highly artificial. To achieve his *sfumato*, Leonardo in fact relied precisely on the trace of the artist's hand, smudging pigment with his brush and even with his fingers.[51] The prints he left on paintings are visible even to the naked eye. Just taken as representations, moreover, *sfumato* paintings sacrificed the colors of nature, denying that there are ever clear, dry, sunny days. Among the reasons why Leonardo favored *sfumato* must have been that misty scenes suited the new oil medium, with its translucent glazes laid one atop the other, and that he simply liked the way *sfumato* looked: when he recommended that the battle painter pay attention to smoke and dust, after all, he was not primarily reflecting on the nature of perception, but showing his interest in a distinctive subject matter. In the end, *sfumato* and contour are simply two competing pictorial systems, each with its own values: contingency versus perfection, interiority versus apprehensibility. Seeing them this way has the attraction of letting us follow a messier history, in which artists from Sofonisba Anguissola to Orazio Gentileschi to Canaletto to Boucher to Ingres did not embrace *sfumato*: *sfumato* was not necessarily the direction of progressive painting; it was not inherently modern.[52]

Nor was Leonardo's *sfumato* simply a mode of naturalism; it was a maneuver or set of maneuvers against another kind of painting. Accounts of *sfumatura* tend to exalt Leonardo, imagining him alone in the studio, laboratory, or field, painting in a way that depended on nothing more than his own direct experience. But *sfumato* is a past participle form of the verb *sfumare*; the very term recalls an act that was done *to* an object.[53] If *sfumato* is the blurring or smudging or enshadowing of something already made, it becomes a kind of twin to circumscription, the line drawn around an already established, even an already painted, form.[54] The history of *sfumato* was agonistic, and its contest was played out not only between artists who favored different techniques but also within individual works.[55]

As a motif, *sfumato* can seem a presence, a representation of cloud or shadow or smoke; as a practice, though, it is also an absence, or the pursuit of an absence, an attempt to negate the contours that had in various ways been fundamental to Quattrocento painting. The fact that it was neither possible nor desirable to eliminate contour entirely – Leonardo himself continued to compose with pen, the most linear medium – oriented *sfumato* toward an unreachable goal. What it mostly did was to disguise or qualify contours the painter had established, the lines he initially made on the panel or canvas.

One means of doing this was to absorb the contour into another form. Leonardo tended to set figures against a dark background (fig. 35), with the idea that they would project forward in relief.[56] Yet these backgrounds frequently have the effect not only of establishing a light–dark contrast but also of making it difficult to see the contour line, obscuring it into the surrounding gloom. What is more, Leonardo used the technique both for backgrounds and for interior modeling, notably in his portraits, where a nostril or a chin casts a shadow on the flesh below (see fig. 18).

Another means of working against contour was to shade toward an edge, such that the contour became the darkest version of a hue that continued but faded out beyond it. We see this, again in the portraits, when we look just inside the contour that establishes the shape of the face, where a grainy dry paint gives the effect of a line that has slightly bled, losing its clarity or integrity. Elsewhere – the sides of the nose, for example – a softer glaze could simply replace contour altogether. This is a technique that Leonardo used more and more extensively in his late career: the Virgin and Child in the late panel now in the Louvre have no jaw line at all (fig. 36). It also became a rule in Leonardo's *Treatise*: "Do not make definite or finite the shadows that you can distinguish [only] with difficulty and the edges of which you cannot recognize."[57]

Finally, Leonardo undermined contour in his representation of veils. In the late Louvre panel, some of the clearest contour lines run along the sleeves of Saint Anne's drapery. Yet the panel also gives the sense that just inside these contours, we see through the surface they bound, into the distance. Inside her left forearm, a *pentimento* is visible. But are the little

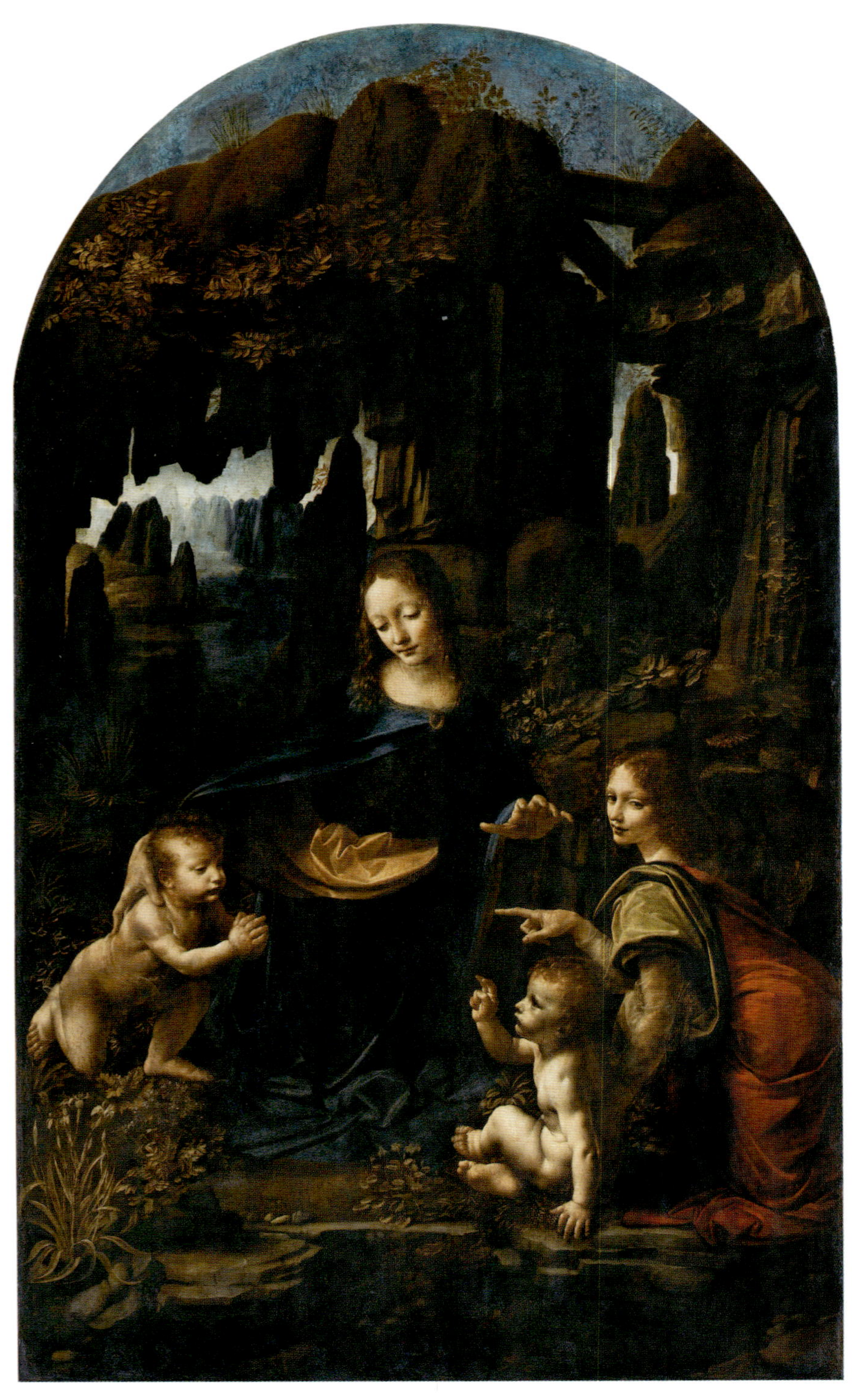

35 Leonardo, *Madonna of the Rocks*, oil on panel, Louvre, Paris

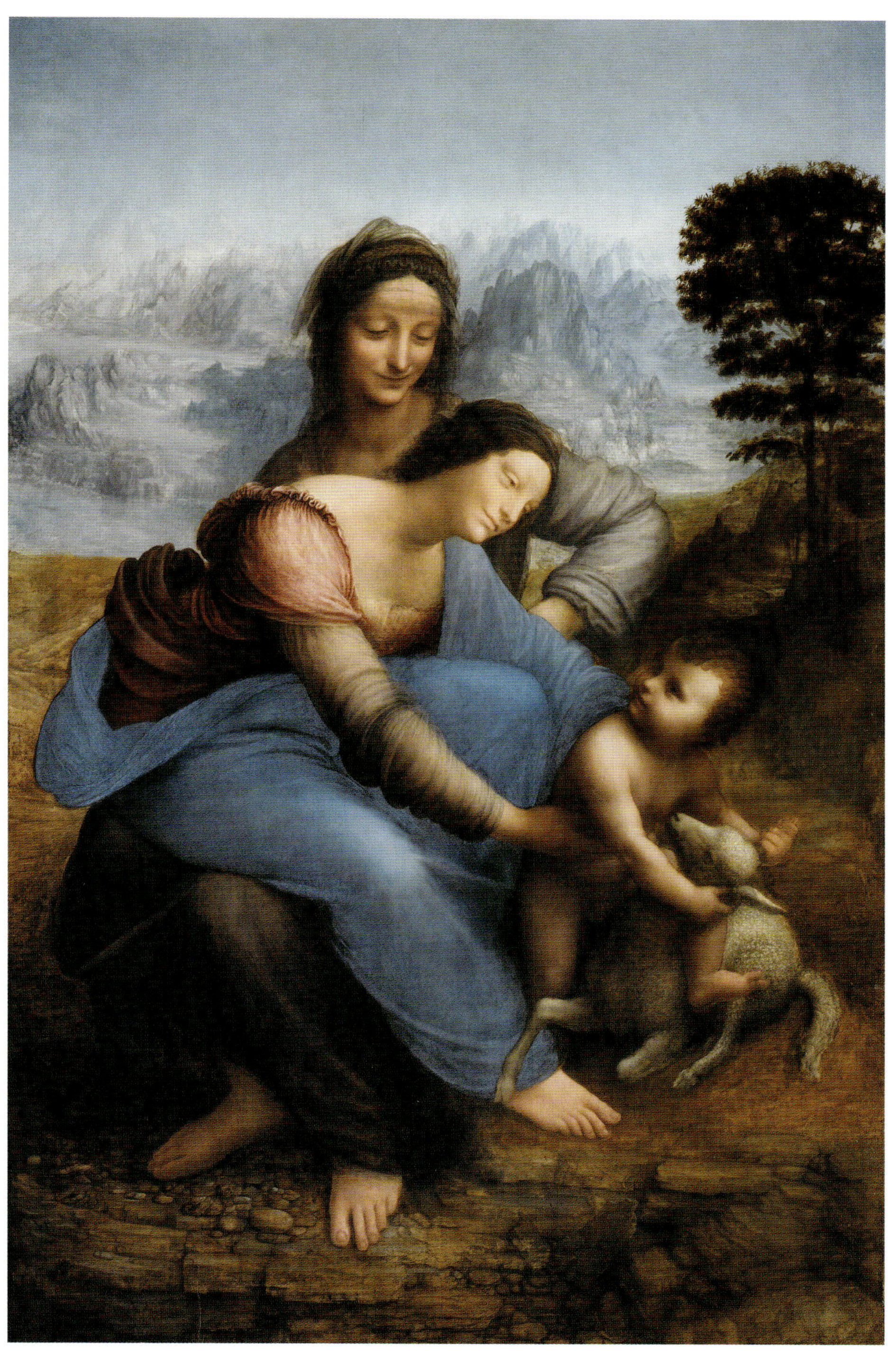

36   Leonardo, *Virgin, Child, and St. Anne*, oil on panel, Louvre, Paris

loops of paint at the point where the arm joins the torso also *pentimenti* or are they folds of semi-transparent fabric? In the veil around the Virgin's head, the contour lines do not quite contain the brown paint that represents her hair, as though they are not really contour lines at all. Some of this may be a matter of the painting's state rather than an indication of Leonardo's ultimate intentions, though we see him already using the veil to compromise contour in the *Mona Lisa*, where a line that at first seems to define the extent of her head then tapers and splits and peters out, ultimately denying that it was a contour after all.

Superfluous Contours

Michelangelo's first paintings – at least, the earliest surviving paintings whose attribution has won a strong scholarly consensus – date from the period when Leonardo's attack on contour was taking its most forceful form. In Florence that attack was remarkably successful, winning over the likes of Raphael, Fra Bartolomeo, and Andrea del Sarto, who would become the most attractive local advocate for *sfumato* paintings in the decades to follow. That makes Michelangelo's manner, with its sharp rejection of the practice, look as adversarial as Leonardo's.

It might also look conservative, a retrenchment in the techniques he had learned in the Ghirlandaio shop. Yet Michelangelo's approach to contour was anything but an endorsement of Quattrocento methods. Alberti may have described circumscription as the first part of painting but, as we have seen, that writer also thought that the visibility of the contour line compromised the painter's illusion.

In the surviving drawings for the Cascina project (figs. 37–39), by contrast, Michelangelo has gone over and over the contours, doing so after the pose of the body had been clearly established. In a figure study now in the British Museum, he used a pen to redraw his outlines. In the two sheets now in Haarlem, he shifted from a lighter to a darker chalk [58] Athough he modeled interior forms with the cross-hatching technique that Ghirlandaio had pioneered, the contours are so strong as to counteract

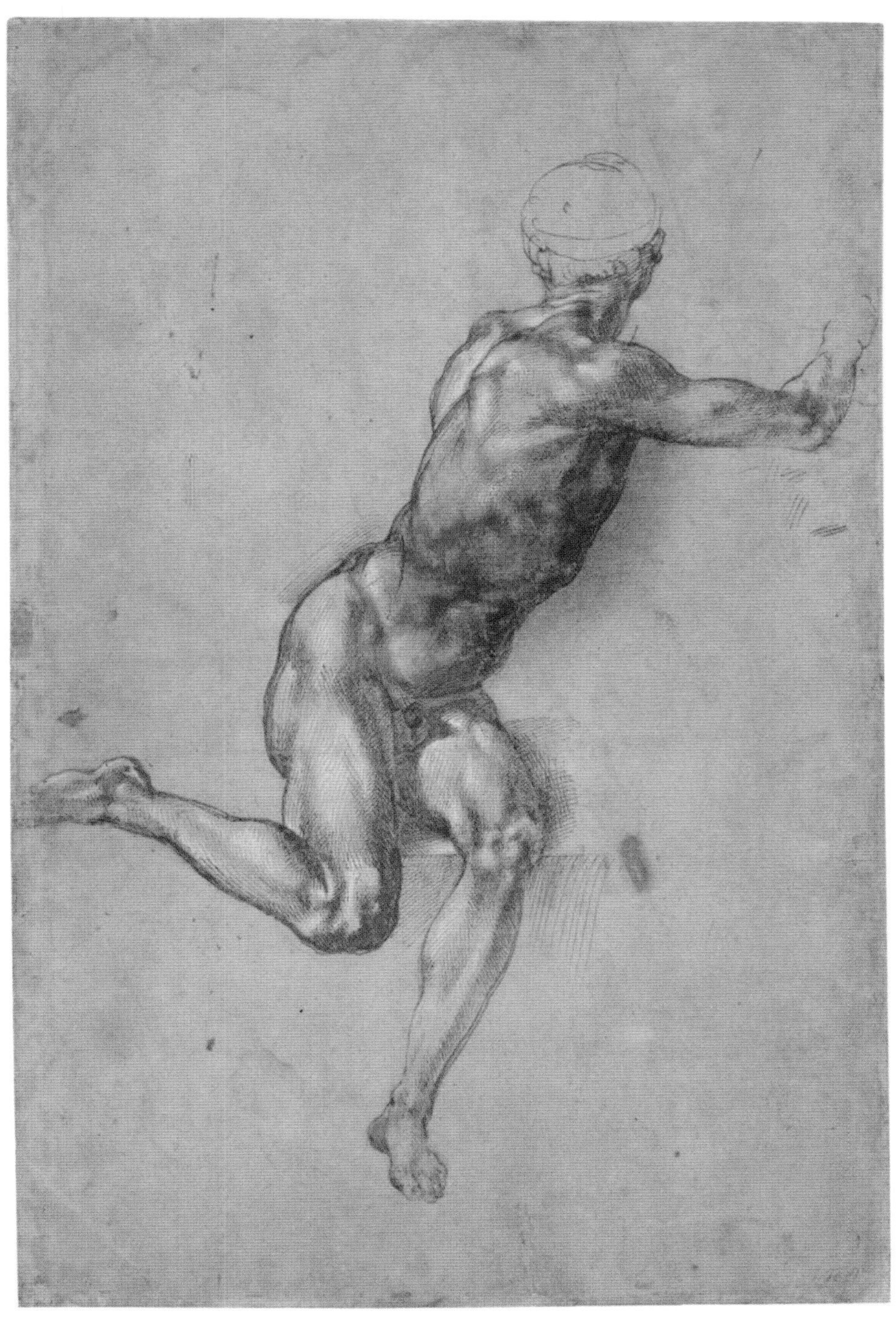

37   Michelangelo, figure study for the *Battle of Cascina*,
pen and ink with grey and brown wash and white heightening over lead point
and stylus on paper, British Museum, London

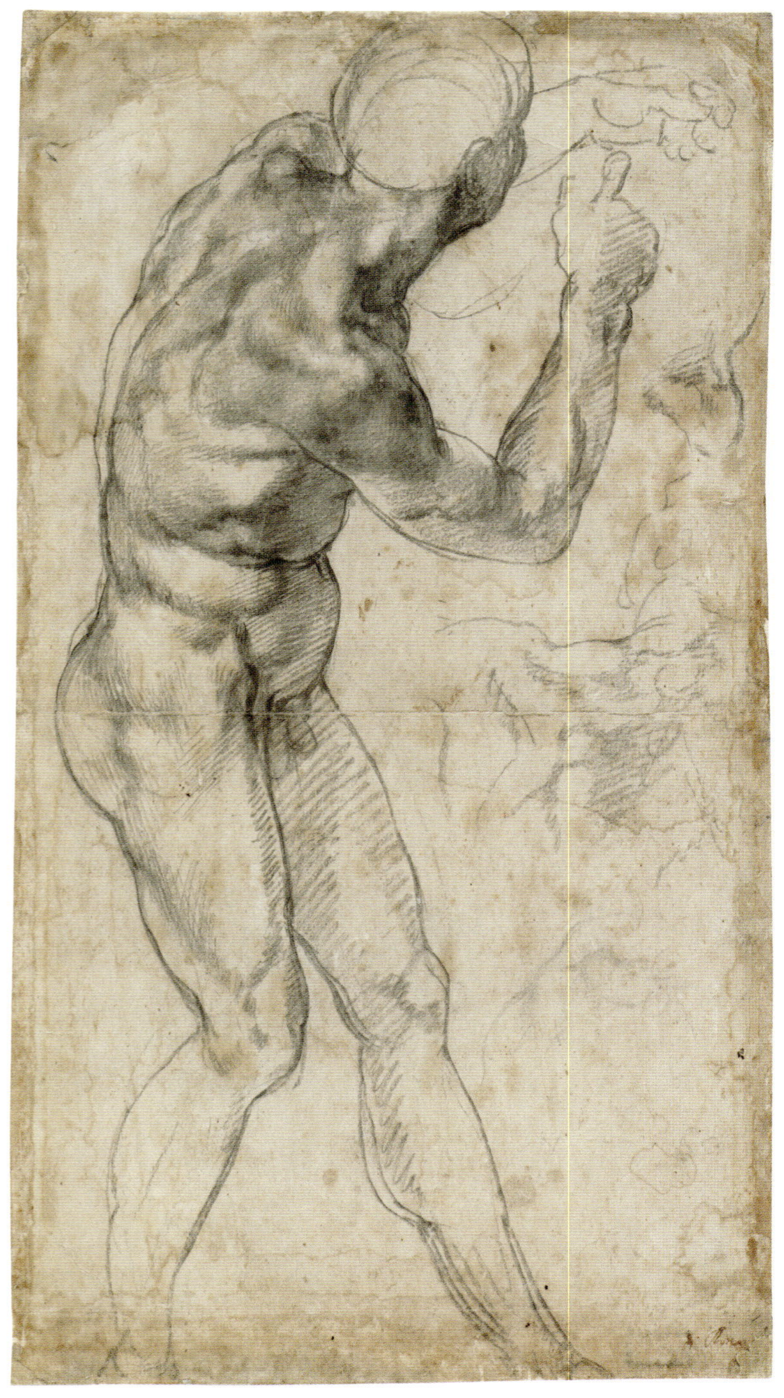

38   Michelangelo, figure study for the *Battle of Cascina*,
black chalk with white heightening on paper, Teylers Museum, Haarlem

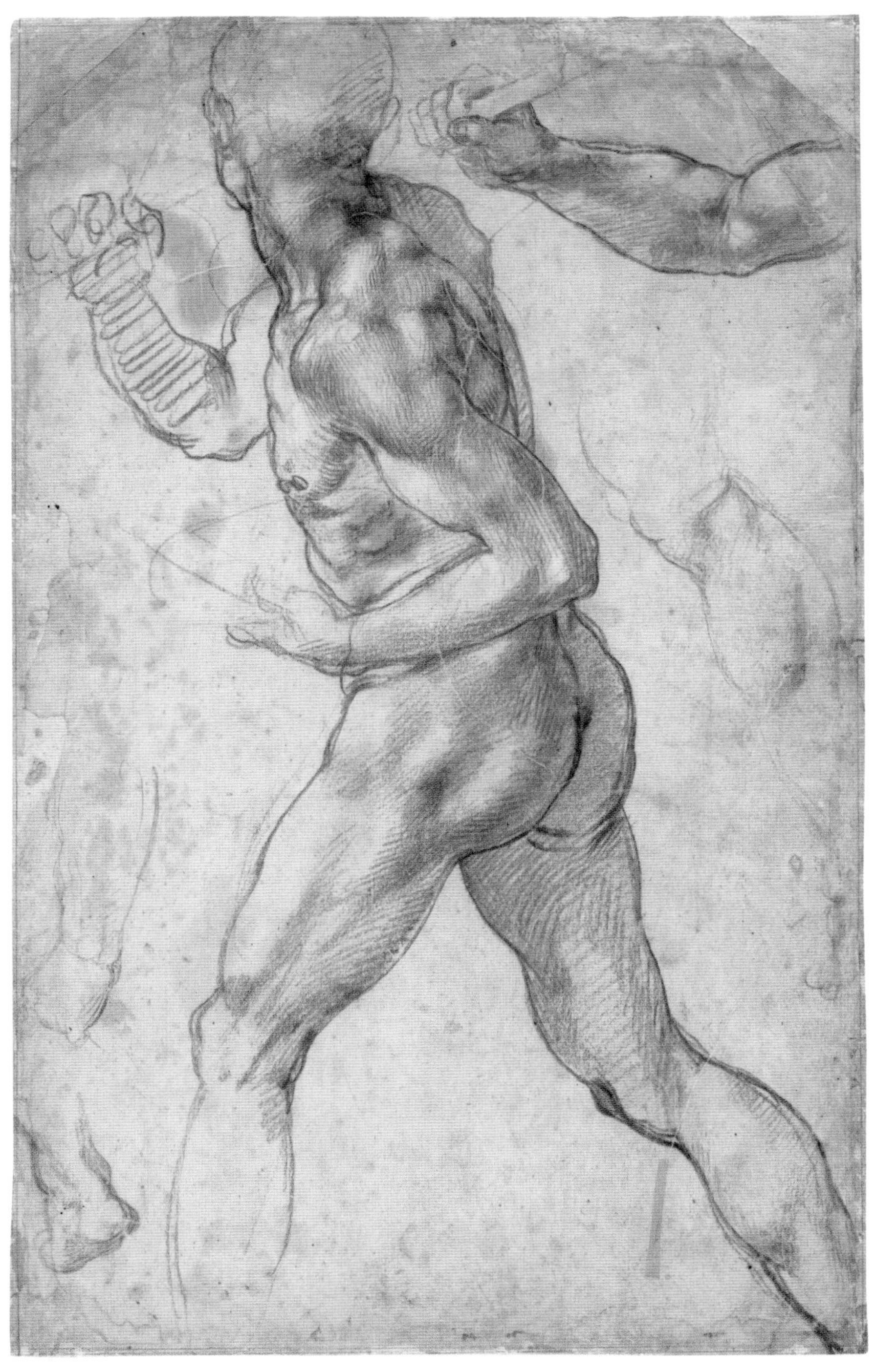

39 Michelangelo, figure study for the *Battle of Cascina*,
black chalk with white heightening on paper, Teylers Museum, Haarlem

that modeling, reflattening the figure even as it emerges into relief. Nor is there any reason to believe that those contours are just a function of drawing, that Michelangelo would have abandoned such devices in the painting he was ostensibly planning. The Doni Tondo, too, has hard, dark outlines. There, in fact, the forms that surround the bodies transform themselves from a means of picture making into a motif. The figures' costumes include a variety of curious bands and straps: a girdle clenches the pink cloth beneath the Virgin's breasts; a strap marks the connection between her torso and her right arm; her hair, like that of her son, is controlled by a kind of diadem. These are motifs that interested Michelangelo enough for him to carry them from work to work: the bands in the Doni Tondo are comparable to the cloth straps that wrap Christ and his bearers in the unfinished 1500–01 *Entombment* (fig. 40) and the sling that runs around the torso of his *David*. The skin-tight armor that the Cascina soldiers would have worn, not to mention the narrative that has them putting that armor on, would have drawn attention in that painting, too, to a group of forms that follow the body's contours so closely as to become nearly coterminous with them.

Michelangelo's approach to figural drawing remained remarkably consistent over the decades.[59] It may not be unreasonable, then, to look at Michelangelo's preparatory drawings for the *Cascina* in conjunction with his own most famous statement on contour, which appears in a poem he later addressed to his friend Vittoria Colonna. Published with a commentary by Benedetto Varchi, the first stanza took on a life of its own, coming to represent nothing less than Michelangelo's theory of art:

> Non ha l'ottimo artista alcun concetto
> c'un marmo solo in sé non circonscriva
> col suo superchio, e solo a quello arriva
> la man che ubbidisce all'intelletto.

(The greatest artist does not have any concept that a single piece of marble does not circumscribe within its superfluity, and only a hand that obeys the intellect attains this.)[60]

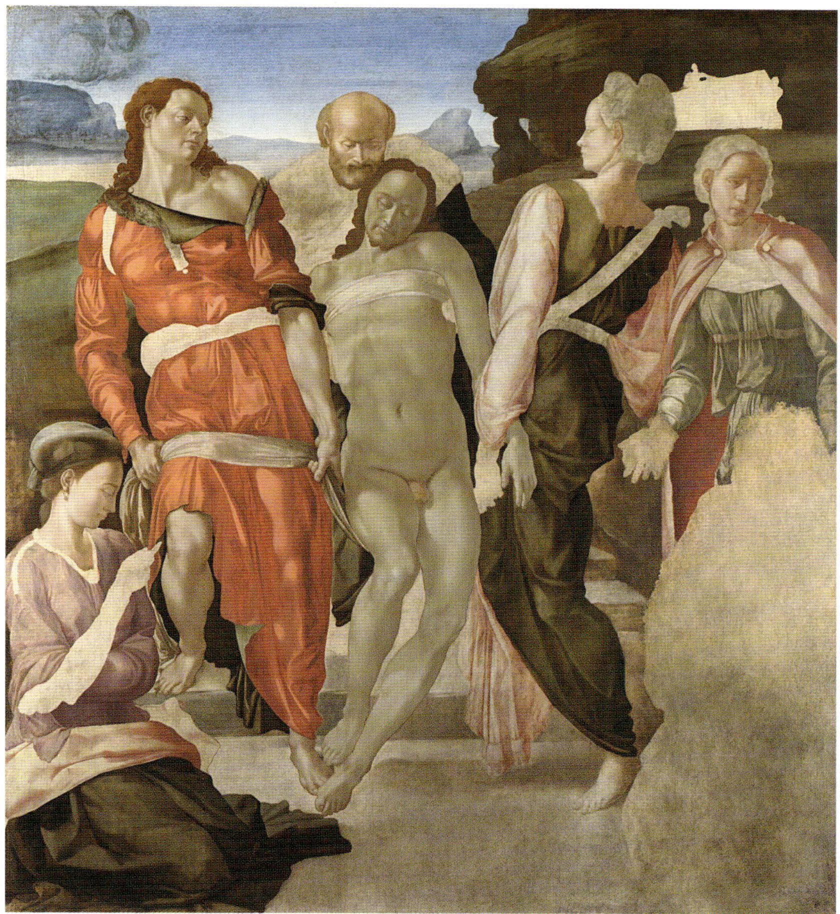

40   Michelangelo, *Entombment*, oil on panel, National Gallery, London

Most scholars writing today, in our age of Conceptual Art, have focused
on the dynamic relationship that the poem envisioned between the idea
in the artist's head and the hard, intractable thing before him. What merits
equal attention, however, is the other key term in the poem's opening
lines, one emphasized, like *concetto*, through end rhyme: "The greatest artist
does not have any concept," Michelangelo writes, "that a single piece of
marble does not *circumscribe*."

Although the poem ostensibly concerns sculpture, the language of
circumscription belonged more to the literature of painting and drawing,

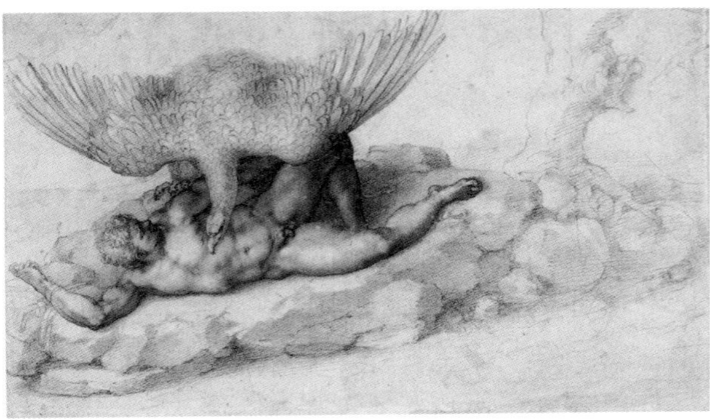

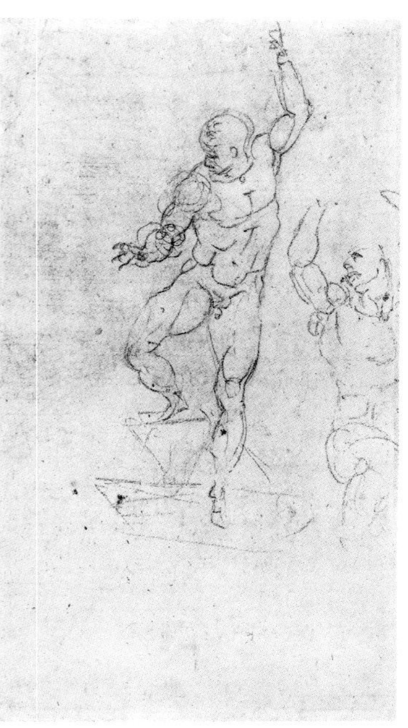

41 (*above*)   Michelangelo, *Tityus*, black chalk on paper,
Royal Collection, Windsor

42 (*right*)   Michelangelo, *Resurrected Christ*, black chalk on
paper, Royal Collection, Windsor

and the artist regularly reinforced the outlines of his figures on paper. A
telling example from the period leading up to the years when the poem
was written is Michelangelo's *Resurrected Christ* (fig. 42), which the artist
generated by tracing the body of *Tityus* on the other side of the sheet
(fig. 41). This form, which is constituted almost exclusively by its
circumscription, makes the contours of the *Tityus* – who is bound to his
rock not with chains but with thin bands – all the more conspicuous, and
copyists of the drawing would only strengthen them.[61] Michelangelo
employed such effects throughout his career and they are notably pronounced in the drawings from the period of the *Cascina*.[62]

It is also sometimes said that Michelangelo's drawings manifest a
specifically sculptural interest, but his poem, at least, could be read in just
the opposite way, treating sculpture in terms of drawing. The combined
evidence, moreover, points to one way in which Michelangelo differed
profoundly from Leonardo: whereas Leonardo repeatedly set out to define
the limits between various arts, Michelangelo pursued a single set of

concerns across media. It seems to have been around 1505–6, shortly after Michelangelo created the strongly outlined forms of the *Cascina* drawings and the *Doni Tondo*, that he first conceived the sequence of prisoners or slaves for the Julius tomb. In the marbles he eventually carved, the band that surrounds an already constituted figure would become an explicit and unmistakable part of the work's subject (fig. 43). Indeed, what is most remarkable in Michelangelo's famous sonnet, where his work in painting, sculpture, and drawing are concerned, is the notion that circumscription lay just beyond the figure, as a kind of excess. Such an idea is already latent in some of the Quattrocento conceptions of outline that have been considered here: the cut that marked the end of a *giornata*, for example, fell by necessity outside the painted figure, as did the incision that the gilder used. With Michelangelo, though, the contour that enters the picture, the contour that becomes a motif, is something different.

Michelangelo long associated the theme of binding visually with force. In subjects like the *Slaves* or the *Tityus*, an element wrapping a highly muscled figure prevents him from moving. But in a number of Michelangelo's poems, the idea he pursues is not merely that art can show force, but that art is force: binding and unbinding are what art does. One example:

> Sì come per levar, donna, si pone
> in pietra alpestra e dura
> una viva figura,
> che là più cresce u' più la pietra scema;
> tal alcun' opre buone,
> per l'alma che pur trema,
> cela il superchio della propria carne
> co' l'inculta sua cruda e dura scorza.
> Tu pur dalle mie streme
> parti puo' sol levarne,
> ch'in me non è voler né forza.

(Just as it is by removing, lady, that one places in hard and alpine stone a living figure, which grows more where the stone diminishes, so the superfluity of one's own flesh, with its coarse, rough, hard bark, hides some good works in the soul, which trembles under this burden. You alone can so remove my extreme parts, for in me there is neither will nor force.)[63]

The poem turns on the comparison between acting on a person and making a sculpture. Yet the implied artist does not exactly shape anything; rather, he reveals what sounds like an already conceived and formed figure by stripping what surrounds it, and in this way comes to resemble the beloved or spiritual guide who excavates the forceless lover's own soul.

Michelangelo could not have made this kind of comparison had he not been familiar with the conventions of Petrarchan poetry. Yet the ideas he expresses here with knowing poetic form – that the artist's object is the figure, that that figure is bound, that the artist's labor is a kind of force – are not themselves inherently poetic. In the course of comparing painting and music, Leonardo at one point wrote that music consists of "harmonic moments," which are "constrained to be born and to die"; these moments, he continued, "encompass the proportionality of the members, and out of this harmony is composed, just as the contour line encompasses the members, out of which human beauty is generated."[64] The remark is dense, even opaque, and there is little agreement in the specialist literature even about the precise meaning of Leonardo's words.[65] What is safe to say, though, is that Leonardo, in seeking a musical analogy for the contour line that encompasses the members of the body, located it in something "constrained." The contour line does not merely define; it restricts.[66] When Michelangelo's contour line metamorphosed from the dark chalk that outlines the Cascina soldier into the cloth strips that wrap the Doni Virgin into the binds that immobilize the Julius prisoners, his art was making visible a set of connections that others, too, had intuited.

Leonardo may have regarded *sfumato* as a way of rendering movement, but this was also a claim for contour, its opposite, both because the contour suggested the repositioning of the body and because the contour line lured the eye along its length. In the very year that Michelangelo received the Cascina commission, Pomponius Gauricus had published a text in Florence exhorting artists "to examine nature diligently, considering her elegant and

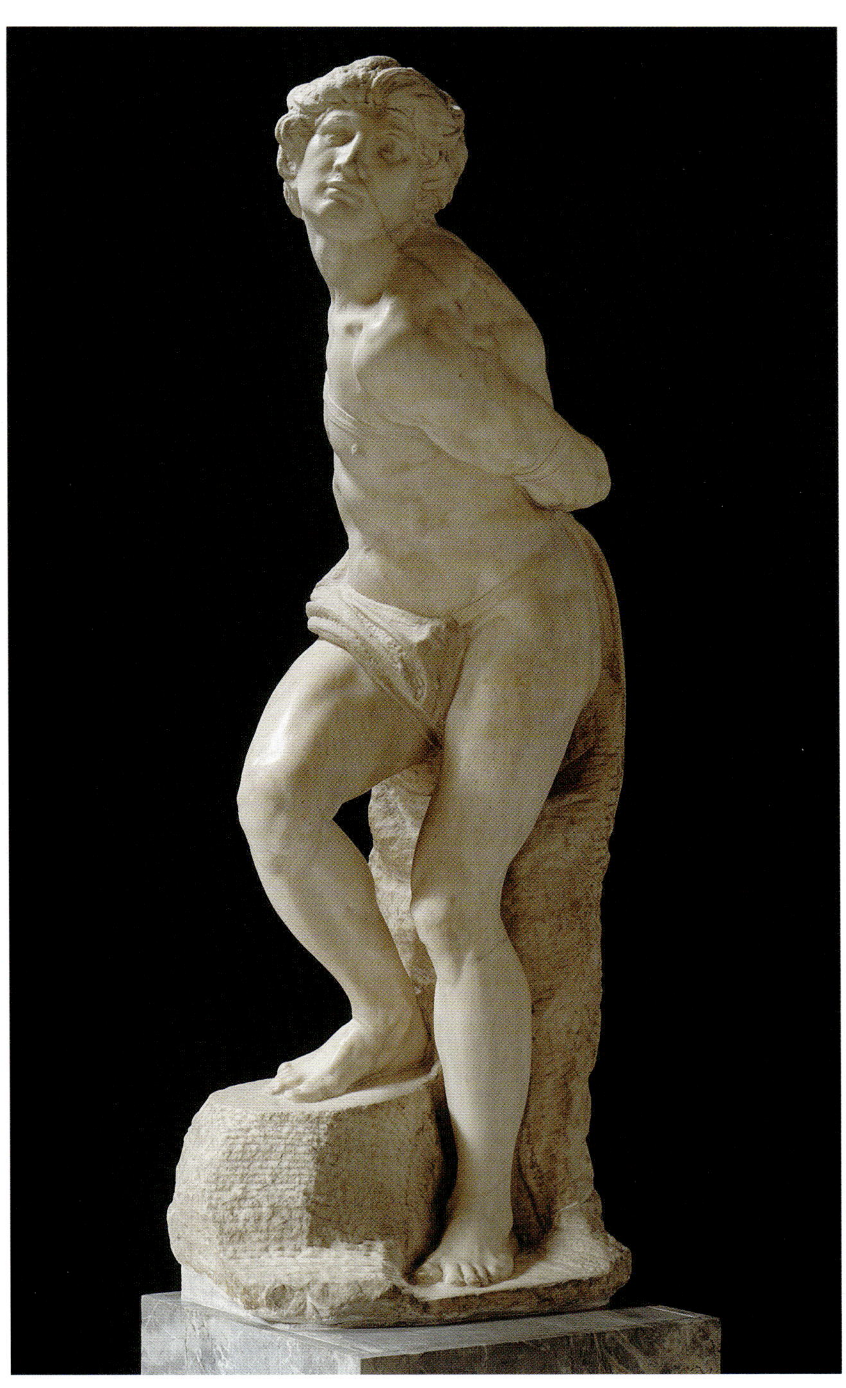

43   Michelangelo, *Rebellious Slave*, marble, Louvre, Paris

beautiful bodies, when they make their circumscription of the body, and to animate those things with gesture and harmony."[67] In the *Cascina*, Michelangelo set out to show the reversibility of this idea. The contour could animate but it could also fix the figure, paralyzing it into a pose.

The Autonomous Figure

Such an idea of binding and unbinding would only work for the artist who understood his vehicle to be the depicted figure. The history of the Julius tomb suggests that, by the second decade of the sixteenth century, Michelangelo was thinking along just such lines: the slaves initially conceived for the bottom story of the monument became independent works, and the bands that circumscribed them came to look like declarations of their severance from a larger whole. If the *Cascina* cartoon, for its part, has a mythical place in the history of Renaissance art, that is in no small part for its crystallization of the idea that it was figures, not compositions, that ambitious artists made.

The dismantling of the *Cascina* cartoon into its constituent figures is central to its history. Vasari's 1550 *Life* of Michelangelo reports that the cartoon was torn up by the artists who studied it in the Medici Palace, and Benedetto Varchi reports, similarly, that the "fame of this most marvelous cartoon . . . was spread throughout Italy, as, after many years, was the cartoon itself," by the artists who had come to Florence to study it.[68] This happened, Vasari initially states, during an illness of Giuliano de' Medici, which would place the event in 1516.[69] In his later, revised version of the *Lives*, however, Vasari changed his story, blaming the sculptor Baccio Bandinelli alone for the act of destruction and moving up the date: during the tumult that accompanied the expulsion of Piero Soderini in 1512, Bandinelli sneaked into the Medici Palace and tore the cartoon into pieces. Vasari then went on to list the motives that various people familiar with the incident had ascribed to Bandinelli, among them "the affection he had for Leonardo da Vinci, whose reputation had been diminished by Michelangelo's cartoon." It is impossible to know which of Vasari's stories, if either, is true. What can be documented, though, is that for most of the

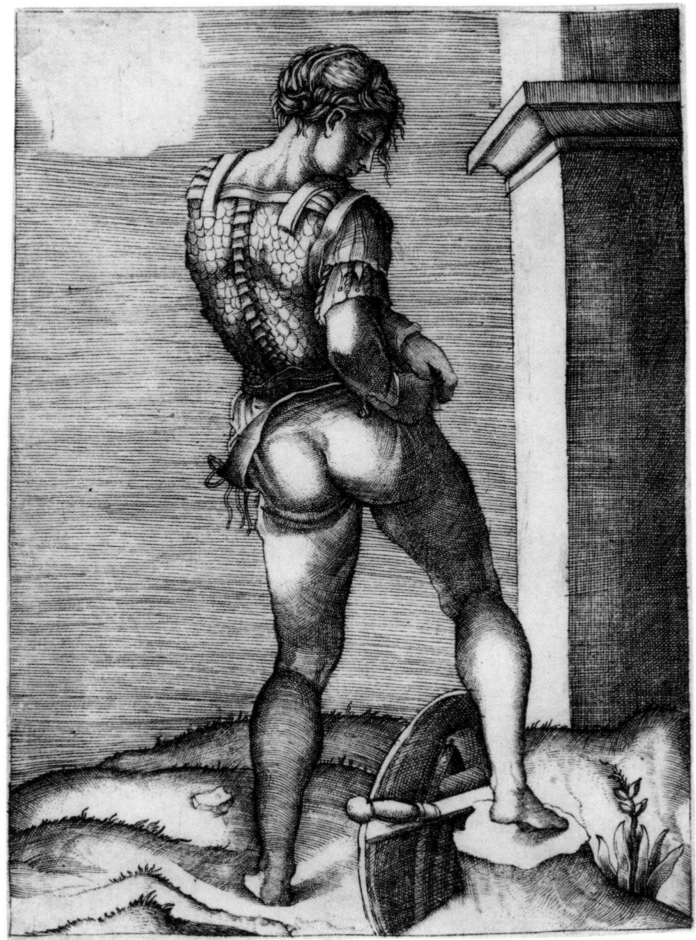

44   Marcantonio Raimondi, after Michelangelo, *Man Pulling on Breeches*, engraving

sixteenth century, the cartoon was known only in pieces: Raffaello Borghini had one in his villa outside Florence, Uberto Strozzi had several in Mantua, and others appear to have made their way to Turin and Madrid.[70] Astonishingly, none of these survives, but the history would have added to the sense that Michelangelo's legacy was fragmented and figural, something reinforced by engravings that Marcantonio Raimondi and his followers produced (fig. 44).[71]

Surviving records of the larger composition, paradoxically, allow the same impression. When writing of the *Cascina*, art historians typically illustrate a monochrome painting in Holkham Hall, traditionally ascribed to Aristotile da Sangallo (see fig. 12). This has its own problems, starting with the fact that more than a dozen surviving drawings by Michelangelo for the Cascina project show figures that the Holkham Hall painting does not include.[72] That painting, moreover, differs from Michelangelo's compositional drawings in its treatment of the figures, separating them more decisively from one another.[73] Then there is the matter of the date. Sangallo seems to have carried out the Holkham Hall painting in 1542, that is, decades after the destruction of the cartoon.[74] It cannot, then, be a direct reproduction but must derive from one or more intermediary studies; at the time of making, it would have come across as a reincorporation but also as a reinterpretation of something long since dispersed.[75] It may be significant that Aristotile made the painting one year after the

45 (*below left*)   Michelangelo Buonarroti, *Last Judgment* (detail of fig. 1)

46 (*below right*)   Aristotile da Sangallo, after Michelangelo, *Battle of Cascina* (detail of fig. 12)

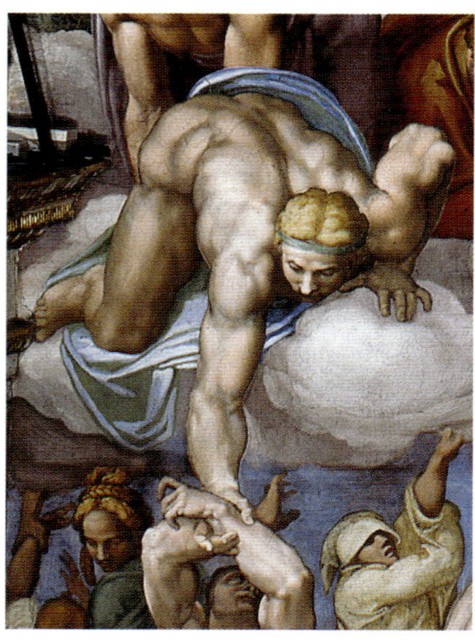

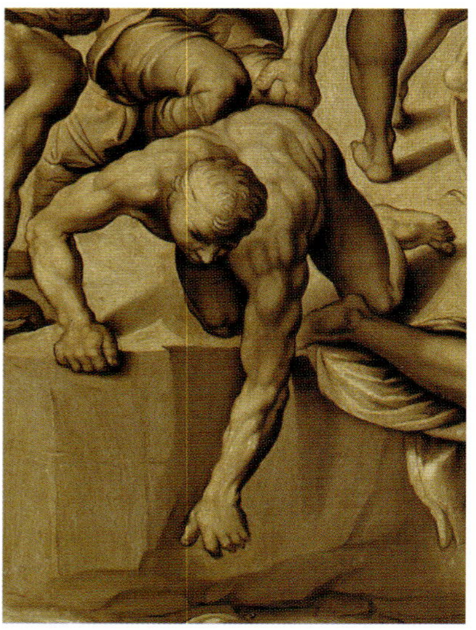

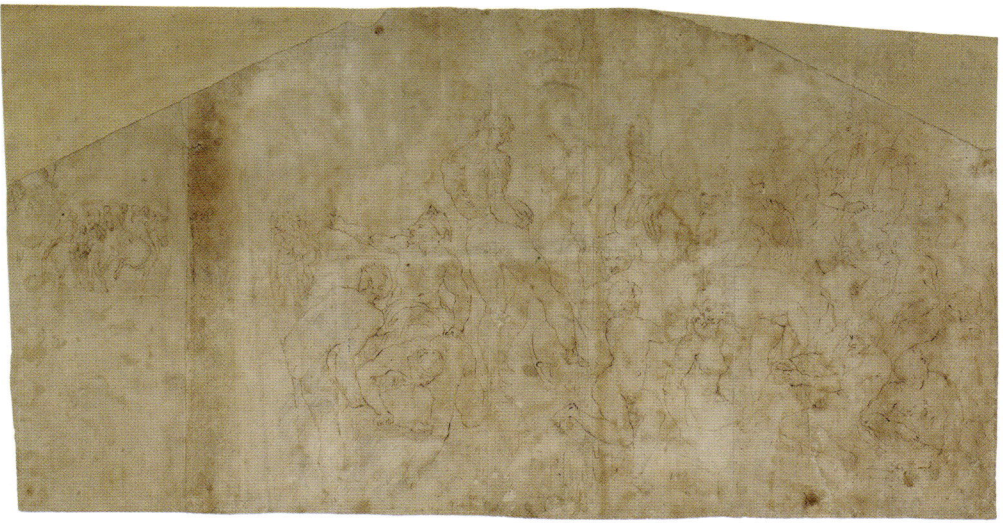

47 Anonymous copy after Michelangelo's *Battle of Cascina*, ink on paper, British Museum, London

unveiling of Michelangelo's *Last Judgment* (fig. 1): perhaps he thought that that fresco's images of climbers (figs 45, 46) and fighting figures would renew interest in Michelangelo's first plan for a monumental painting. Yet we might wonder also whether, in 1542, charges like that which Gilio would print were already in circulation, that the painter Michelangelo had concerned himself with the figure at the expense of history. As noted earlier, it was onto the *Last Judgment* that later writers projected Michelangelo's confrontation with Leonardo.

The Holkham Hall painting is not the only late sixteenth-century work to take up the *Cascina* as a composition. A drawing now in the British Museum (fig. 47) is close to it in form, omitting just one of the figures shown there. In the left background, however, it also shows the approaching enemy, a detail that could indicate that the drawing was carried out independently of the Sangallo and that the 1542 painting does not record everything that was in the original carton.[76] What is most interesting in the present context is that the figures in he British Museum drawing consist almost entirely of contours. As such, the sheet bears

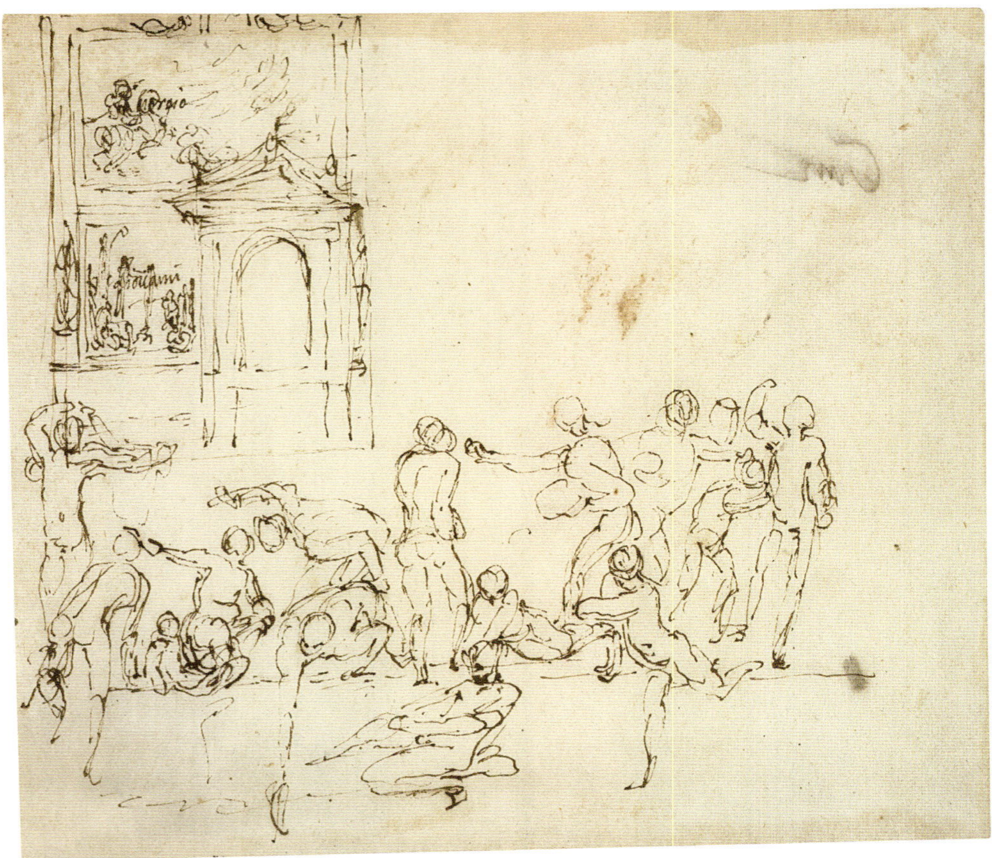

48   Anonymous drawing after Michelangelo's *Battle of Cascina*, pen and brown ink
over black chalk on paper, Albertina, Vienna

comparison with another contour drawing, now in the Albertina (fig. 48).[77]
Remarkably, its maker changed the positions of nearly all of Michelangelo's
figures. Wilhelm Köhler regarded it as a kind of homework assignment for
a young drawing student; Thode called it "an arbitrarily playful rearrange-
ment of the figures in the Grisaille." The great Michelangelo scholar
Charles de Tolnay referred to the work as a "copy" after Michelangelo, a
more surprising description, unless we decide that it is in the figure rather
than the composition that the copyist believed Michelangelo's authorship

to lie.[78] This may have been precisely the point of Michelangelo's forceful assertion of the contour in the face of Leonardo's haze.

Subordination and Subjectivity

Leonardo worked on the *Anghiari* for nearly a year, but he appears to have focused almost exclusively on the central scene of the "Battle for the Standard" and it is unclear how much progress he made. His pace conforms to the image that contemporaries left of his uncommonly slow working manner: Matteo Bandello, writing of Leonardo's progress on his previous mural assignment, the *Last Supper* in Milan, described the painter staring at the wall for hours at a time. "I have also seen him come directly to the Grazie and, having ascended the scaffolding, take the brush, apply one or two strokes to one of those figures, then immediately depart and go elsewhere."[79] Vasari had heard, similarly, that "the Prior of that place kept pressing Leonardo, in a most importunate manner, to finish the work; for it seemed strange to him to see Leonardo sometimes stand half a day at a time, lost in contemplation."[80] Ugolino Verino wrote around 1502 that Leonardo "is incapable of removing his hand from the panel and so, like Protogenes, takes many years to finish one."[81] All of these writers may have been playing to a cliché, but the descriptions offer a strong contrast with Michelangelo, who would later describe oil painting as an "arte da donna" (a woman's art), and who, after the *Cascina* assignment, largely avoided painting in any medium but fresco, which required him to finish the day's work before the plaster dried.[82]

The very medium in which Michelangelo worked, then, was one that he associated with virility and boldness. We might even say that Michelangelo's conception of fresco in this period laid the groundwork for what would come to be called *bravura* painting, a mode that drew attention to its own fast, virtuoso performance. Early artists and writers associated *bravura* style with the figure of the *bravo*, the mercenary soldier, likening the painter's handling of the brush to swordplay.[83] There were other means by which artists could invite such comparisons as well.

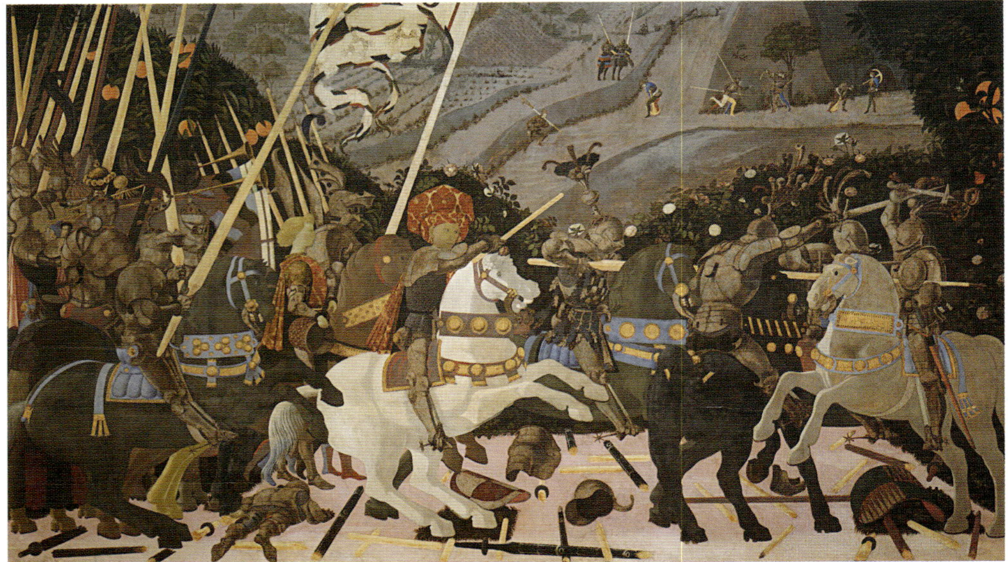

49   Paolo Uccello, *Battle of San Romano*, tempera and oil on panel, National Gallery, London

Benvenuto Cellini wrote that the clay modeler who followed the example of Michelangelo, raising and lowering the arms of his figure, bending and straightening its limbs, demonstrated himself to be a man of merit ("valentuomo"). Baldinucci described Michelangelo "giving [a model] a new attitude and resolving it, with *marvelous bravura*" into the opposite of what it had been before.[84] The figures Michelangelo painted for the *Cascina* mural would, in their daring poses no less than their fresco medium, have implied a confidence worthy of a soldier.

A soldier of high rank? The word that fifteenth-century Italian writers used to denote the ground – the figurable surface – of a painting was "campo," literally "field." The significance of this becomes especially apparent in paintings like Paolo Uccello's battle panels (fig. 49), in which the lances on the ground at once collapse the depiction (wooden objects) with its means (orthogonals) and open the painting up beyond its own borders, such that it flows into the beholder's space. It is as though a surface on which figures emerge in relief has been tipped backwards, as though

the support against which figuration happens and the field on which figures fight are one and the same.[85] If the *Cascina* similarly were imagin-
atively extended to include the position from which the artist painted it,
that position would have to be slightly elevated: the gaze of the soldiers
who look out at us do not run perpendicular to the ground plane; they
look up slightly. This is just what Pomponius Gauricus recommended in
the treatise he published in Florence the year Michelangelo began work
on the *Cascina*. Gauricus suggested that when an artist set out to make
battles, he should employ the kind of perspective one gained when looking
down from a height. What Gauricus was after was a sort of clarity, one
that would be lost if the viewer were positioned – as in Leonardo's scene
– below the action, or looking at the conflict head-on.[86]

In its circumstances, imagery, and reception, that is, the *Cascina* created
a scenario where the relationship of artist to figure resembled that of the
commander to his combatant. Michelangelo was not just recreating a
history, casting actors who would repeat a performance that had taken
place at some time in the past; he was composing a picture that implied
the actor before it. We might recall the fragment of poetry Michelangelo
added to some drawings of David the year before the *Cascina*: "David with
his sling and I with my bow, Michelangelo."[87] This was an artist who
thought about his work in terms of combat, and thought of that combat
on analogy with his depicted subjects.

Yet here, as often in Michelangelo, metaphor opens a paradox. When
Michelangelo returned to the image of the bow in his poetry, he used it
to describe the tortured form of his own body at work. "I bend myself
like a Syrian bow," he wrote as he painted the Sistine Chapel ceiling,
adding that "one shoots badly through a crooked barrel."[88] Or consider
how the Cascina figures themselves look if we come back to them by way
of the *Rebellious Slave* (see fig. 43), initially conceived shortly after Michelangelo broke off work on the *Cascina*. Just who is his captor? Our first
answer might be that it is Pope Julius, the successor to Saint Peter,
to whom Christ said in Matthew 16:19, "And whatsoever thou shalt
bind upon earth, it shall be bound also in heaven: and whatsoever thou
shalt loose upon earth, it shall be loosed also in heaven." Or we might

follow Vasari, who understood the slave to have belonged to a triumphal program that celebrated the Papacy's territorial victories.[89] By the time Michelangelo carved the marble, however, the nature of this subjugation had already begun to slide. With regard to the figure of stone whose imprisoning layers have been removed, Michelangelo himself is the one who binds and unbinds. The metaphor of binding opens the possibility that the artist might step into the patron's role, precisely what Counter-Reformation critics feared.

But the metaphor is more powerful than this. "Binding" was among the most common images of Renaissance magic; the man with power to capture or free another became a kind of sorcerer. Particularly influential in the formulation of this theory was Marsilio Ficino, whom Michelangelo knew personally. As the historian of magic Ioan Couliano has written:

> All of [the lover's] means of persuasion are also *magic* means, whose goal is to bind the other to him. Ficino himself, to define this process, uses the word *rete*, meaning "net" or "web." To put it simply: the lover and the magician both do the same thing: they cast their "nets" to capture certain objects, to attract and draw them to them.[90]

We might compare this to Vasari's remark on the *Last Judgment*, which attributes to Michelangelo's contours in particular a magical effect: "This work leads after it bound in chains those who persuade themselves that they have mastered art; and at the sight of the strokes drawn by him in the outlines of no matter what figure, every sublime spirit, however mighty in design, trembles and is afraid."[91] Those less sympathetic to Michelangelo's approach to painting, as the final chapter of this book will show, saw troubling implications in just such figures.

Yet as soon as the contour was taken to imply something about the artist, it raised a host of other associations as well. Michelangelo ultimately gave his *Rebellious Slave* to the Republican exile Roberto Strozzi, with the idea that the struggling prisoner conveyed a desire for self-government; Michelangelo was siding not with the captor but with the man who seeks freedom.[92] This aligned the imagery of the prisoner, however retrospectively, with the republican ideas that stood behind the *Cascina* commission, too. When the artist also took up the theme of binding as a poetic trope, he was never the master, always the subject, captivated by a beloved. This must have been central to the idea of the *Tityus*, a gift drawing that was itself a variation on the prisoner theme, but also to the single figure studies Michelangelo made for the *Cascina*. And does the composition of the *Cascina*, with all those figures seen from behind, not lure the male beholder sooner to join the soldiers than to give them orders?[93]

Ultimately, the bound figure was a figure of mastery. The sinuous line that turned the plane into the window or the ground required exquisite control of the brush or pen. The captive body which that line surrounded, in turn, could seem to make that control into a topic for painting. Yet as a figure, and a figure of a beautiful, powerful soldier, control was always in the end reversible: the image of mastery created a subject position with which the artist or viewer could equally identify. This was the paradox of the *figura sforzata*.

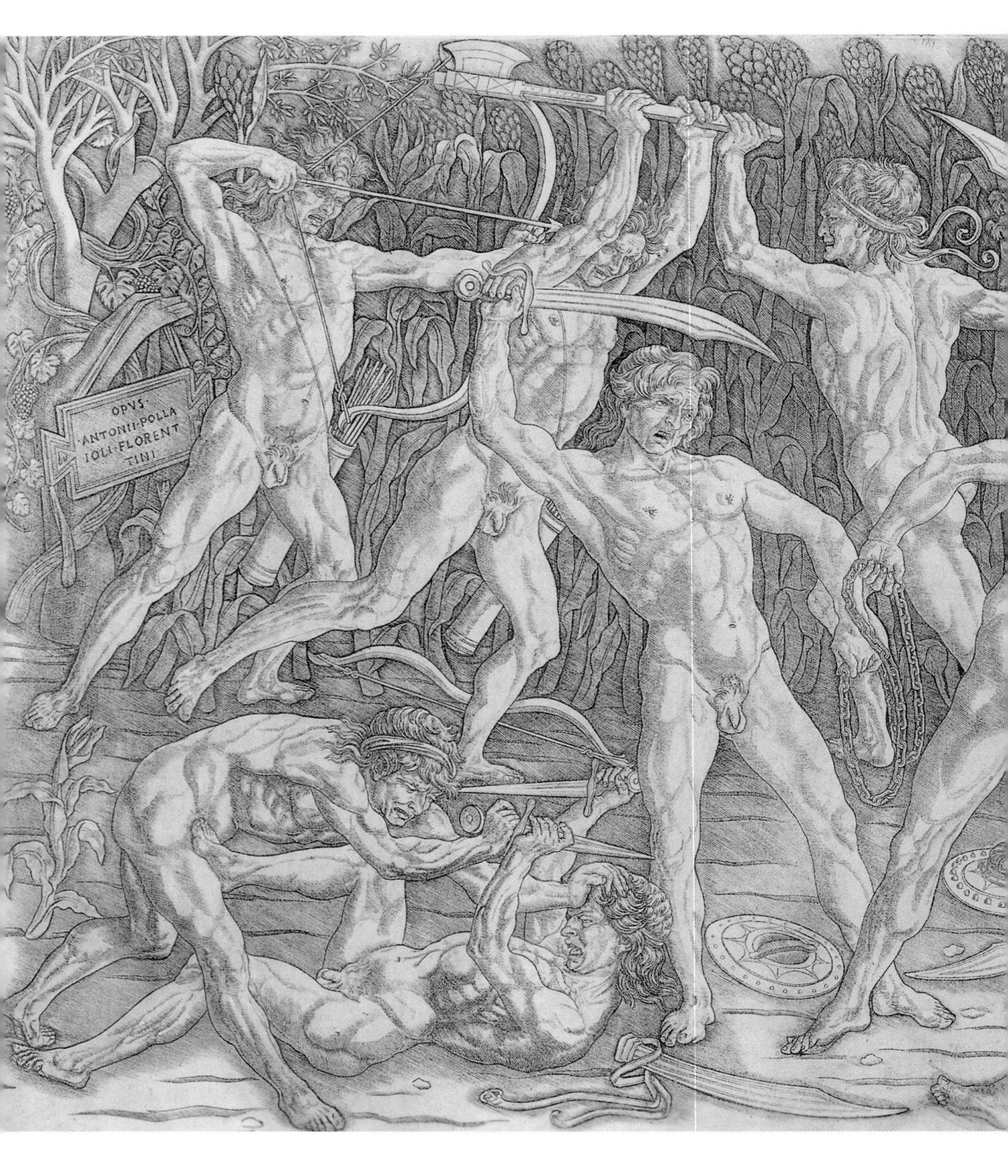

OPVS·
ANTONII·POLLA
IOLI·FLORENT
TINI

3

FLEXION

What Did Artists Invent?

The Renaissance medium that most explicitly constructed a role for the artist-as-inventor was engraving. By the middle of the sixteenth century, engraved prints – and occasionally prints made with other techniques as well – bore inscriptions that assigned distinct roles to the man who incised the metal, the man who owned the plate or initiated the production, and a third person who did neither of these things.[1] Such sheets allow a definition of invention that looks much like what Florentine academicians, later in the century, would come to call "disegno": the inventor, typically, was the person who provided a design in the form of a drawing.

Yet if we look to the origins of this division of roles, we find a somewhat different conception of what invention might comprise. The earliest print to bear an inscription distinguishing the roles of the engraver and the inventor seems also to be the earliest reproduction of Michelangelo's *Cascina* (fig. 51).[2] Vasari tells us that the engraver Marcantonio Raimondi was so close to his teacher, Francesco Francia, that he acquired the last name "de' Franci"; the F in the monogram may simply refer to this. Still, we might wonder if the final "F" did not rather play some role in the reconception under way in these years of what it meant to "make" a work.

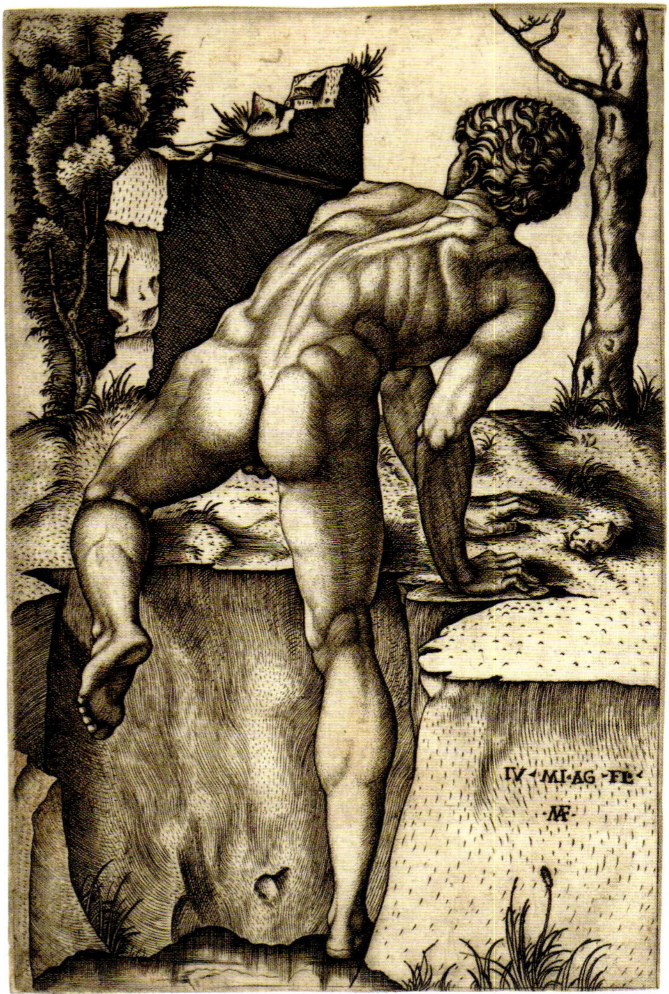

51   Marcantonio Raimondi, engraving after a figure from
Michelangelo's *Cascina*

Earlier prints used forms of the verb *facere* to point not to the engraver
but to the designer; later in the century, an "F" after an artist's name or
initials would typically indicate that that person had cut the plate.[3] Con-
tributing to the change was Michelangelo, who had signed his St. Peter's
Pietà "Micael Angelus Flor Faciebat": much has been made of his use of

the imperfect, which suggests a previously ongoing rather than completed process; it certainly indicates that he regarded "making" as a matter of carving and not just of composing.[4]

The first line of the engraving's inscription has received less comment. The three abbreviations on the right must stand for Mi[chel] Ag[nolo] Flo[rentinus], and the IV could be a date – the cartoon by Michelangelo that served as Marcantonio's ultimate source is from 1504, the legendary moment when he worked alongside Leonardo.[5] Marcantonio was interested in medals and, when medals from the period bear dates, these frequently refer to the event they record, not the moment of their own making. More likely, though, is that the IV represents a not-yet-conventionalized reduction of "invenit." It may in fact be the case that the engraving is the first ever to use a form of that word.[6] And if that is true, then the print has an even more dramatic distinction, being the earliest artwork in any medium to declare itself an invention of an artist.

If the print attributes to Michelangelo an invention, of just what does his invention consist? At numerous points in his career, Michelangelo supplied drawings for others to execute in more public media, but he does not appear to have done that here: rather, Marcantonio presumably based the print on a drawing he himself had made a few years earlier, when he was in Florence. In late sixteenth-century prints that employ the term "invenit," the word commonly refers to an overall composition. But that is not the case here either, for Marcantonio has in fact extracted one figure from a larger group, inaugurating the practice of serially reframing individual members of the assembly that Michelangelo originally composed, establishing multiple contexts for the single Michelangelo figure in the process (fig. 52). It is not even true that "invenit" in this case credits Michelangelo with all the constituent elements of a larger work: from Michelangelo, Raimondi and his imitators took only the figures, deriving landscape and other motifs from other artists, or making them up themselves.

In the years the Cascina was underway, literate viewers of painting often associated invention with the generation of subject matter. Isabella d'Este, for example, was content to have Giovanni Bellini paint "some history or

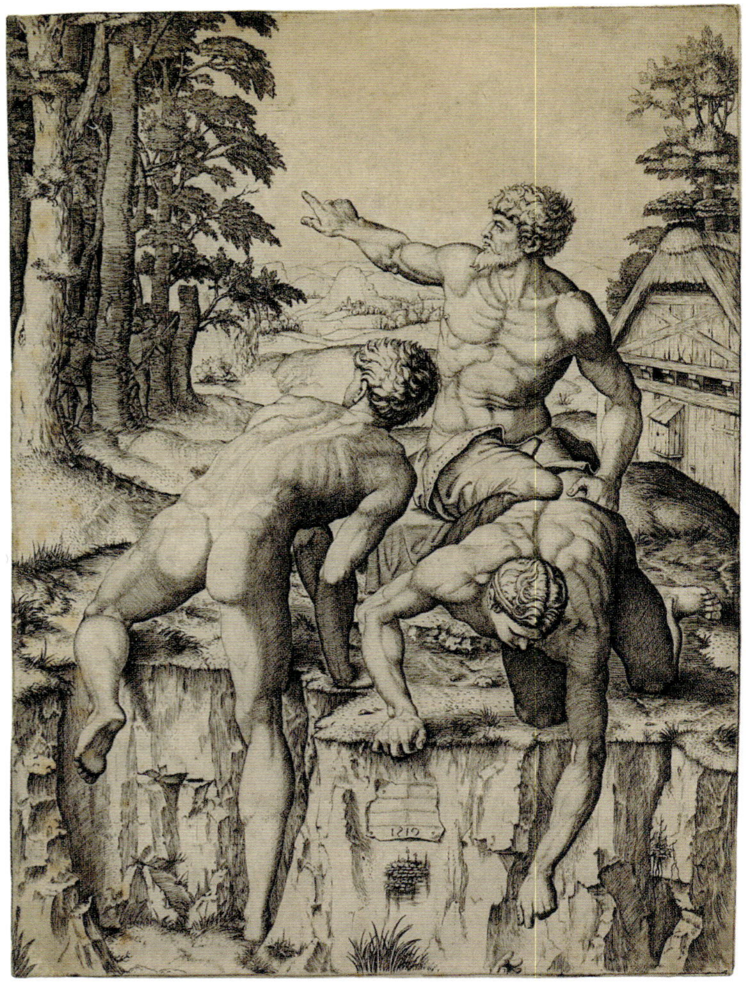

52   Raimondi, *The Climbers*, engraving

ancient fable," so long as, "using his invention, he makes one that represents an ancient thing with a beautiful meaning."[7] This seems close to the way that followers of Michelangelo would come to use the same language: in a public letter of 1582, for example, Bartolomeo Ammanati wrote that "we all know that most of the men who employ us do not give us any invention whatsoever, but leave everything to our judgment, saying 'here

I would like a garden, here a fountain, here a pool, and so forth.'"[8] Paolo Veronese, hauled before the Inquisition for filling his painting of the *Last Supper* with "scurrilities and other inventions" ("scurrilità e simili inventioni"), stated that he had been commissioned "to decorate the picture as [he] saw fit" and that he had consequently done as his superiors had, referring pointedly to the example of Michelangelo in the Sistine Chapel.[9]

Sources like this demonstrate that although Michelangelo was not the first Renaissance artist to be associated with invention, his example was particularly empowering to imitators. They also show how different the "invention" associated with the Raimondi print was. In naming Michelangelo as its inventor, the engraving cannot be attributing the subject to him, since the subject is one thing that Raimondi took the liberty to change. No viewer would have understood the image of a single nude man in a wooded area with a broken wall to be a representation of the *Battle of Cascina*. The conventional title for the related three-figure print is simply "The Climbers." Michelangelo's function, the inscription suggests, amounted to a narrow responsibility for the figure alone – and not even for the represented character so much as for the naked pose. Both the Latin *invenire* and the Italian *inventare* could refer to a discovery no less than a contrivance; what was novel in Michelangelo's painting was not a person or object that no one had seen before, but a novelty he had found through experimentation with a set of given forms.

This is different from Ammanati and Veronese but it is also different from Alberti, who had identified the pictorial "invention" with the material – especially the literary material – from which the painter built his composition. The most relevant part of Alberti's discussion may in fact be that when he introduces the topic of invention in Book Three of *De pictura*, the quality by which he proposes that it be measured is force: invention has such force, he maintains, that even without being painted it can give pleasure.[10] With such a remark in mind, Marcantonio's Michelangelo, the art embodied in the singular flexed athlete, may seem to reduce invention to a kind of essence.

★ ★ ★

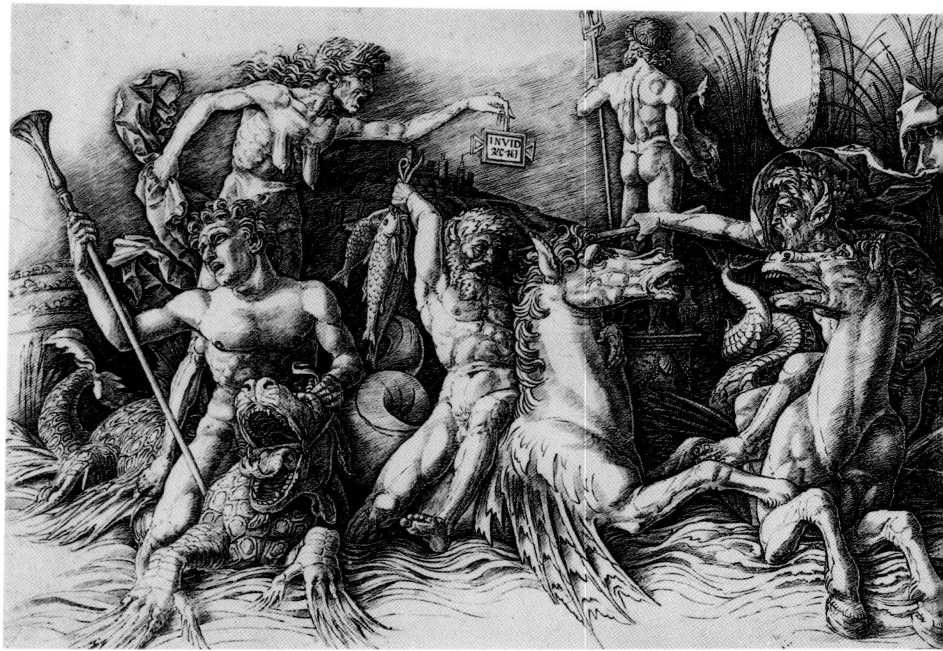

53   Andrea Mantegna, *Battle of the Sea Gods*, engraving

Pollaiuolo and the Mechanics of Invention

The engraving that Raimondi completed after Michelangelo's *Battle of Cascina* may have been the earliest to declare itself a document of invention, though similar ideas must have been part of the appeal of the medium from the beginning, and nowhere more than in printed battle scenes. Among the more impressive early Italian engravings was Mantegna's two-plate *Battle of the Sea Gods* (fig. 53). A hag at the left holds a plate that identifies her as a personification of Envy, and the other characters in the scene are now generally taken to represent the ancient Telchines, a mythological race famed for their works in metal.[11] Mantegna must here be asserting that rivals would be driven to monstrous envy by his art. And he would have believed his artfulness to reside not in the plate's execution (for which Mantegna was probably not responsible) but in its invention, a collection of monsters and unexpected poses. Battling figures, in this case, make artfulness, and artistic competition, into a pictorial subject.

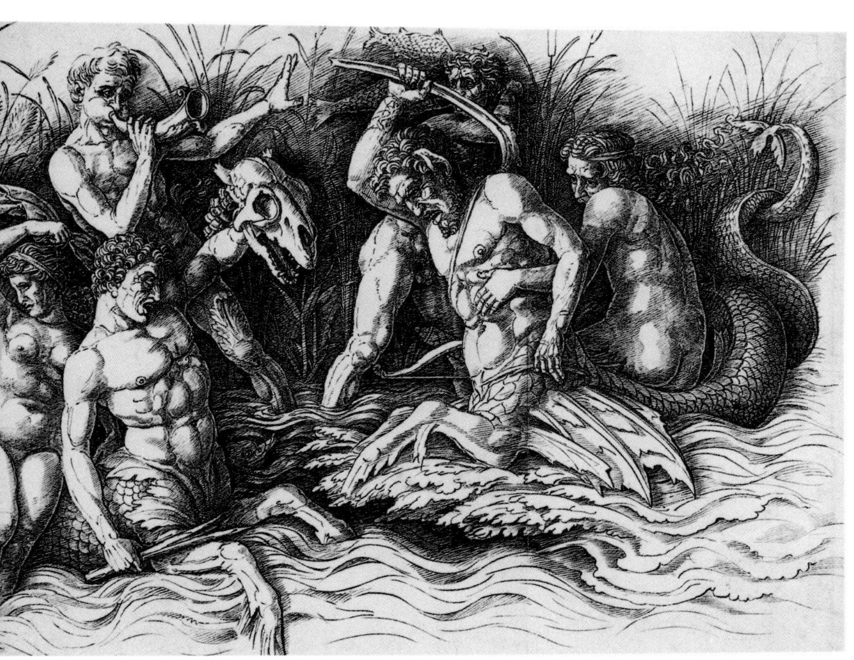

With its violent theme and undisguised ambition, the work could well
have served as model for Leonardo and Michelangelo both: the hybrid
animal forms out of which Leonardo builds his figures' armor seem in
particular to refer to Mantegna's paradigm. Equally influential, probably,
was an engraving that Antonio Pollaiuolo made in Florence, perhaps a few
years after Mantegna's, one that has come to be known as the *Battle of the
Nudes* (fig. 54). The compositional procedure that lies behind this print
bears comparison with the Albertina *Flagellation* sheet, which may also have
been by a goldsmith (see fig. 4). There, the two lower figures appear to
offer alternative possibilities for a single painted or sculpted character, as
do the two above them. The artist is doing something rarely seen before
1400, using a drawing to compare how the same character would look if
treated in different ways, now with an arm lowered rather than raised, now
with a leg bent at the knee rather than straightened. The page illustrates
a mode of invention that consists in changing a pose, or in posing per se.

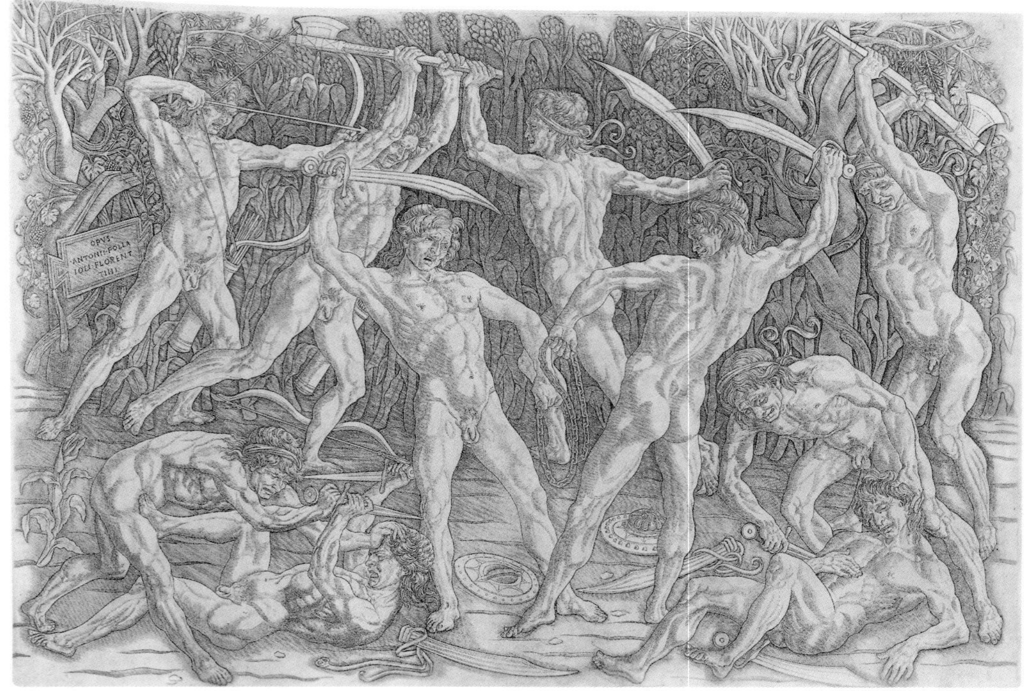

54   Pollaiuolo, *Battle of the Nudes*, engraving

This is the kind of practice about which Alberti wrote in *Della pittura*, when asserting that the pleasing picture is one in which bodies and their poses differ from one another, in which "some [figures] stand straight and show their entire face, with hands lifted and fingers raised, one foot planted, while others have their face the other way, their arms back down and their feet joined." The point, he continues, is that each of these figures has its own act and its own "flexion of members."[12] What is remarkable about this comment is that it concerns not the study but the finished work. It allows the same kind of appreciation for a narrative painting and for something like the Albertina sheet, a figure-by-figure regard that seeks not what connects neighbors but what distinguishes them. The pleasing picture at this point sounds less like a composition than a collection. And the painter multiplies the figures in that collection by bending them. If

Pollaiuolo's *Battle of the Nudes* seems disjointed, that effect results in part from the engraver's reliance on strong contour lines, in part from an approach to making art that focuses on flexion.[13]

It may be that the print was intended to serve as an ethnographic illustration, depicting a specifically African scene.[14] However, with the later direction of Florentine art in mind, it also seems possible to say, more simply, that Pollaiuolo here concerned himself with depictions of force. The man at the top left, drawing a bow, does not actually seem to be aiming it at anything; he appears to be operating the bow for its own sake, as though he were demonstrating how it works. The two figures to the right of this bowman make the handle of an axe into a kind of lever, the left hand of the frontally oriented figure serving as a fulcrum around which competing pressures are applied.

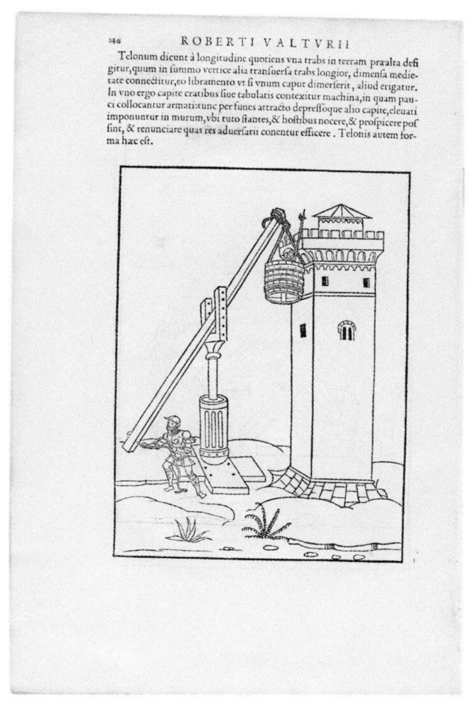

55   Roberto Valturio, *telone*, from *De re militari* (1483 edn.), woodcut

When the print was made is still debated but it is safe to say that Pollaiuolo conceived it in the period during which the production of treatises on machines was especially lively.[15] In many of those, the lever was a central preoccupation: it is the basis, for example, of the *telone* (fig. 55) in Roberto Valturio's widely read *De re militari*, completed in 1455 and published by 1472.[16] Francesco di Giorgio wrote "ragione dela lieva," or "demonstration of the lever," above one of the diagrams in his *Trattato I*, underway at the same time.[17] The same author, in the 1470s, was copying the earlier works of Mariano Taccola, who had written about and depicted the lever both in his 1449 manuscript *De rebus militaribus* (now in Paris) and in the probably earlier manuscript *De ingeneis* (now in Florence). Today we associate the device especially with the legacy of Archimedes, but that is a connection that few in Pollaiuolo's own day could have made.[18] If they saw the motif in his print as a lever at all, this was because an extensive late Quattrocento mechanical literature, not just an ancient Greek writer, made the device into a central leitmotif.

Leonardo, no less than Michelangelo, came to locate artfulness in the bent figure, and did so in the context of violent imagery.[19] Unlike Michelangelo, Leonardo had read Valturio and knew Francesco di Giorgio personally; what he sought were words and images to describe what happened at the locus of opposing forces. In this, he was elaborating a connection between the figure and the simple machine that Pollaiuolo had already visualized.[20]

Mechanical Flexion

Alberti dedicated his Italian text *Della pittura* to Filippo Brunelleschi. One reason for this must be that he associated Brunelleschi with the practice of linear perspective that is the topic of his treatise's first book. Yet when it came to singling out an actual undertaking of Brunelleschi's, Alberti did not mention a contribution to painting per se but instead praised the dome of Florence cathedral, "done without the aid of beams or elaborate wooden supports, a demonstration of unquestionable artfulness" ("fatta sanza alcuno aiuto di travamenti o di copia di legname, quale artificio certo").

This focus – not on harmonious spatial design or the use of classical vocabulary that we now celebrate as the hallmarks of Brunelleschi's architecture, but on ingenious invention – is consistent with the way that other Quattrocento writers commemorated the architect. The inscription that Carlo Marsuppini composed for Brunelleschi's tomb referred to "the many machines invented by him with divine ingenuity."[21] When Francesco di Giorgio referred to the legacy of Brunelleschi, he did not even describe him as an architect but as "a most learned inventor of devices."[22] Antonio Manetti's biography of Brunelleschi offers a similar picture.

Leonardo was in the shop of Andrea Verrocchio while that artist was producing the metal globe to go atop Brunelleschi's dome. The practical problem of installing this object would doubtless have prompted conversations about the ideas that had garnered Brunelleschi his fame; Vasari believed that in 1478, Leonardo had offered to raise the entire Baptistery so that a new lower story could be added to it; later, Leonardo would do drawings of machines that Brunelleschi had invented.[23] Brunelleschi's legacy may even lie behind Leonardo's fascination with automata: the principal example of the wind-up machine in fifteenth-century Italy was the clock; in studying such mechanisms, it cannot have escaped Leonardo that Brunelleschi had been particularly celebrated as a clock-maker.[24]

For those who wished to emulate Brunelleschi's demonstrations of ingeniousness, the easiest path was drawing: from the period 1440–1500 we have hundreds of pages illustrating mechanical novelties. Their components were mostly standard – rope, chains, toothed wheels, axles, trusses – though it is doubtful that many were ever built.[25] Indeed, it may be more appropriate to think of these on analogy less with the modern instructional diagram than with the hybrid creatures that sometimes appear in the same pages. They assert the same inventive license that painters were claiming, a combinatory conception of freedom that they modeled on the fabrications of poets.[26]

In the earliest Italian mechanical drawings, it is rare to see the machine's operators or any other reference to the world of labor.[27] The presence of figures has even been used to distinguish autograph manuscripts by Francesco di Giorgio from those produced by later copyists (fig. 56).[28] At least in Italy, then, one broad change that differentiates the mechanical drawings that immediately preceded Leonardo's is the human presence they began increasingly to show. The shift may itself reflect the new culture of invention and experimentation, a concern less evident in earlier drawings primarily devoted to recovering the lost technological knowledge of the ancients.[29] Yet, if this is the case, how did technological invention and experimentation extend to the figure itself?

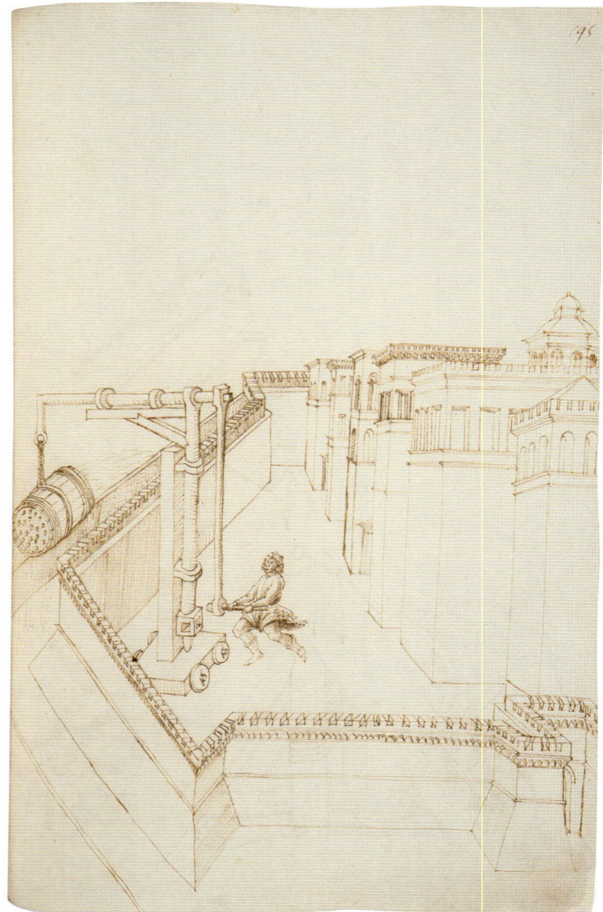

56   Copy after Francesco di Giorgio, "Braccio di
brandeggio di corpi incendiari," Codice Magliabechiana,
II.I.141, fol. 195r, Biblioteca Nazionale Centrale, Florence

One basic consequence of adding a figure to the drawing of the
machine is that the drawing itself becomes readable in multiple directions.
Some drawings point not only to the mechanics of the artificial parts but
also to the force expended by their human operators. We see this, for
instance, in Valturio's illustration of the *telone*. Others reverse this dynamic.
Then we might ask whether the difference between these two categories

is really so clear. To show a laborer hooked into a machine required the artist to think not just about the machine's movements but about the body's.

Leonardo's own machine drawings, with and without figures, concern themselves above all with the principles of force and its application, the effects of torque and tension. A good example is a drawing on the lower half of a sheet now in the Pierpont Morgan Library (fig. 57), labeled "modo di torciere una trave per fare i chavellettj" ("manner of bending a beam for making trestles"). Anchored underground, the machine provides for a board to be inserted into a brace at one end over a fulcrum in the center. Lifting a lever against a peg that provides a second fulcrum forces the beam into a curve. A second peg in the frame where the force is applied holds the bent beam in its new position while the lever is readjusted. The hatching lines create a *chiaroscuro* that allows the beam to be read more easily against the ground plane – the same kind of effect Leonardo would employ in his figural paintings – though they also evoke the direction of pressure. If the cross arm were removed from the brace on the left, the board would spring up in the manner of a catapult, along the vector indicated by the hatching just below that end of the board. The empty peg holes (to which the inscription above the contraption refers) serve as reminders of the progress that the machine's operators have already made, incrementally manipulating the board into its present state.

A drawing like this makes clear that machines can imply agency, even when no operator is depicted. A question posed by drawings that show machines together with figures, in turn, is the direction of that agency. Scholars who have written about a Leonardo drawing in Windsor, showing a cannon foundry (fig. 58), have tended to dwell on Leonardo's fascination with artillery and with large casting operations. (The drawing dates to around 1485–90, the period of Leonardo's monumental bronze Sforza monument.) But of course this can not be a description of an actual foundry: the workers are nude. Perhaps the cannon here serves primarily as a representation of weight – a chief preoccupation of late medieval mechanics – in which case the primary subject of the drawing would be, again, the human body's actions in the operation of a lever.

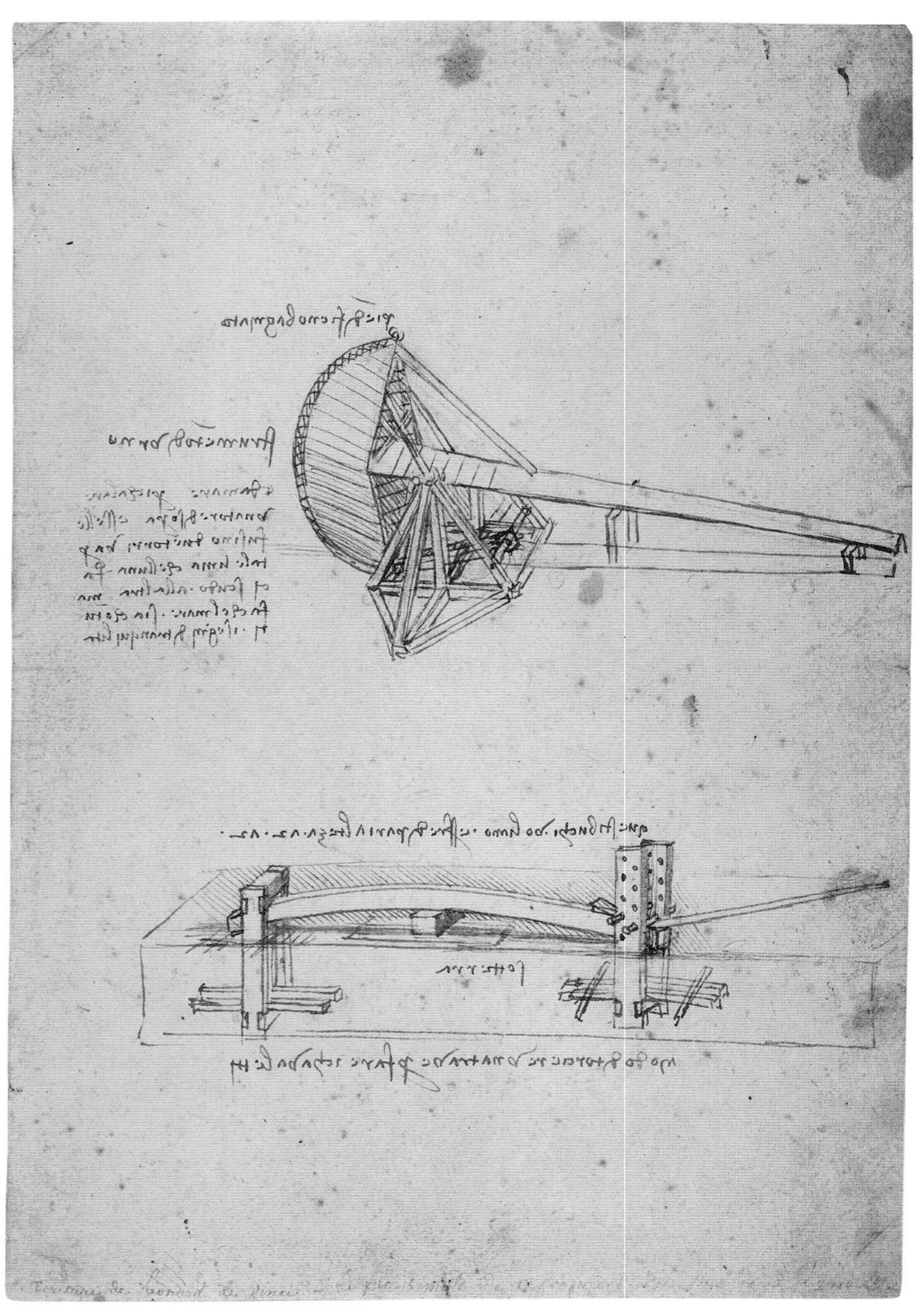

57   Leonardo da Vinci, two designs for machines, pen and dark brown ink
over black chalk on paper, Morgan Library and Museum, New York

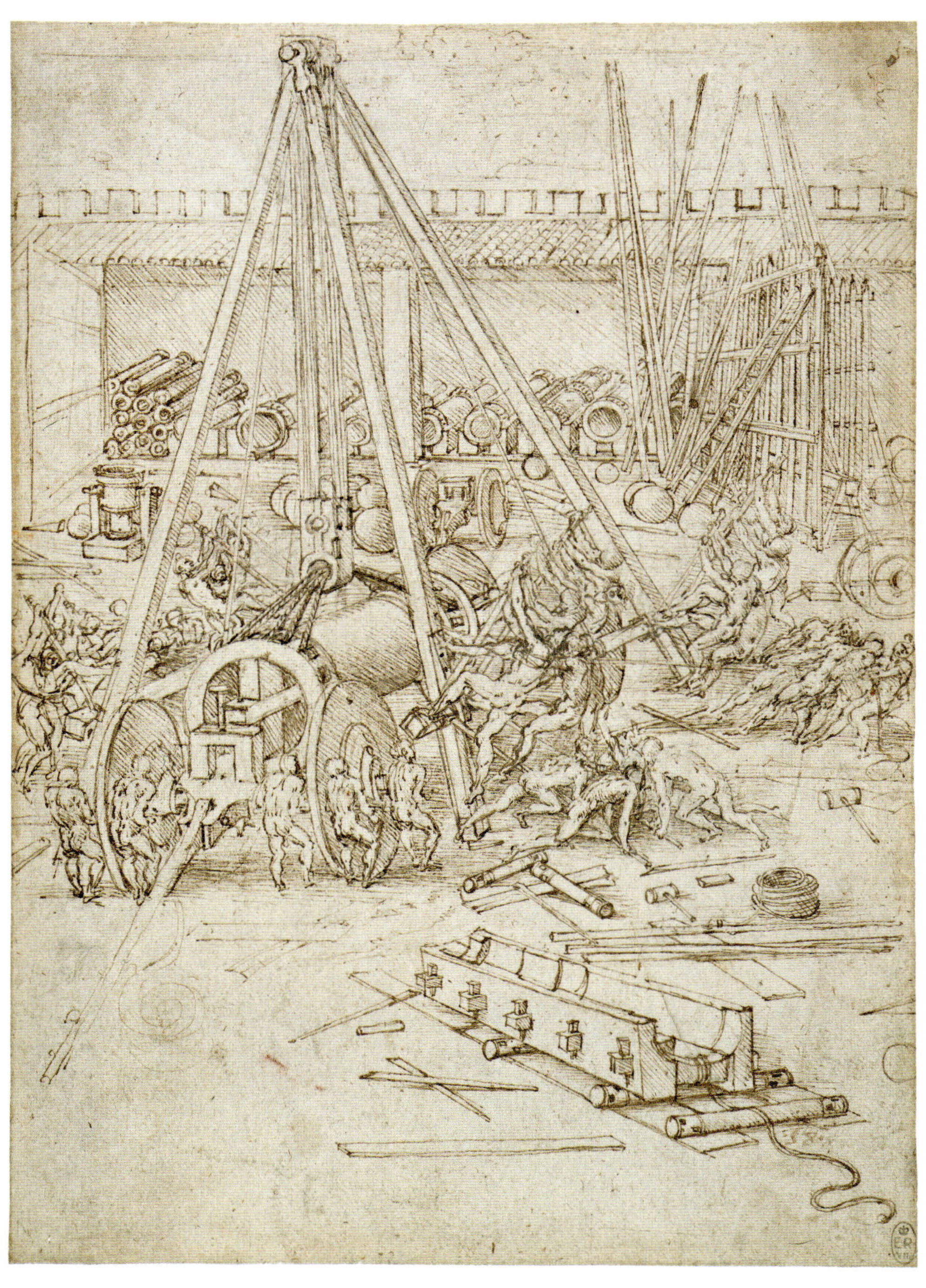

58   Leonardo, *Cannon Foundry,* pen and dark brown ink over black chalk on paper,
Royal Collection, Windsor

This would bring it much closer to the diagrams from the mechanical literature that Leonardo surely knew, a chief difference being that Leonardo expands the field of investigation to include not only the moving weight but also the moving body. His drawing is both a depiction of engineering and an image of labor, but it is especially a demonstration of the inextricability of the two. The sheet describes how bodies operate machines and also shows how machines require specific movements from bodies.

One reading of the Windsor drawing would be to say that it depends on an analogy. Some of the earliest Renaissance engineering illustrations come from doctors; engineers like Taccola approached their machines as though they had "anatomies," and their drawings subject machines to dissection.[30] The important point for the longer history that this book follows, though, is that such drawings *instrumentalize* the human bodies they portray.

Machines on Walls: Piero, Filippino, Pinturicchio

Mechanical inventions must have been of interest even to many artists whom we do not know to have been active as engineers; in the years leading up to the Council Hall commissions, simple and complex machines came to play prominent roles in a range of mural paintings.

Piero della Francesca's *True Cross* cycle in Arezzo, completed by 1465, was a major touchstone; to Leonardo and Michelangelo both, this would have been of interest in part for its inclusion of monumental battle scenes. In choosing which parts of the story to tell, Piero and his patrons largely recapitulated the episodes Agnolo Gaddi had painted in Santa Croce the previous century.[31] One scene which Piero adds, however, depicts men in contemporary dress operating a rope and pulley (fig. 59). A certain justification here may come from the *Golden Legend*, according to which St. Helen had a Jew named Judas thrown into a well to starve after he refused to reveal the location of the True Cross. "On the seventh day, Judas, weak from hunger, asked to be drawn from the well, and promised to

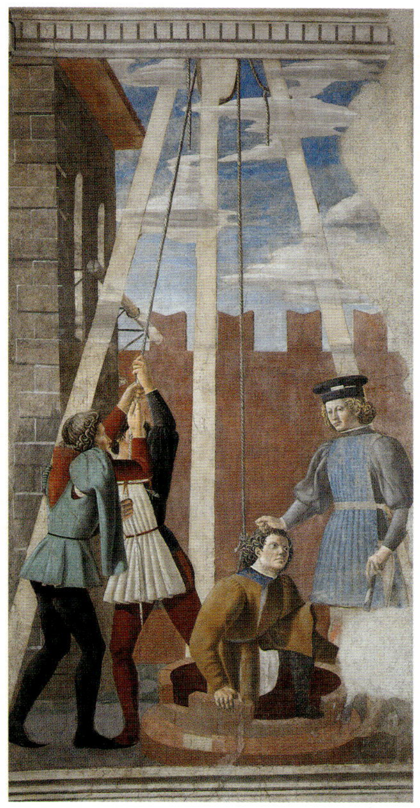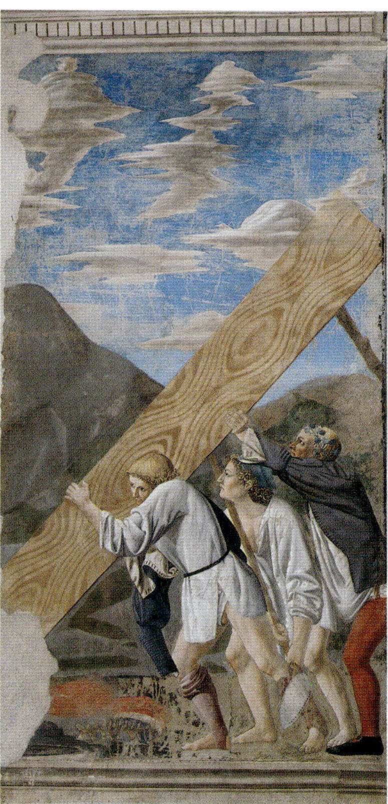

59 (*above left*)   Piero della Francesca, *Judas Lifted from the Well*, from the *Legend of the True Cross* cycle, fresco, San Francesco, Arezzo

60 (*above right*)   Piero della Francesca, *Burial of the Cross*, from the *Legend of the True Cross* cycle, fresco, San Francesco, Arezzo

reveal [the Cross's] whereabouts." Yet this is not what Piero shows. Helena is absent altogether; what we get is an event unnarrated in the text. Piero not only gave the scene its own framed space but also paired it with the scene of the burial of the Cross, reconceived so as to maximize its representation of physical labor (fig. 60). The book Piero wrote on perspective demonstrates his attention to the Brunelleschian legacy in Florence. Here he takes a pictorial theme that had largely belonged to the

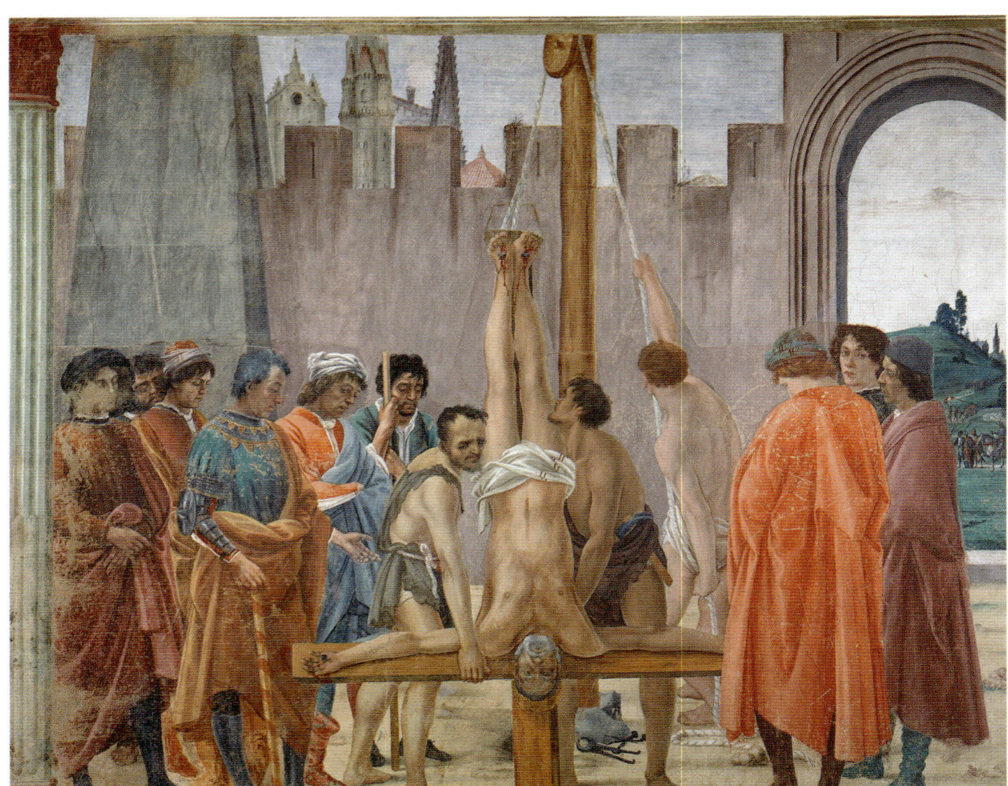

61   Filippino Lippi, *Crucifixion of St. Peter*, fresco, Brancacci Chapel, Santa Maria del Carmine, Florence

domain of technical manuscripts and brings it into an entirely new context.

Chapels like Piero's counted among the most prestigious commissions artists could receive: painters from surrounding cities surely traveled to Arezzo to see the new images. And in the decades that followed, a number of ambitious muralists found ways to incorporate superfluous machines into their own projects. A prominent Florentine example that both Leonardo and Michelangelo would have known is Filippino Lippi's 1481–2 *Crucifixion of St. Peter* in the Brancacci Chapel (fig. 61). Filippino was

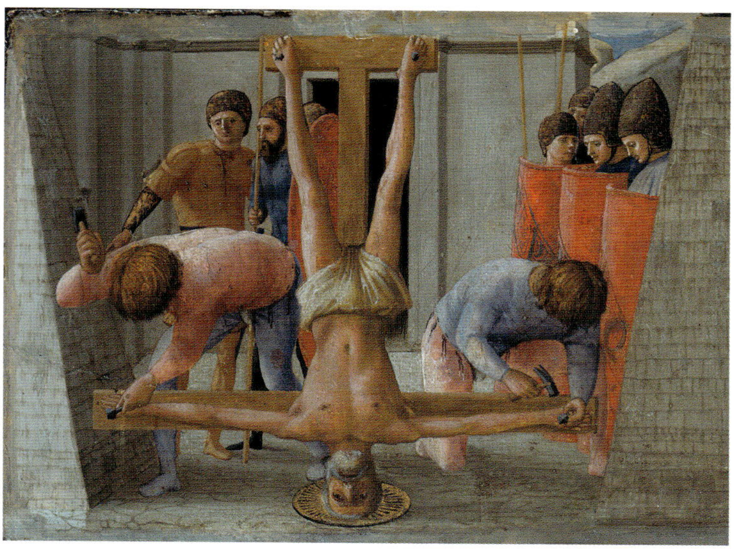

62   Masaccio, *Crucifixion of St. Peter*, tempera on panel,
Staatliche Museen, Berlin

adding to a cycle that Masaccio had helped to paint in the 1420s, but he
transformed the conventional formula for this subject – a formula used by
Masaccio himself on a panel now in Berlin (fig. 62) – by imagining a pulley
system used to raise the cross. As with Piero, the fresco commission presented an opportunity to show both an ingenious device and the work
required to operate it. A decade later, Filippino would return to the idea
when depicting the *Martyrdom of St. Philip* (fig. 63): this time the laborers
have abandoned the pulley in favor of a lever, using a broken capital as its
fulcrum.

Nowhere do we see machines taking over paintings more agressively
than in Pinturicchio's *Penelope and the Suitors* (fig. 64), originally painted
in the Palazzo del Magnifico in Siena on the occasion of the wedding of
Lord Pandolfo Petrucci and now in the National Gallery in London. The
fresco belonged to a cycle of virtues, and the point was surely to celebrate
the ruse by which Penelope put off the suitors shown at right, promising
to marry one when she finished weaving a burial shroud, then unweaving
it every night. Yet the main character in the painting is the enormous loom

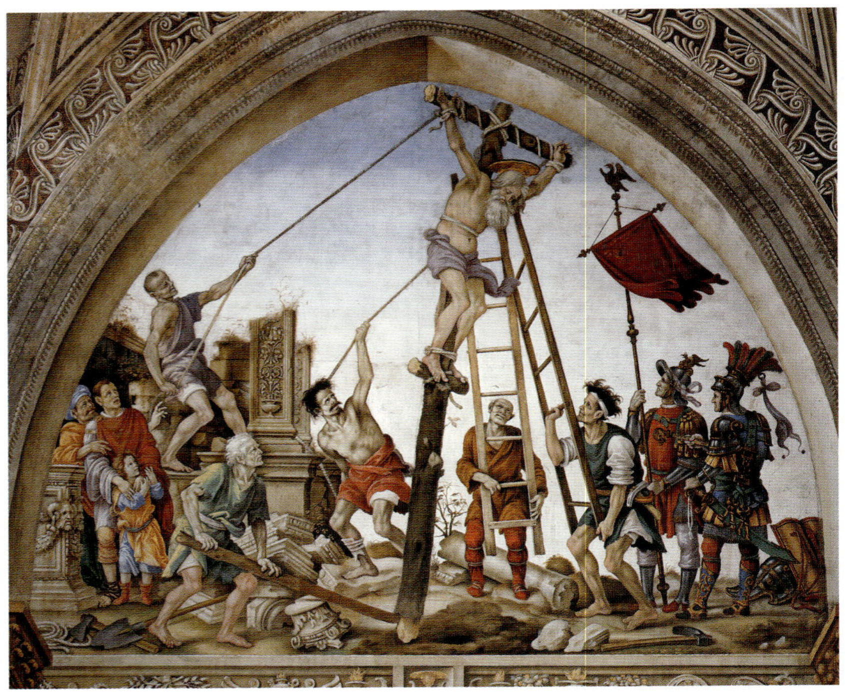

63   Filippino Lippi, *Martyrdom of St. Philip*, fresco, Strozzi Chapel,
Santa Maria Novella, Florence

at which Penelope sits, its frame unfolding to fill the entire room. The birthplace of Mariano Taccola and Francesco di Giorgio, Siena was, more than any other Renaissance city, the home of the machine drawing, and like many works in this genre, Pinturicchio's painting challenges the viewer to follow the connections between parts and whole – between the heddle, suspended from cloth pulleys, the treadles and cords that move this, and the shroud that wraps around the cloth beam – trying to see just how (and if) it all works. Indeed, it is difficult to imagine Pinturicchio rendering such an object without an actual drawing before him. Among the most remarkable details of the painting is the ship in the background, rendered with careful precision, as knowingly depicted as the boats in Leonardo's nearly contemporary naval studies.[32] Its presence introduces an element of continuous narrative: we see Ulysses arriving through the door at right, at the end of his journey, but we also see what he was doing while Penelope

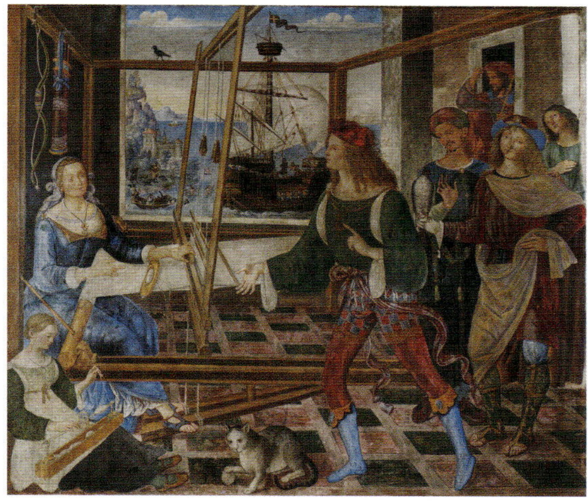

64   Bernardino di Betto, called Pintoricchio, *Penelope and the Suitors*, detached fresco, National Gallery, London

wove. The painting, that is, invites comparison between the roped machines that Penelope and Ulysses respectively operate. And there is one more instrument in its collection: hanging above Penelope's right shoulder is the bow that only Ulysses could string.

What I have proposed vis-à-vis Pollaiuolo's *Battle of the Nudes* is that artists could invoke the theme of figure and machine even when reducing the machine to its basic elements. And that, too, is the case in painting no less than on paper. The 1475 *St. Sebastian* by the Pollaiuolo brothers (fig. 65) shows a group of archers in the process of trying to kill the saint. At least five of the six appear already to have fired off one round, and the fact that they have to shoot repeatedly points ahead to their ultimate failure in that attempt. Still, the point of the painting is not just to show Sebastian's invincibility or suffering: the Pollaiuoli used this choice of narrative episode to focus attention on bodies engaged in the loading and discharging of weapons. Once we regard the painting as a depiction of physical operations, it becomes more difficult to dwell on the antithesis between the saint and his opponents. Sebastian is essentially a variation on the figures who surround him; he wears dress nearly identical to the man with the loincloth in the central foreground.

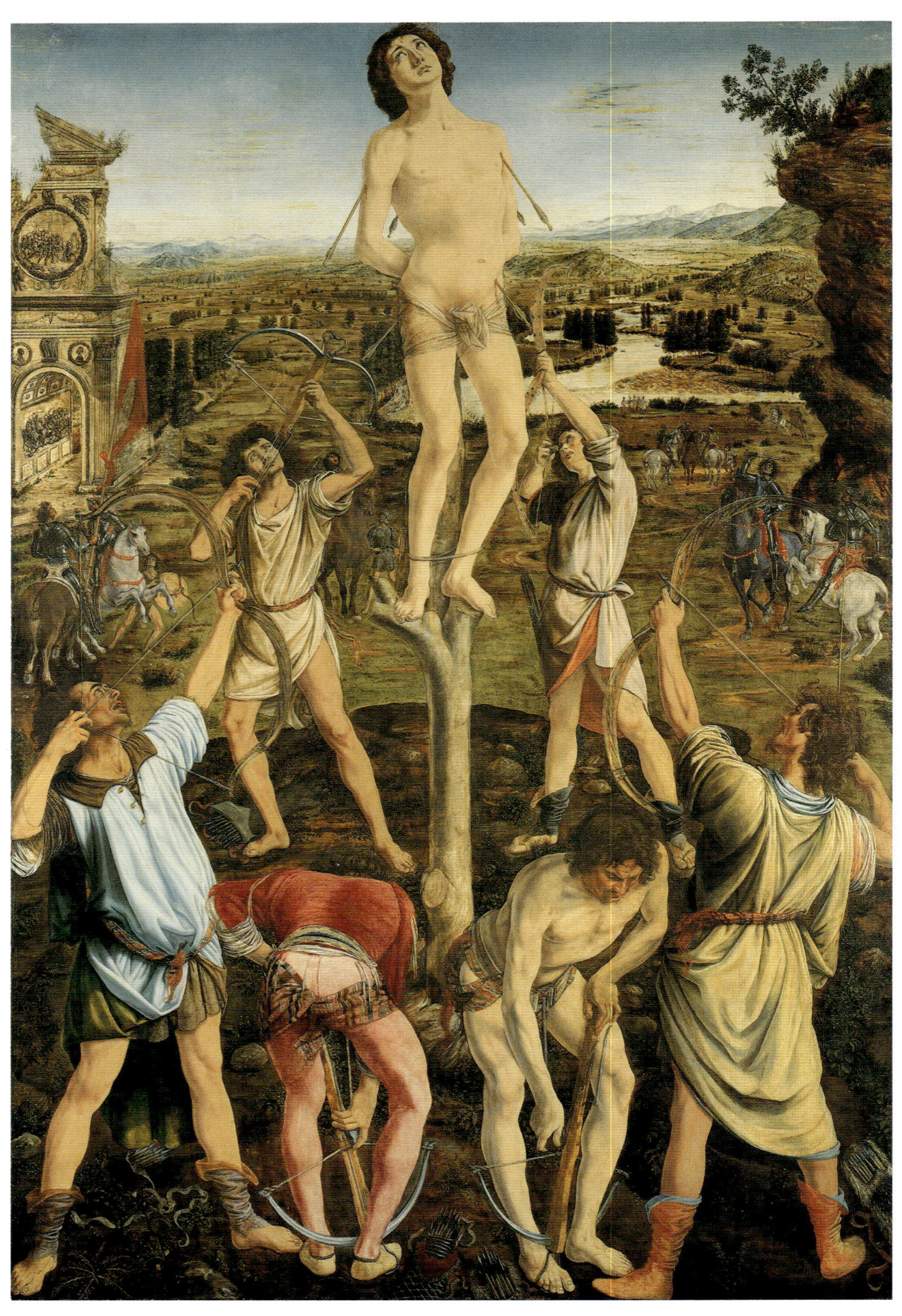

65   Antonio and Piero del Pollaiuolo, *St. Sebastian*, oil on panel,
National Gallery, London

The bending bows underscore the idea of flexion, but also function as a measure of the effort each figure expends, registering force with its own form. Note especially the red face of the figure just to the right of the center in the foreground. We might even say that the Pollaiuoli compare the human body to the bow, thinking of its functions on analogy with the machine. Bodies and bow are both things to be bent; Sebastian is particularly bow-like, his position determined by the fixing of ropes, though the point really bears on all seven of the primary actors.

Leonardo on "violence"

The Pollaiuiolo brothers were hardly the only painters to take up the metaphor of body as bow. Michelangelo, as we have seen, adopted it when painting the Sistine Chapel ceiling. Later, he made a finished drawing in red chalk of archers, most of them shooting without bows, as though the bending of their bodies was all that mattered. No one devoted more reflection to the topic, however, than Leonardo da Vinci. Leonardo himself became preoccupied with the bow between 1483 and the early 1490s, while attempting contemporaneously to design a colossal, functioning crossbow for Lodovico Sforza and to write a treatise on military engineering that would supersede Valturio's (the standard text in the period).[33] But Leonardo's reflections on the weapon took him outside the domain of military functionality. When Valturio wrote about the bow, he dwelt on its use through history; in Leonardo, by contrast, the bow becomes a leitmotif, by way of which Leonardo sought to understand a notable variety of processes and principles.

As the mechanism that introduced motion into the arrow, the crossbow in the first place illustrated what Leonardo thought of as "violence" (*violenza*):

> The blow given by a light weight is made as potent as the potency of its cause. Thus, an arrow weighs three ounces. A force made by a weight of 400 pounds pulls the cord of the crossbow back to the latch, and in its undoing, the said force is transmuted and attaches itself to the arrow.

Thus, so long as an arrow weighs three ounces, it carries with it in its course the nature of such weight as was its cause.

Every weight that is expelled through violent motion adds to itself during its flight such potential as was the cause of its course.[34]

Leonardo's language here Italianizes the Latin term that Renaissance philologists had used to render the Greek *kinesis bia*, a force or motion contrary to nature.[35] Ultimately, he is invoking the kind of antithesis that Aristotle drew in *Physics* 215a, where he wrote that "every motion must be either natural or forced, and there can be no such thing as forced movement if there is no natural movement, for forced movement is movement counter to that which is natural, and the unnatural presupposes the natural." More narrowly, what interests Leonardo here is the transformation of weight into force and back again: a weight applied to the string creates a force, which in turn becomes a counterforce that attaches itself to another weight (a three-ounce arrow.) The mechanism of the crossbow allows Leonardo to diagram "nature" and "violence" in opposition to one another: the weight that charges the bow is a "nature," the motion that unleashes the arrow is a "violence."

But it is important to note that the opposition is purely schematic, that it could be modeled by the crossbow in exactly the opposite way as well. In its structure, after all, the crossbow is a kind of sibling to the machine for bending beams. In operating the crossbow, it is not just the arrow but also the limbs of the machine (Leonardo calls them the "molle," the springs) that move. Violent motion is present – violent motion is required – even before the trigger is pulled.

This recognition allowed Leonardo to reverse the dynamic we have just seen him describe. On folio 842v of the Codex Atlanticus, he shows, in the middle of the page, something like a conventional crossbow, seen in plan (fig. 66). The text beside it reads, "I ask you: if this crossbow, or rather, if this crossbow's cord, is pulled from a to c by a weight of 400 pounds, how much weight will it take to move the said cord from a to b, that is, halfway between a c?"[36] The text makes clear that the orientation of the crossbow is significant, for its cord has to be understood as being dragged

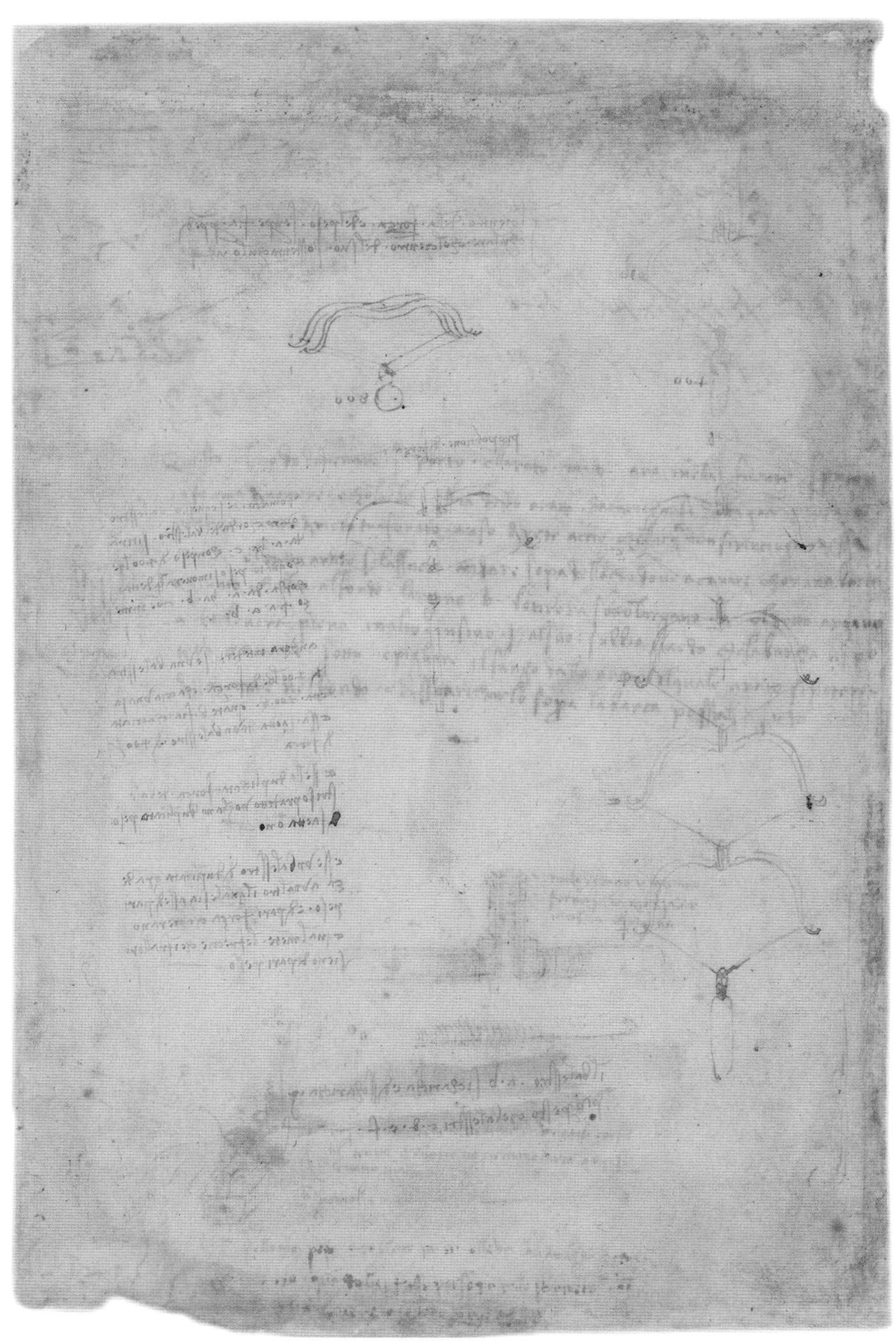

66   Leonardo, Codex Atlanticus, fol. 842v, Biblioteca Ambrosiana, Milan

downward by weight. It also shows that the relation between weight and force – the heading on the top of the sheet is "De forza e peso" – can be explored even without an arrow. Indeed, it can be explored even by considering just a fragment of the bow. The remaining six crossbows on the page all lack a barrel, and we might even doubt that Leonardo was still thinking of them as crossbows had he not labeled them – "balestri." The interest is entirely in what weight does to the crossbow's arms. Along the right side of the sheet, four crossbows have been hooked together in such a way that the weight at the bottom acts up through the entire chain. Although Leonardo's note here refers to the speed with which such bows could "discharge" themselves, the experimental arrangement has made it impossible for any of them to fire anything.

Another sheet dis- and re-assembles the elements of the crossbow still further (fig. 68). The paragraphs in the top right column suggest that the goal here was to consider "the proportion of force and motion," beginning with these two questions:

> I ask: if a crossbow propels an arrow 400 braccia, will a crossbow that is proportionally formed with four times the force and size propel the arrow four times as far?
>
> I ask: if a crossbow of equal weight is mounted in these various sizes over a single length, what effect will this have on the distances it propels an identical arrow?[37]

Leonardo must have puzzled over this in the course of trying to scale up this crossbow. Yet the drawing below is more an investigation by analogy than a step in the direction of any practical design. What this looks like is a group of crossbow arms that have been mounted above one another on a single staff in such a way that those higher up the chain bear increasingly more weight. While Leonardo is still concerned with proportion here, what is growing by increments – at least in the drawing – is the weight attached to the same arm, not the arm itself.

At the top of the next column, he returns to the topic of violent motion:

Force.

The force in bodies cannot be created without force or weight together with motion.

Force.

Force is caused by violent motion by means of weight or another force.[38]

Here, as before, Leonardo is thinking primarily in terms of displacements. But whereas initially violent force was what moved an arrow upward, now it is what drags an arm down.

All of this is the verso of the sheet, though a shadow comes through from the recto, where we find Leonardo abandoning military concerns altogether and thinking about a motor for a flying machine (fig. 67). Now its *schematic* structure becomes especially visible. In the first place, the crossbow form is what Leonardo's inscription refers to as the "fondamento del moto," the basis of motion. In the device on the lower left, the arms of the crossbow have become springs that, gradually discharging their tension, cause cords to turn wheels. In the larger drawing that takes up most of the page, a similar motor has been inserted into the framework of the flying machine itself. The crossbow's arms still move cords, but those cords now extend and retract the joined bones of the wing structure above – a wing structure that we might see as an enlargement of the very same crossbow. Suddenly, the concern on the verso with the mechanical consequences of scaling take on a surprising incidental significance: Leonardo realizes that his research into monumental war equipment might teach him something about how a small bowed device can drive a larger but similarly structured machine, lifting the machine, rather than an arrow, into the air.

Of course, it is possible to see the wings of the flying machine not only as enlargements of the crossbow but as anatomized human arms. On other sheets, a human body takes the place of the crossbow–motor. It is perhaps not surprising, then, that Leonardo ultimately compares the actions of the crossbow to that of the human body. He does this indirectly in a drawing like that on folio 1070 recto (fig. 69), where figure and crossbow are

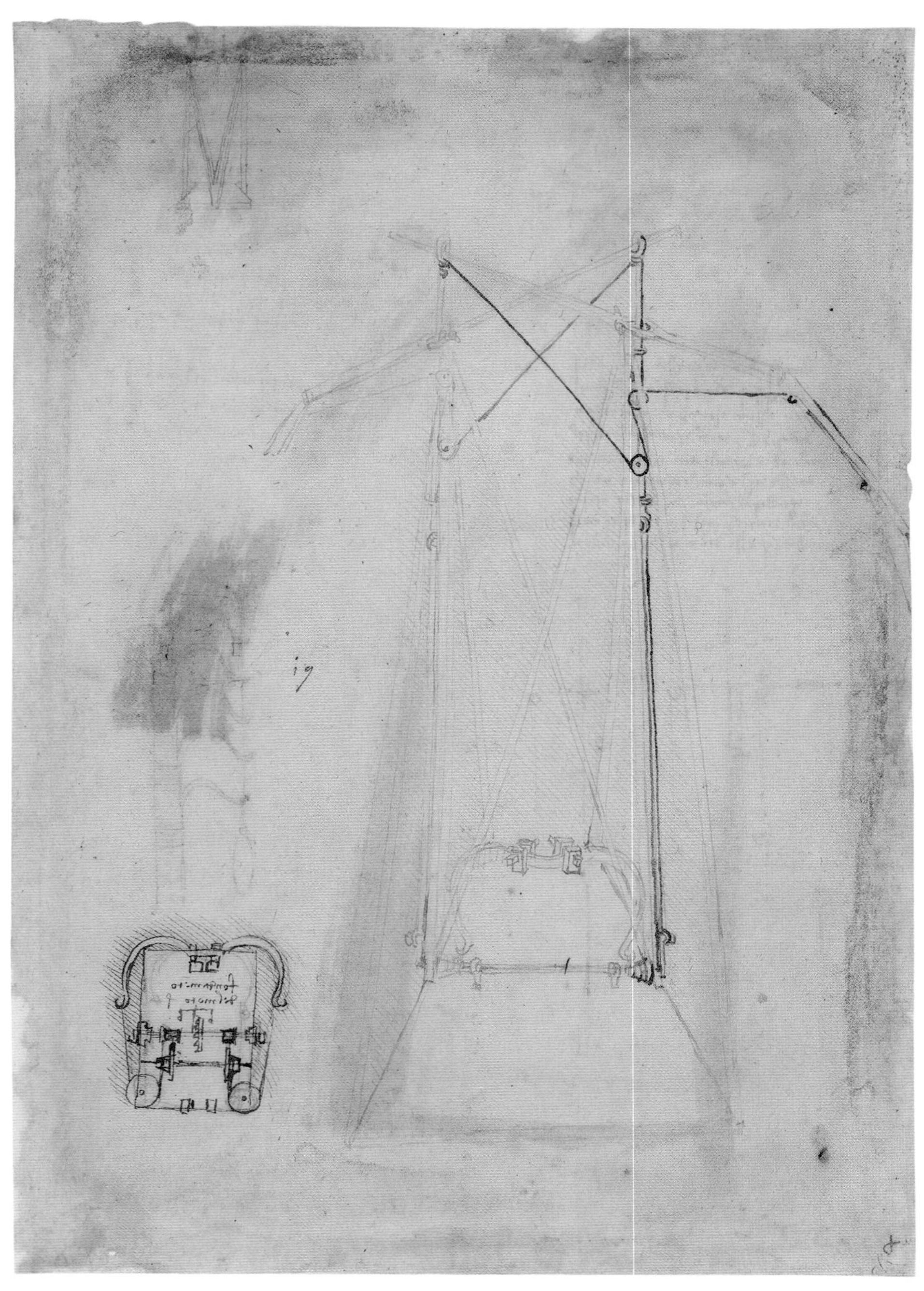

67   Leonardo, Codex Atlanticus, fol. 863r, Biblioteca Ambrosiana, Milan

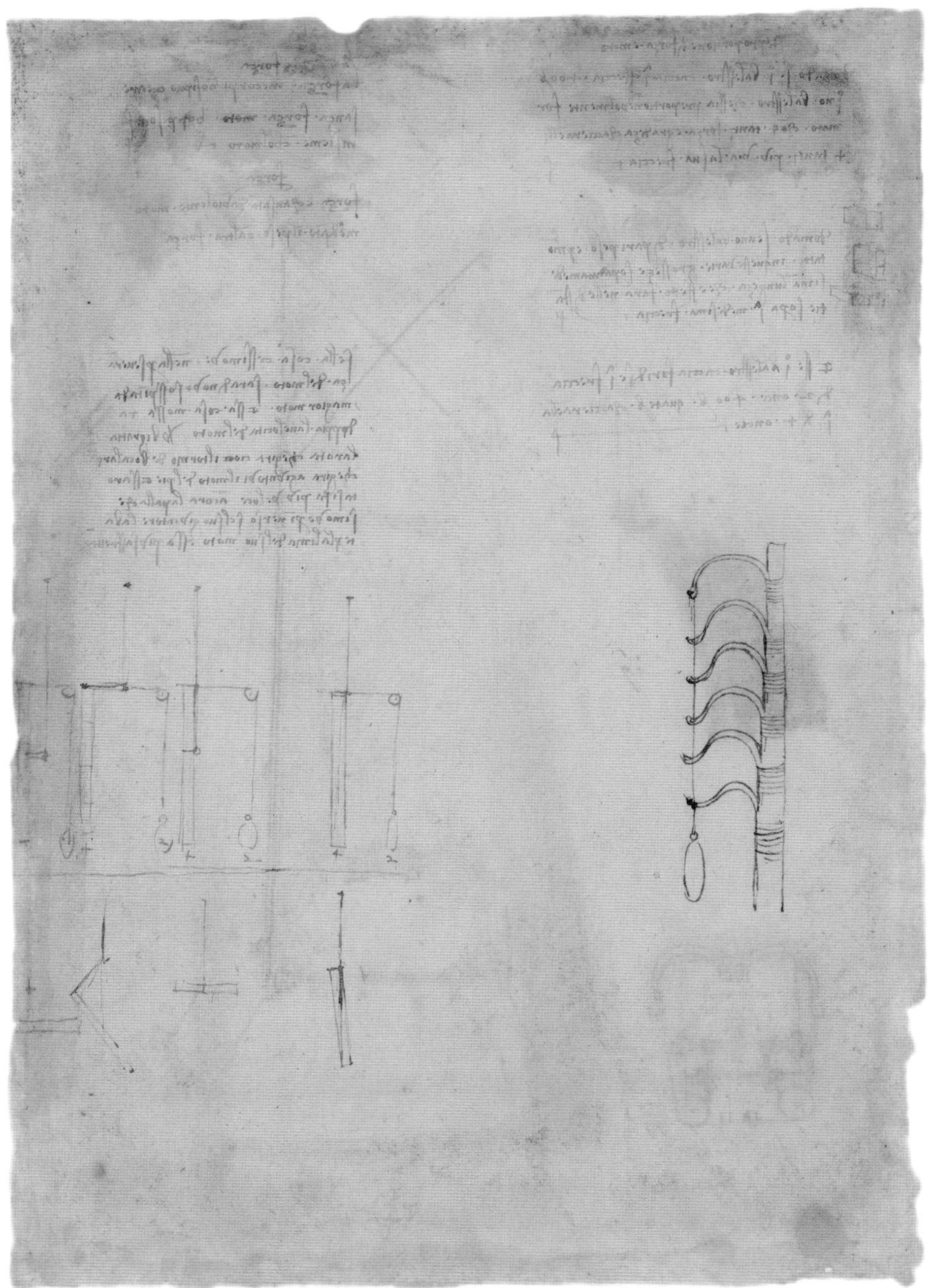

68   Leonardo, Codex Atlanticus, fol. 863v, Biblioteca Ambrosiana, Milan

incorporated into one great machine: the expenditure of human energy loads one crossbow after the next. It is a machine for converting, translating, human force into the crossbow's. And he does this directly – for the first time, to my knowledge – on folio 576 verso of the Codex Atlanticus, where he writes:

> If a man generates force with his shoulder in a place that resists this, the weight of that force will return to his feet, and if the thing beneath his feet consents, it will be moved by the force extending from the man and through the weight of that man. But if at the same time the thing touched by the shoulder consents and that consent returns with its motion in favor of the motion caused by the said man, which he then makes with his shoulder, will it not be lacking then at his feet? Certainly it will, and I give this example. A crossbow stands bent by a force of 400 pounds, in an exchange of cord between two pilasters, and it opens such that each pilaster feels 200 pounds of the force; whence if one of those pilasters has such weight that it resists that 200 pounds, the crossbow ought to stand firm in its force and not toss that pilaster to the ground as it does.[39]

Leonardo is essentially comparing the force transmitted from the bent wood of the crossbow to the force transmitted by the exerted man. It is but one of the instances in which Leonardo treats the human body as a *mechanical* subject.[40]

Leonardo was working through these ideas in Milan, probably in the 1490s. But the same principles ultimately guided his conception of the *Anghiari*, particularly the "Battle for the Standard," a dramatization precisely of force and its resistance, with men bending a piece of wood. But it is also in the *Anghiari* project more broadly that we see him most explicitly bringing reflections on the mechanics of movement into the design process. The verso of one sheet now in Venice bears further comments on the "motors" of animate and inanimate bodies, on "natural" and "violent" movement. By now, the latter term has come to look like a near synonym for "artificial," though it is hardly incidental that Leonardo developed his theory of violence by meditating on a weapon. That becomes all the more

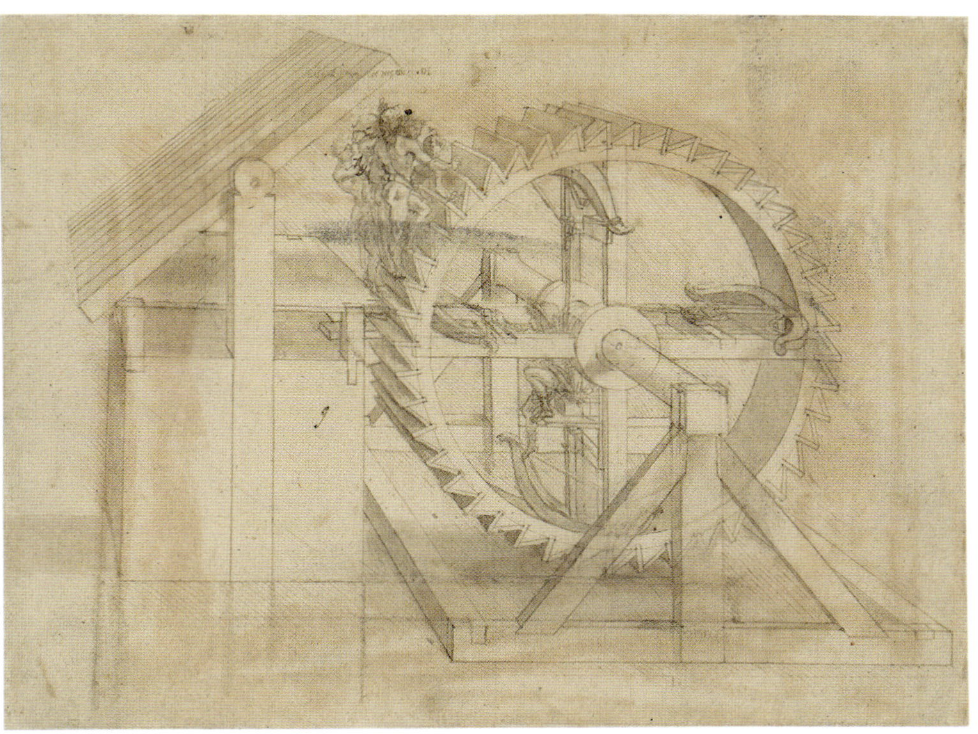

69   Leonardo, Codex Atlanticus, fol. 1070r, Biblioteca Ambrosiana, Milan

clear on the recto of the Venice sheet (fig. 70), which contains, at the top, some sketches of horsemen and foot soldiers in a skirmish, presumably an early idea for the *Anghiari*. Below this, individual figures swing weapons – or, in one case, bend under the blows of a weapon. These are the immediate descendants of the figures Leonardo earlier showed working with machines. And should we have any doubt that he also thought of them in conjunction with the text on the back of the page, we need only look at the way that the posthumously compiled *Trattato della pittura* isolated and explained such actions:

The apparatus of force in every movement wants to be carried out with twistings and bendings of great violence, and wants the return to be easy and comfortable. In this way the operation will have a good effect.

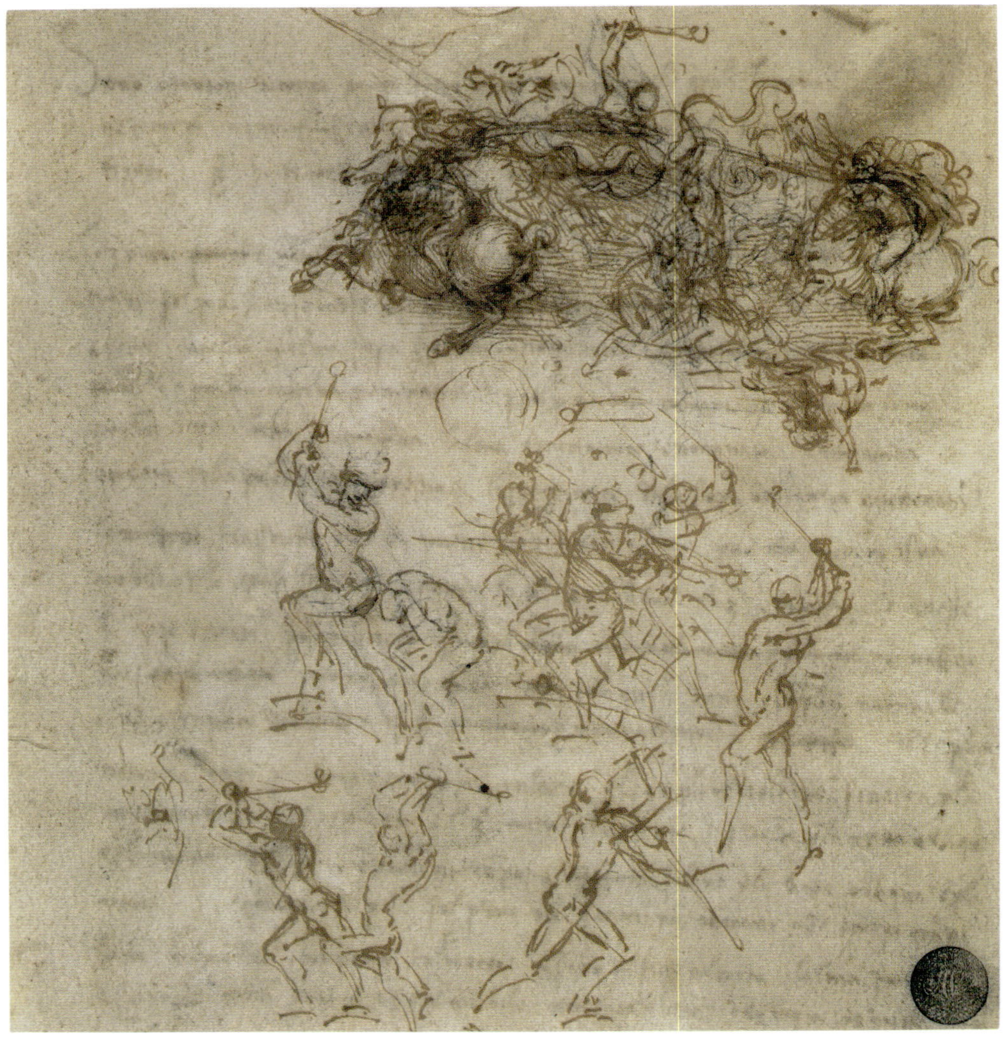

70   Leonardo, studies for the *Battle of Anghiari*, pen and brown ink over black chalk on paper, Gallerie dell'Accademia, Venice

When a crossbow does not have violent tension, the movement of the thing thrown from it will be short or nil. For wherever there is no violent undoing, there is no motion, and where there is no violence, that violence cannot be destroyed. For this reason the bow that has no violence cannot shoot if it does not acquire violence, and, once acquiring it, does not chase that violence from itself. Thus a man who is not twisted or bent has acquired no potential.[41]

As we have already seen, the comparison between the bow and the bent human figure was not entirely new. But what it allowed Leonardo to do was to bring an Aristotelian language of mechanics to bear specifically on the performance of human gesture. At first, Leonardo had used the concept of violent, counter-natural force primarily to describe the impulse that drove the arrow from the bow, the charge that arrow carried with it on its flight. By the time of the *Anghiari*, however, the orientation of force had been reversed. No longer was "violence" an unleashed force – no longer was it manifest primarily in the shooting of the arrow – but the exact opposite of this, the tightening of a form that empowered it to act. Where figuration was concerned, counter-natural *violenza* is what displaced a body from its natural position such that that body wanted to return to its original, natural state.

Signorelli

In the past, it was common to present Leonardo as a man out of time, one whose writings and experiments could be understood only in relation to themselves. But Bertrand Gille's remarkable 1964 *Les Ingénieurs de la Renaissance* reoriented scholarship on Leonardo's technological studies by demonstrating the degree to which the artist's formation as an engineer depended on reading and on exchanges with contemporaries; historians of technology now tend to characterize Leonardo's depictions of war machines or of devices for pulling and lifting as the products not of a lonely experimenter and inventor, but of a well-traveled and well-informed court artist, not to mention a reader of the most recent mechanical theory. A similar point could be extended to Leonardo's terminology, noting that the language Leonardo learned to employ when reflecting on mechanical problems must have come in no small part from early Renaissance practitioners and writers. Giovanni Fontana was describing a pulley system in terms of "violence" already by 1440.[42] The physics behind Leonardo's "apparecchio della forza" was a shared topic of discussion, even if Leonardo's way of articulating the comparison between the bow and the body is particularly vivid and memorable.

Some of the sources for Leonardo's writings must have belonged to an oral culture that is now only partially measurable. But the converse is also true: to the degree that Leonardo's science represents a larger culture, the fact that he wrote so extensively makes him especially valuable as a witness. His discussions of violence, however, offer a perspective on the broader visual culture. Leonardo's way of seeing, his "period eye," helps us notice things in works by his contemporaries that we might otherwise miss. To see the way that the Anghiari and Cascina scenes shed light on a more broadly shared set of artistic interests and practices, let us look at the nearly contemporary paintings of Luca Signorelli.

Signorelli had clearly studied the Pollaiuolo bothers' *St. Sebastian*, and he painted his own monumental version of the subject as an altarpiece (fig. 71) for a funerary chapel in Città di Castello in 1498.[43] Like the earlier panel, this drew particular attention to the jointed movements of the men in the foreground, yet in Signorelli's rendering their weapons become far more marvelous machines. The anachronistic specification that Sebastian's tormentors would have employed this sort of crossbow is notable in a painting made in the very years when Leonardo was formulating his ideas on "the apparatus of force." Indeed, the movement of ideas now becomes all the more difficult to untangle. Could Leonardo, too, have seen the Pollaiuolo painting, taking an interest in the same detail that fascinated Signorelli? Was the specific comparison he made, between body and crossbow, one that was already in circulation, to be taken up more or less independently by all three artists? Even more than its predecessor, Signorelli's painting presents a cycle of charge and discharge, a conception of movement keyed to violence and its undoing.

Given these interests, it is not surprising that Signorelli devoted such attention to figure drawing. An early study of the nude shows one of the "Forze" of Hercules, the hero's slaying of the giant Antaeus (fig. 72).[44] A slightly later nude man seen from behind (see fig. 5) establishes a type that Michelangelo would use with only slight variation in the *Cascina*.

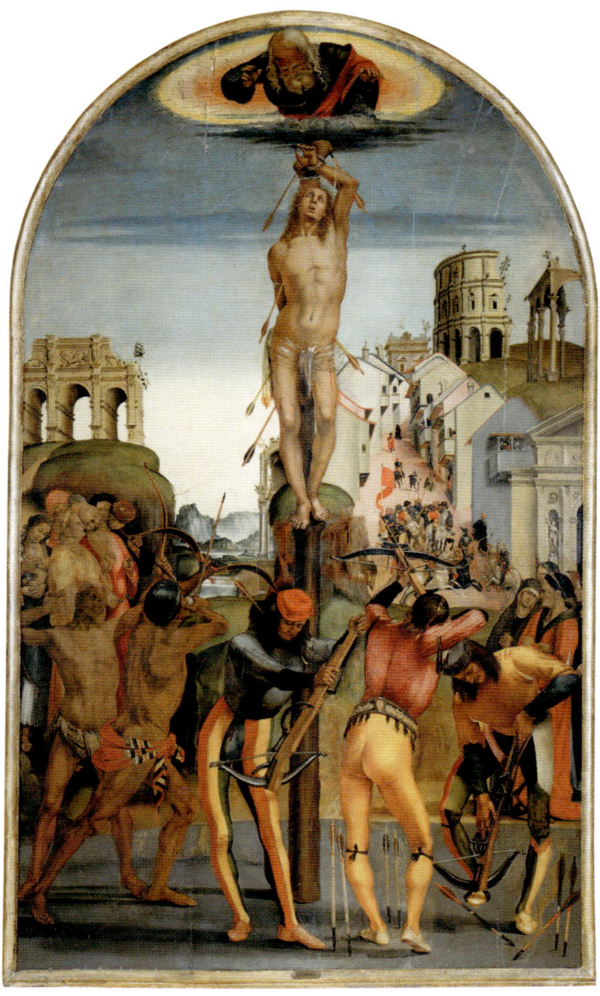

71   Luca Signorelli, *St. Sebastian*, oil on panel,
Pinacoteca Comunale, Città di Castello

(compare fig. 44) Presumably based on a posed assistant, the purpose of its gesture is unspecified, though it bears comparison with that of the man loading the crossbow in the *St. Sebastian*.[45] What can safely be said is that the drawing isolates the figure to study its flexion. Strong contours establish the swing of the hip and the rotation of the torso, a line that runs from the lower back through the neck showing the bending of the spine. A

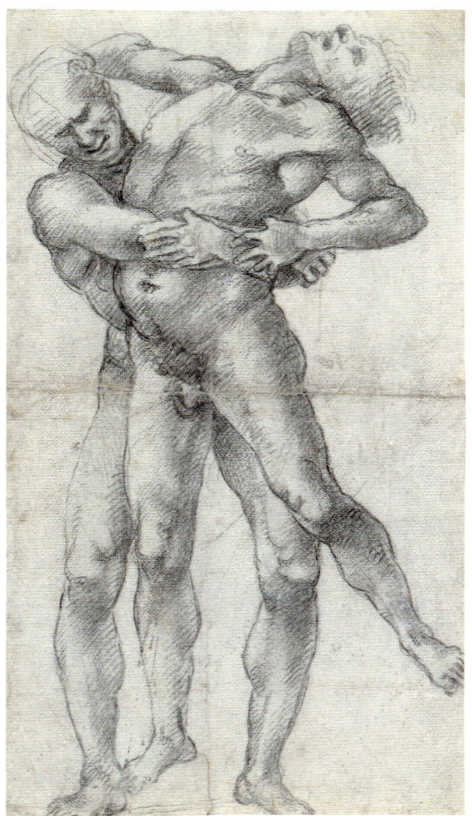

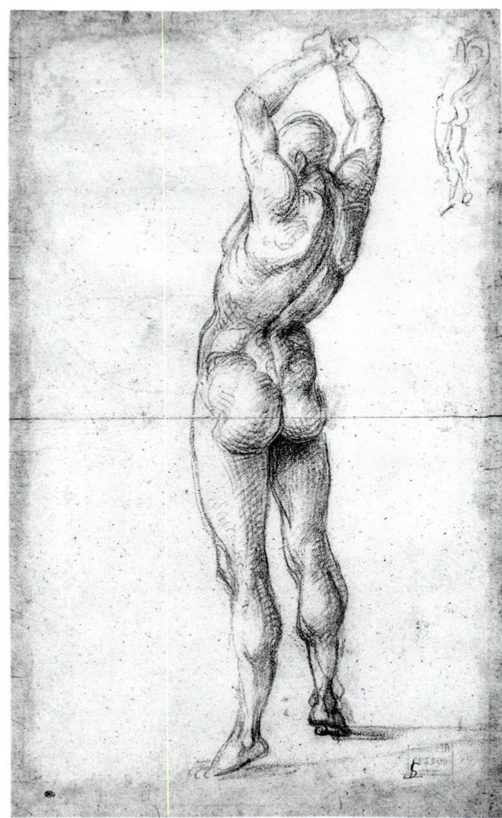

72 (*above left*)   Signorelli, *Hercules and Antaeus*, black chalk on paper,
Royal Collection, Windsor

73 (*above right*)   Signorelli, figure studies, black chalk on paper, Louvre, Paris

pentimento places the left leg in a different position, or rather, shows just
what happens to the leg when it bends at the knee. Similar studies would
continue to occupy Signorelli throughout his late career. One, of a man
preparing to swing some kind of weapon (fig. 73), dates to the years after
Leonardo's *Anghiari*, and resembles the figures that would anchor the
theoretical reflections in the later *Trattato*.

It was just one year after the completion of the *St. Sebastian* that
Signorelli began working on his masterpiece – the most admired mural

cycle completed in Italy in the years just before *Anghiari* and *Cascina* – the frescoes for the Chapel of San Brizio in Orvieto Cathedral. The altar wall of that space contrasts a scene of music-playing angels whose sound helps move the Blessed into a state of rapture with an image of the entrance to Hell, the foreground of which shows a group of demons wrestling with the nude bodies of the Damned (figs 74 and 75). The wrestling theme, which Signorelli also explored in drawings, is then expanded and monumentalized in the large bay immediately to the right (fig. 76). The central motif there, of a demon torturing a man with a rope, brings out the double meaning of "violence" that Leonardo's meditations had already suggested.[46] It is a sadistic vision of human suffering, but also a demonstration of the sort of counter-naturally turned body that Leonardo had attempted to describe with a newly technical Aristotelian language. Both readings provide ways of thinking about Signorelli's choice to render the demons as muscular anthropomorphs.[47] The fact that they have human form makes

74 and 75   Signorelli, altar wall frescoes, San Brizio Chapel, Orvieto Cathedral

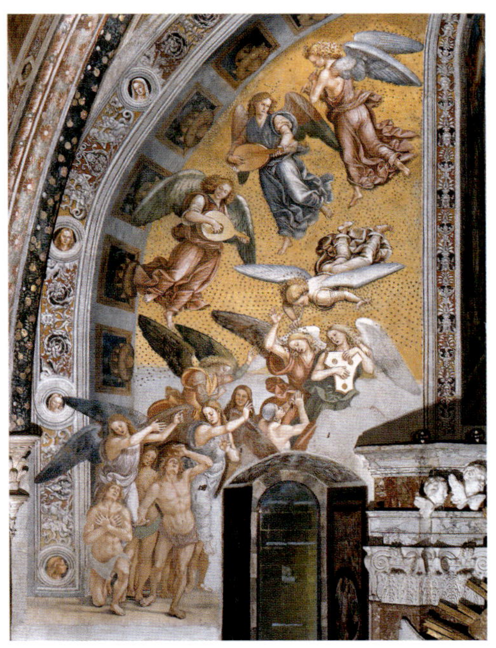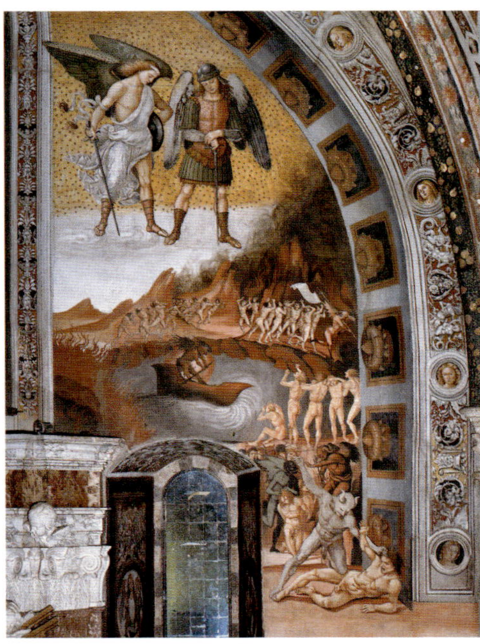

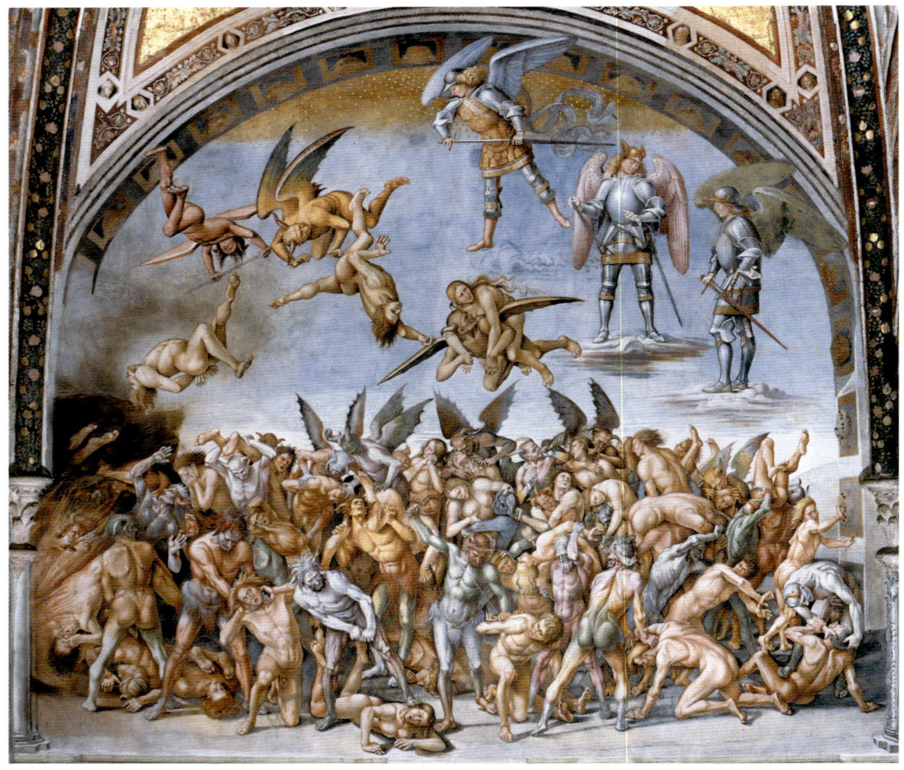

76   Signorelli, *The Damned*, fresco, San Brizio Chapel, Orvieto Cathedral

their actions considerably more menial than we might have expected from demons, and the presence of the rope recalls the imagery of machinery that had found its way into fresco cycles like those of Piero della Francesca and of Filippino Lippi.

The adjacent bay (fig. 77), which Signorelli painted subsequently, shows a similarly dramatic range of human flexions, now without counter-natural pressures. This, like the scene of the Damned, essentially amplifies and expands the *Last Judgment* theme Signorelli had started with. It departs from all previous representations of the *Last Judgment*, though, in its specification that the resurrected dead have skeletons beneath their skin.[48] The theologians with whom Signorelli consulted when painting would easily have justfied the detail, referring to Ezekiel's vision of the Plain of

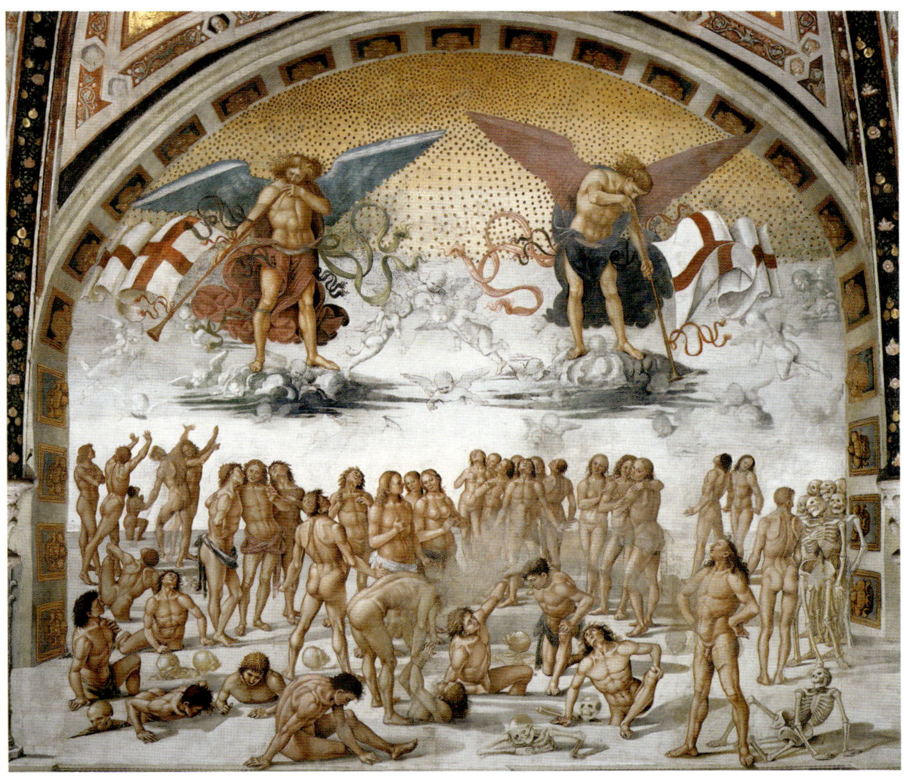

77   Signorelli, *Plain of Dry Bones*, fresco, San Brizio Chapel, Orvieto Cathedral

Dry Bones.[49] But within the broader cycle, the novelty has a different effect, making us aware not only of the woodenness but also of the *jointedness* of the other, enfleshed, bodies throughout the space.[50] The resurrection of the dead was a common subject for automata, and the revelation of the bodies' armature here reminds us that machines, including the automata that Leonardo constructed, were similarly hinged (compare fig. 78).[51]

Across the way is the best-known bay in the chapel, showing the deeds of the Antichrist (fig. 81). Signorelli imagines him as an uncanny double of the Christ whom all viewers would have been accustomed to seeing on chapel walls, whose difference from his true counterpart might initially be missed were it not for the devilish creature who stands at, or perhaps

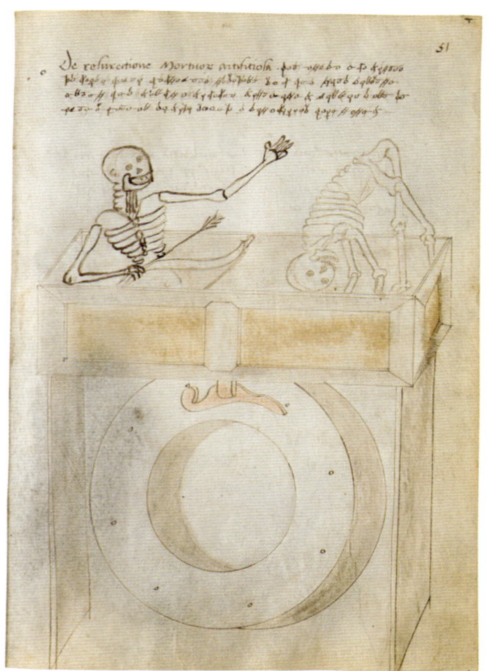

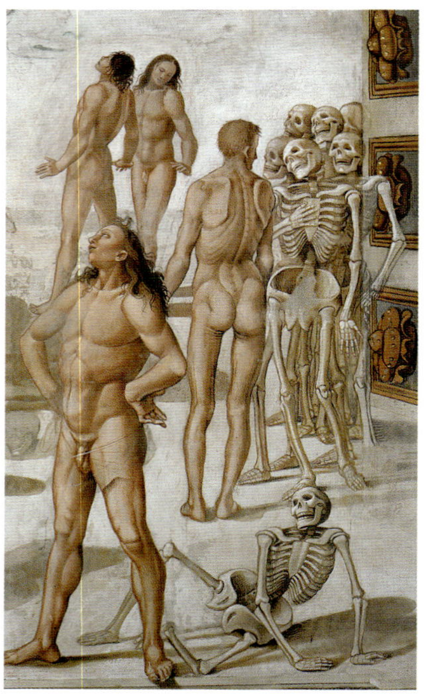

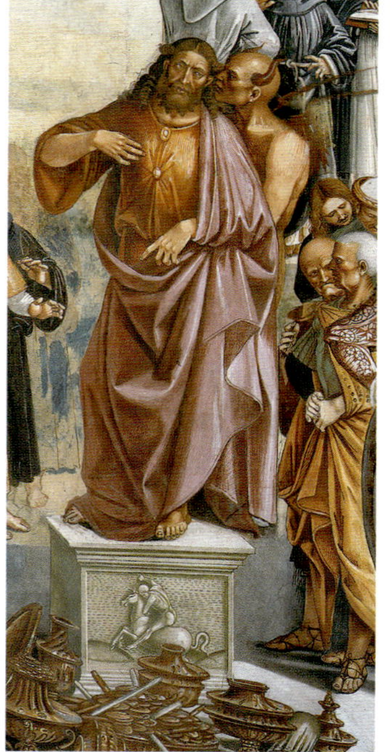

78 (*above left*)   Giovanni Fontana, automaton, *Bellicorum instrumentorum liber*, fol. 51r, Bayeriches Staatsbibiothek, Munich

79 (*above right*)   Signorelli, *Plain of Dry Bones* (detail of fig. 77)

80 (*left*)   Signorelli, *Preaching of the Antichrist*, (detail of fig. 81)

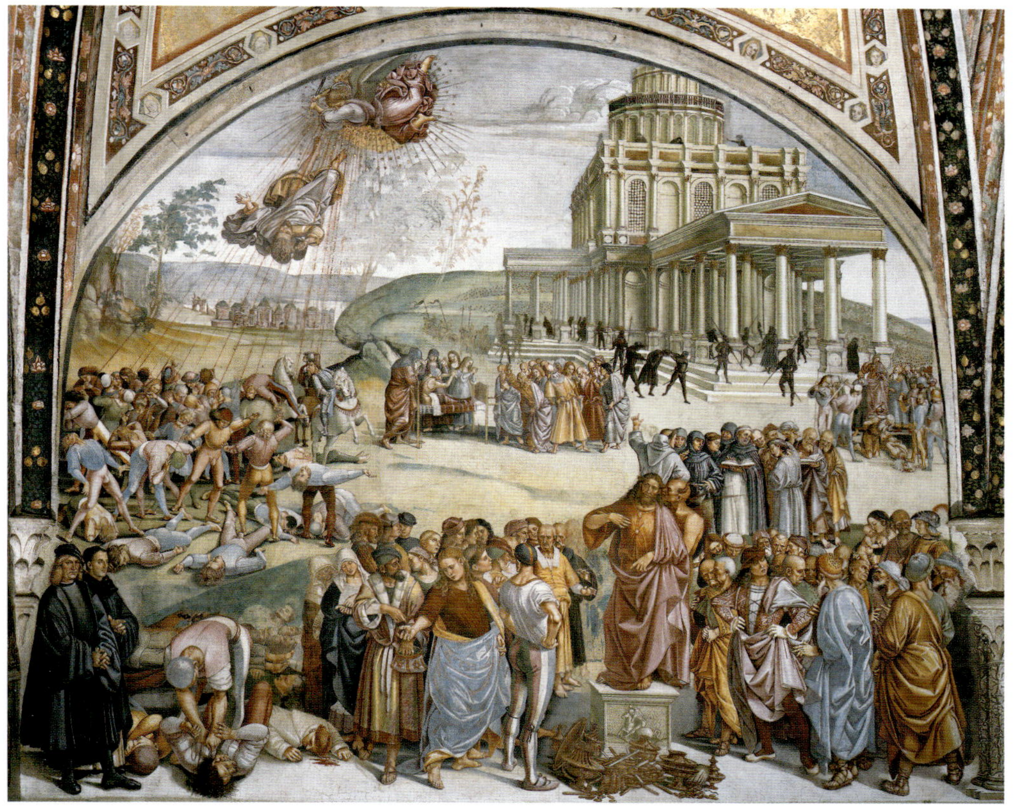

81   Signorelli, *Preaching of the Antichrist*, fresco, San Brizio Chapel, Orvieto Cathedral

emerges from, his side. What is this demon doing?[52] As we see the entity
moving the speaker's arm, whispering into his ear, feeding him words, we
understand that the man on the pedestal is being *operated*. And yet we are
the only ones who see this: the monster is invisible to the listeners around
the rostrum, who take the speaker to be Christ himself.[53] With dramatic
irony, Signorelli simultaneously shows us a machine and reveals its secret.[54]

On the exit wall, Signorelli painted the destruction that precedes the
Last Judgment (fig. 82). Just as he incorporated Ezekiel's vision of the Plain
of Dry Bones on the adjacent wall, so here may Signorelli be referring to
Ezekiel's prophesy of last days (38:22), when fire rains down from the
heavens, though the Book of the Apocalypse also has God send flames

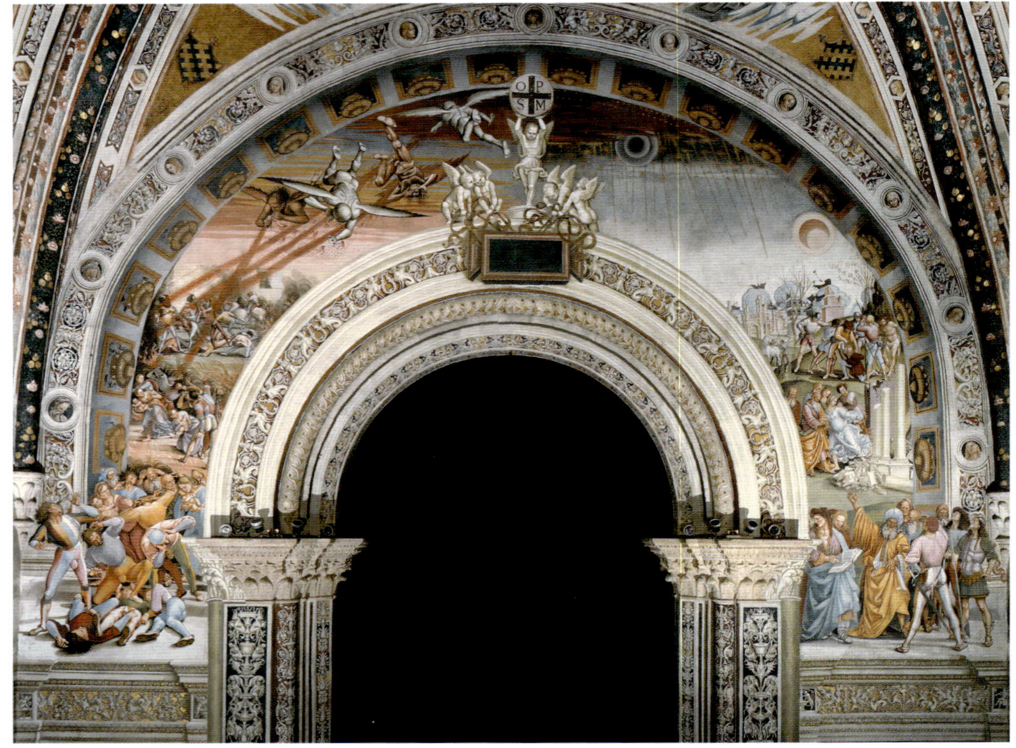

82   Signorelli, *End of the World*, fresco, San Brizio Chapel, Orvieto Cathedral

from the sky (20:9). Either way, the idea of showing not rain, but flying demons breathing fiery rays, is a novelty, one that connects the scene to the wall with the narrative of the Antichrist, who is also destroyed by "lines of force," sent from above.[55] And when these rays strike Signorelli's figures, their bodies do not appear to burn or bleed so much as to turn. Their marionette-like forms recall the Antichrist, a form controlled by an external handler.[56]

Beneath all of this, finally, Signorelli painted an elaborate socle, with portraits, grotesques, and narrative grisailles. These are the most obscure elements of the chapel and with many, there is no scholarly consensus on their subject matter. Suffice it to draw attention to just two of the numerous roundels that take up themes of combat. In the one above the

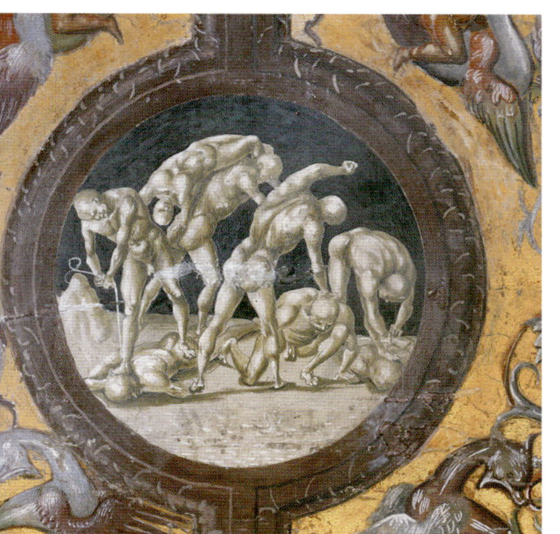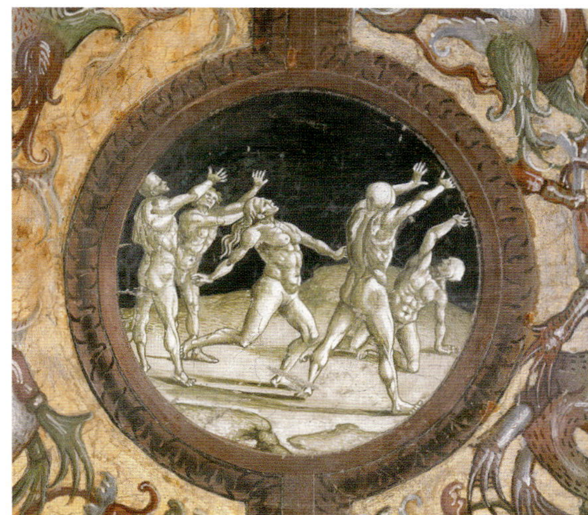

83 and 84   Signorelli, details of frescoed sockels, San Brizio Chapel, Orvieto Cathedral

portrait of an oak-wreathed young man, eight nude men – none of them identifiable – fight with one another (fig. 83).[57] The single piece of equipment the victors have is a rope, with which, once again, one muscular figure turns another. In the scene that occupies the analogous position over the portrait of an older bald man, another group of muscular figures strike dramatic poses (fig. 84).[58] The scene offers no real internal explanation or motivation for their actions. It is as though figures that would have been at home in one of the monumental murals above have simply been transplanted here.

Signorelli brings most of the threads this chapter has been following together. As a student of Piero della Francesca, he would certainly have known the Arezzo frescoes. When he visited Florence in 1483, Filippino's *Crucifixion of St. Peter* would have counted among the newest and most exciting things to see in the city. As we have seen, he paid close attention to Pollaiuolo as well, reemphasizing the elements of the *Sebastian* that had the closest connection to Leonardo. Later in Siena, he painted alongside Pinturicchio, providing frescoes for the very series that included Pinturicchio's *Penelope and the Suitors*: one of these, usually referred to as the

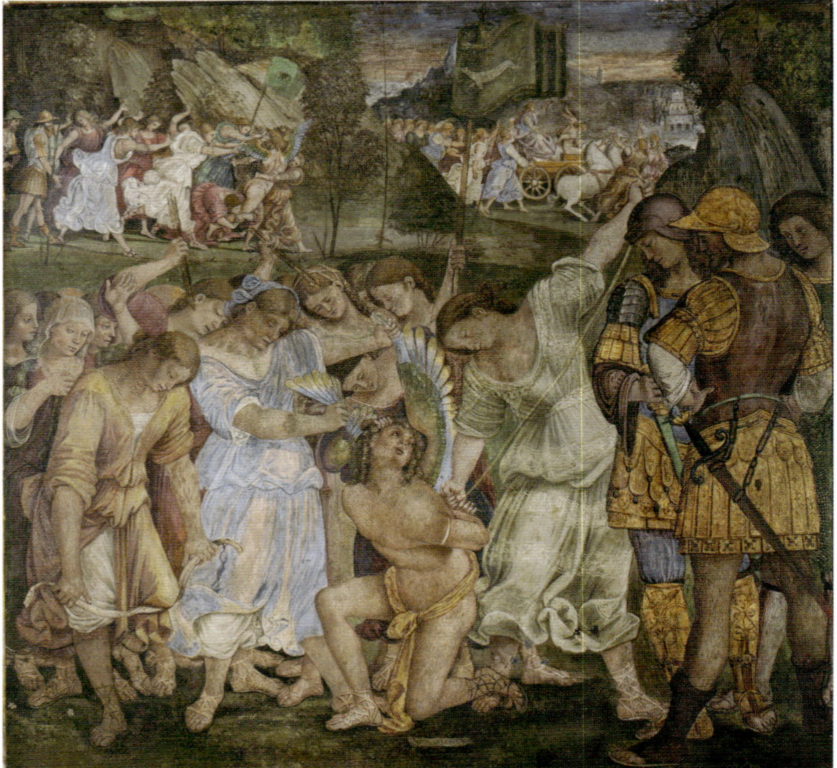

85   Signorelli, *Triumph of Chastity*, detached fresco, National Gallery, London

Triumph of Chastity (fig. 85), shows Love being twisted and bound by a group of powerful women – an erotic variation on the torments that Signorelli had depicted in Orvieto. At left, another woman bends a bow over her knee.

I have been suggesting that all of these connections become meaningful if we allow Leonardo to give us words for them. Still, Vasari tells us that it was Michelangelo who particularly extolled the Orvieto frecoes: in painting the *Last Judgment*, Michelangelo availed himself "of the inventions of Luca in the angels, the demons . . . and other things . . . Michelangelo imitated Luca's method, as all may see."[59] Let us allow for the moment that Vasari is right on this point: we know from the *Carteggio* that

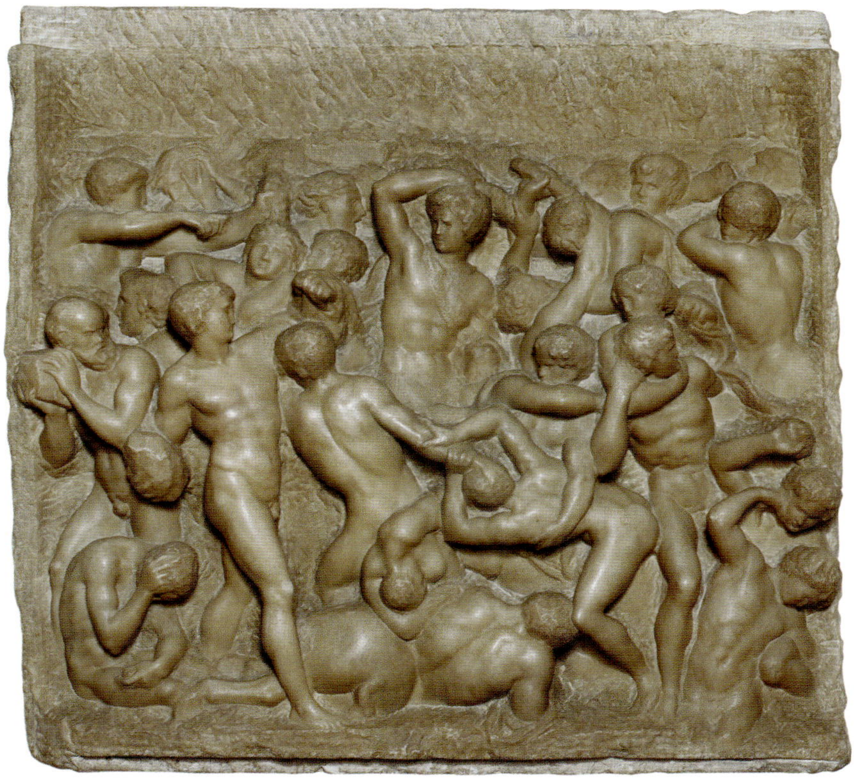

86   Michelangelo, *Battle of the Centaurs*, marble, Casa Buonarroti. Florence

Michelangelo was personally acquainted with Signorelli, and Michelangelo's recent biographers have plausibly speculated that he could have seen the Orvieto frescoes on his journey from Rome to Florence in 1501.[60] Such an encounter with Signorelli might give us one way of thinking about the difference between the *Battle of the Centaurs* (fig. 86), which precedes the Orvieto cycle, and the *Cascina*, which postdates it by just three years and which represents Michelangelo's first project in Signorelli's medium. In the earlier *Battle*, and even in some of the preliminary sketches for the *Cascina*, forms are so entangled as to lose their full legibility as bodies. As his thoughts progressed on the *Cascina*, however, Michelangelo came to sharply individualize depicted actions, both from figure to figure and within the single body. The Council Hall projects, like Signorelli's only slightly earlier murals, betray a fascination with extrinsically no less than intrinsically motivated poses, and with the portrayal of figures where this difference is hard to discern.

Cascina and Anghiari, Revisited

Among a series of counsels for the composition of narrative paintings, Book Two of Leonardo's *Trattato* offers the following advice:

> Remember, painter, when you depict a single figure, to avoid fore-shortening it in its parts as well as the whole, because otherwise you will have to contend with the ignorance of those who are uneducated in that art. But in narrative paintings [*nelle istorie*] do this wherever you have an opportunity, and especially in battles, where necessarily there occurs an infinite number of distortions and contortions of those who take part in such discord or, you might say, most bestial madness.[61]

Leonardo did not have any illusions about the brutality of war, and his final words propose that fighting makes men into animals.[62] The grimacing faces of the soldiers and the detail of one horse biting another in the *Battle for the Standard* radically distinguish his approach from Michelangelo, committed as that artist was to the depiction of male beauty.[63] Yet passages such as this, like his reflections on "violence," show that Leonardo was also capable of taking a more removed, analytical perspective on his subject matter. The idea of soldiers as beasts conforms with a range of earlier, less violent, drawings comparing human and animal forms. And most of the comment above is devoted to drawing two subtle distinctions that have to do not with the nature of war but with painting as such.

The first is between depictions of the single figure and multi-figure compositions. This is intuitive enough even to art historians today, mapping onto the line we now commonly draw between icons and narratives.[64] Whereas modern scholars have taken such oppositions to turn on things like the format of the picture (horizontal versus vertical) and the scale of the figures relative to the picture field (the theatrical picture box versus the dramatic close-up), the *Trattato* instead rests the matter on what the painter does with bodies. Narrative pictures allow for figural contortion and for *scorti* (conventionally translated as "foreshortenings," things that come at you, out of the picture); paintings of single figures do not.

The second distinction is not between paintings but between audiences: the knowing and the ignorant, the learned and the *indotti*. In justifying the injunction to avoid *scorti* in single figures, the *Trattato* does not actually raise any pictorial considerations. It simply observes that if the painter does in such a work employ *scorti*, that work will appeal only to a narrow audience. Indeed, the point seems to be that in battle scenes a broad public will accept a kind of artifice that the sophisticated would value in *any* work. The battle scene is a pretense for a public demonstration of virtuosity.

Evaluating just how true Leonardo's actual practice of painting stayed to this precept depends on what we place in the category of the "sola figura." His early Vatican *St. Jerome* and his late *John the Baptist* in the Louvre both give their protagonists complicated poses and employ at least some foreshortening. In both cases, however, those choices also reflect the fact that the chief character belongs to a kind of narrative – Jerome prays to his crucifix, John delivers a sermon or prophesy. The majority of Leonardo's single figure paintings are portraits. Even in those, we might hesitate to say that Leonardo avoided foreshortening "in the parts as well as the whole." On the contrary, we now tend rather to underscore the role he played in the broader historical shift from a profile portrait format to a composition that addressed or even seemingly responded to the beholder, engaging the axis perpendicular to the picture plane, the sightline of the man standing before it.[65] Still, one might recognize a certain decorous containment of Leonardo's single figure subjects as well – his portraits, notably, avoid dramatic gestures of the sort that Raphael and Titian would soon take up in their own portraits, but which Leonardo reserved for *istorie*.

With Michelangelo, by contrast, it is difficult to draw any useful distinction between the *sola figura* and the *istoria*. He does not seem to have made any paintings at all that contain just one figure. At the same time, he did make highly worked drawings of the complete single human form (see figs. 37–9), and he lent them *storciamenti e piegamenti* that have minimal narrative motivation. If Leonardo's Venice drawing (see fig. 70) powerfully illustrates his idea that battle paintings invite infinite contortions, Michelangelo, treating a bath scene as though it were a battle, keeps Leonardo's distortion but dispenses with the bestial madness.

To explain figural flexion, Leonardo promoted a principle of decorum. Michelangelo undermined it. And this echoed in the way the two artists were studied. While Raimondi and others found it easy enough to isolate the various figures that Michelangelo's design comprised, the rare attempt to do the same with Leonardo resulted in awkward, incomplete-looking works (fig. 87). The distinctive reception of Michelangelo's cartoon mirrored his own own body-by-body composition (see figs. 37 and 51).[66] The closest analogies to this in the heritage of Leonardo are the copies of the *Trattato* (fig. 88), but the figures in this derive from Leonardo's incidental sketches, not from his actual mural design.

Early viewers understood both artists to have taken "force" as a central theme in their murals. Vasari's description of the *Anghiari* dwelled on a soldier who "seeks by the strength of his shoulders, as he spurs his horse to flight, having turned his body backwards and seized the staff of the standard, to wrest it by force from the hands of four others." Of the men at the lower right, he added, "one on the ground has over him a soldier who has raised his arm as high as possible, that thus with greater force he may plunge a dagger into his throat."[67] Cellini wrote of the *Cascina* that although Michelangelo went on to paint the Sistine Chapel, "he never again made anything half as good; his powers (*virtù*) never again attained the force (*forza*) of these first studies."[68]

But if such remarks help establish the historical terms we might use for comparing the *Cascina* and the *Anghiari*, they also underscore just how strongly the role, place, and direction of force in the two pictures differs. Both painters centered their scenes on the staff of a standard – they were painting for the hall of the standard-bearer. But whereas Michelangelo abbreviated his, to the extent that we might not recognize it as a flagstaff

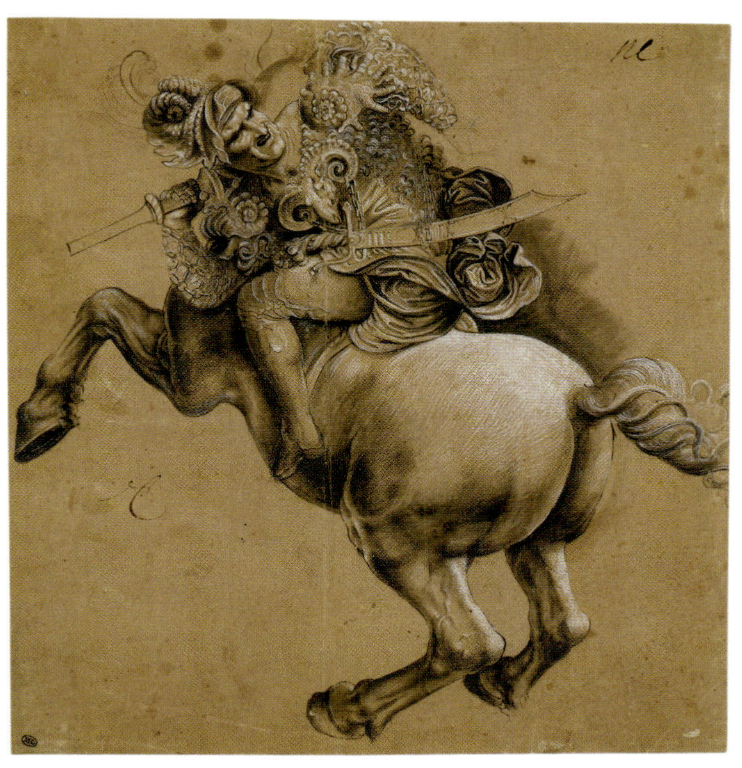

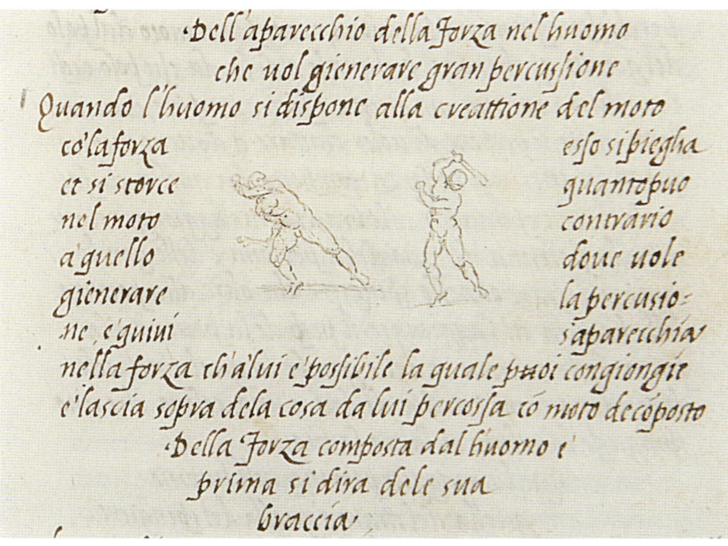

·Dell'aparecchio della Forza nel huomo
che uol gienerare gran percussione
Quando l'huomo si dispone alla creattione del moto
co'la forza   esso si piegha
et si storce   quanto puo
nel moto   contrario
a quello   doue uole
gienerare   la percussione, e guiui   s'aparecchia
nella forza ch'alui e possibile la quale puoi congiongie
e'lascia sopra dela cosa da lui percossa co moto decoposto
·Della Forza composta dal huomo e
prima si dira dele sua
braccia·

87 (*top*)   Anonymous sixteenth-century copy after Leonardo's *Battle of Anghiari*, black chalk and white heighten on paper, Louvre, Paris

88 (*above*)   "Man swinging a weapon, "after Leonardo's *Trattato*, as positioned in the Codex Urbinas

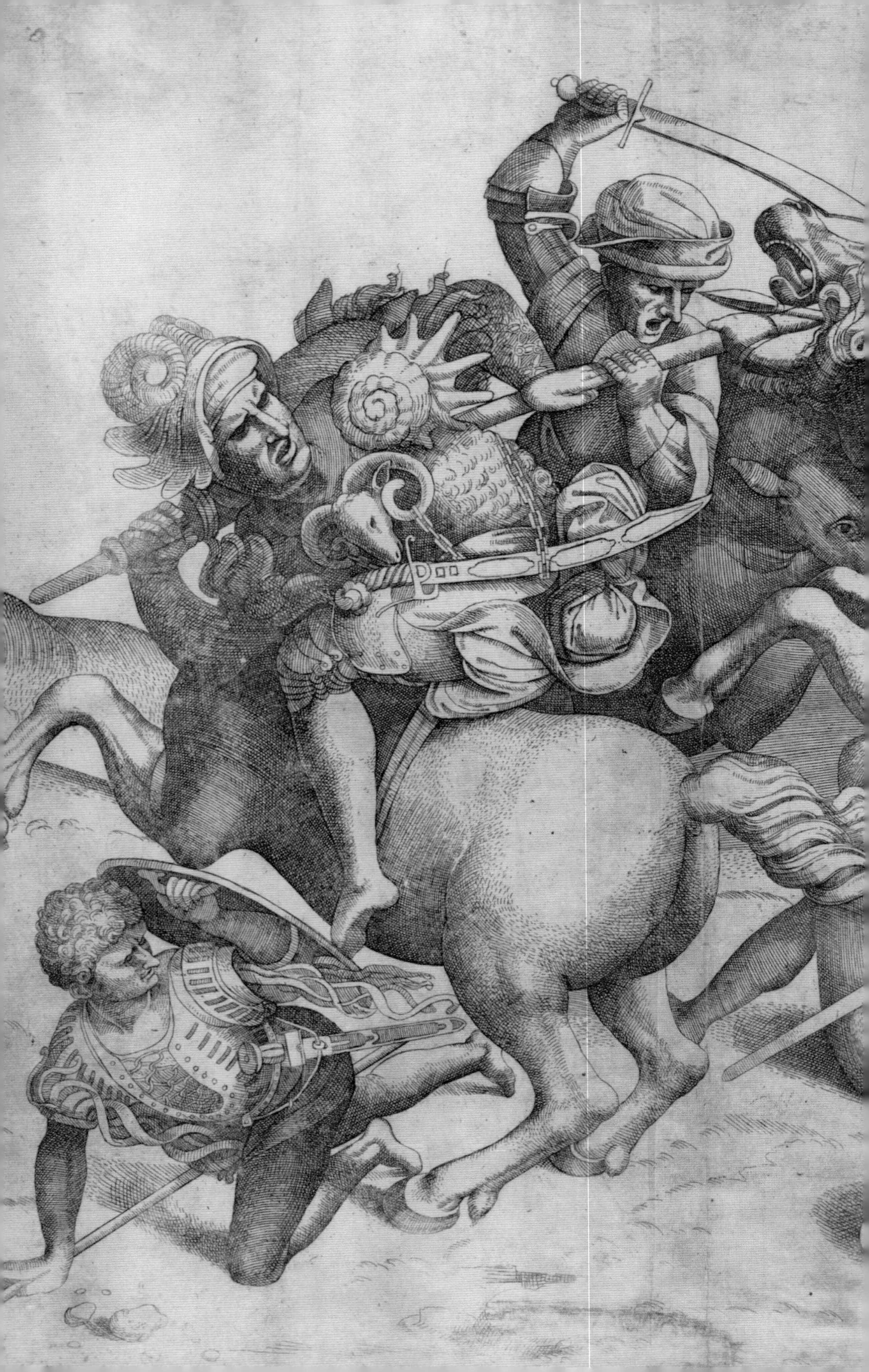

at all – numerous individuals in the Holkham Hall painting hold similar-looking objects – Leonardo organizes everything around the device. Like the axe handle in Pollaiuolo's engraving, and like the bows Leonardo drew in Milan, it provides a flexible form to which contrary pressures are applied, transforming it both into a machine and into a charged double of the bodies themselves. In Michelangelo, there is no such exchange anywhere in the composition. If his figures are expressions of force, that force is not part of an apparatus; Michelangelo has focused entirely on the counter-natural turning of the body, with no implication that something comes out of that. Nothing is explained in Michelangelo by comparing the figure with the machine. In Leonardo, by contrast, the whole painting is a machine, or rather a set of interlocking machines, in which every movement has consequences for every other.

89 Lorenzo Zacchia, engraving after Leonardo's *Battle of Anghiari* (detail of fig. 9)

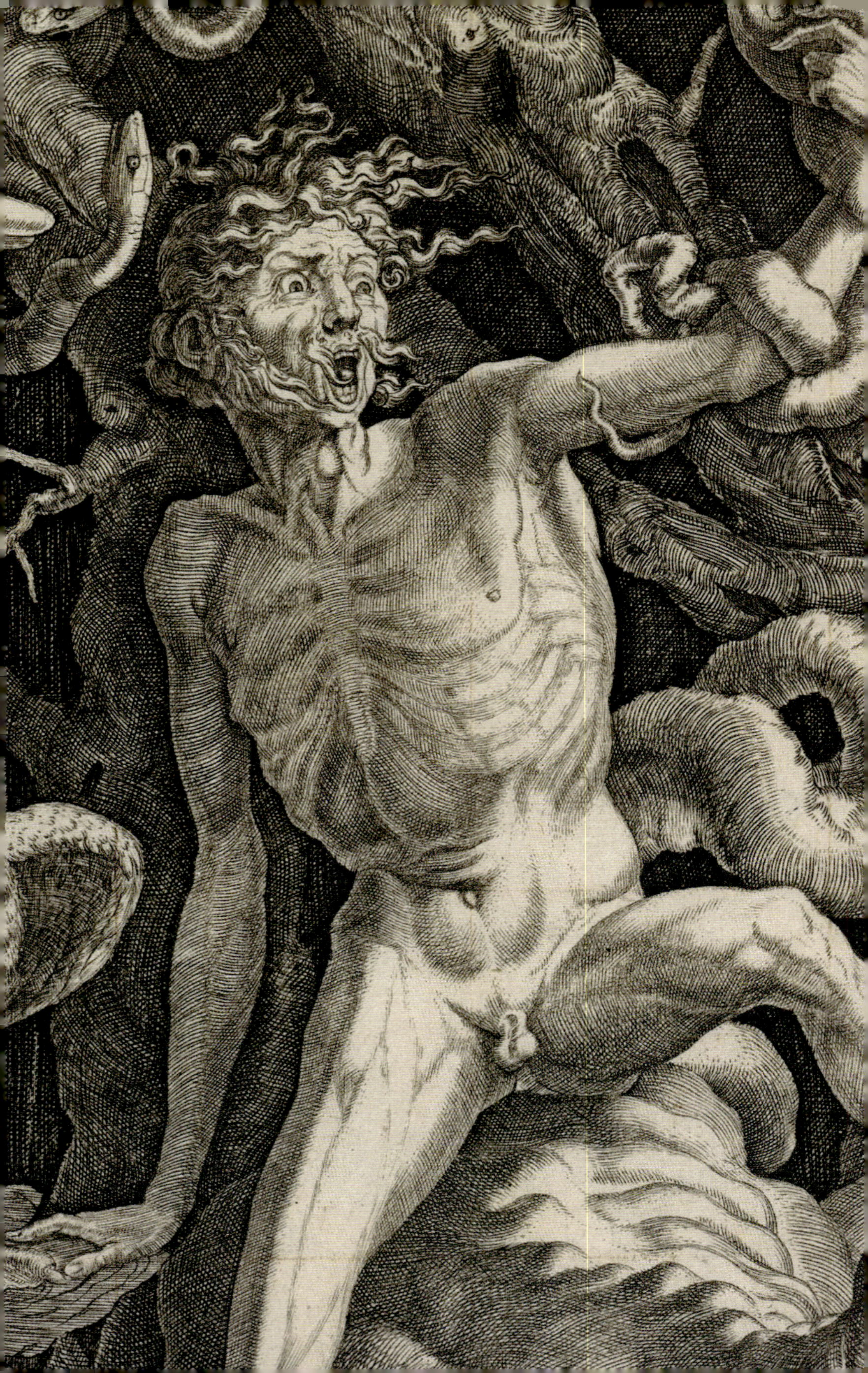

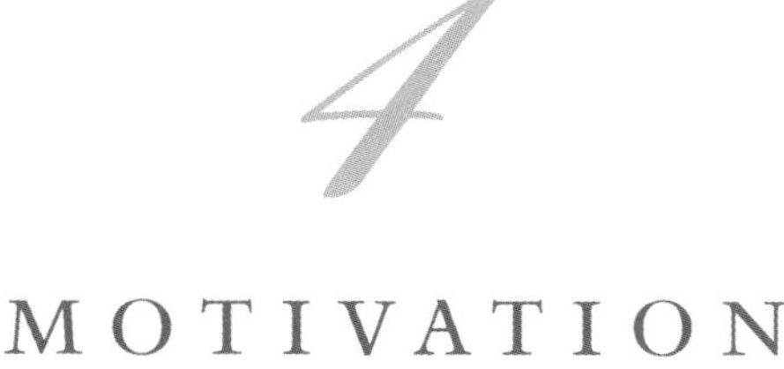

MOTIVATION

Battles and Genre

Raffaello Borghini's 1584 dialogue *Il Riposo* drew on a number of earlier texts, but modern readers have been particularly intrigued by the use Borghini made of Leonardo's *Treatise on Painting*, both because the *Treatise* had not yet been published at the time Borghini read it and because Borghini's appropriations of Leonardo's remarks are uncredited and nearly unchanged.[1] Although he does not mention Leonardo as its author, for example, Borghini includes a close variation on the passage from the *Trattato* that we considered at the end of the previous chapter: "I would thus advise the painter who has to make a single figure to avoid fore-shortenings, both of the parts and of the whole. But in *historie*, and in battle paintings, he can do as he likes."[2] Over five folios at the beginning of Borghini's second book, he dropped in one line of this sort after another. They are extensive but not continous: all are interspersed with other short texts that have no obvious sources in any of Leonardo's writings. What should we make of this?

One possibility is that Borghini's dialogue provides evidence for an otherwise unknown Leonardo manuscript. The versions of the *Trattato* that were in circulation in late sixteenth-century Florence did not contain

90   Jacopo Caraglio, after Rosso Fiorentino, after Michelangelo, *Furia*
(detail of fig. 95)

everything in the long text in the Vatican known as the "Codex Urbinas."[3] And though we can now identify a number of the abridged versions of the *Trattato* that would have been available to Borghini, we cannot yet explain their origin, for they appear to depend not directly on the Codex Urbinas but on an intervening manuscript, a "Codex X."[4] Pehaps Borghini had direct access to Codex X, and the lines in his Leonardo section that do not correspond to lines in the known Leonardo apographs reveal that codex's missing contents.[5]

This is unlikely, however, for several reasons. At the time Borghini wrote the *Riposo*, there was wide interest in the *Trattato* in Florence, and codicological evidence suggests that the owners of various abridgments compared their versions against one another.[6] How could it be that Borghini alone was aware of the missing manuscript, that no one else bothered to transcribe its unique lines? Another problem is that the passages in question are missing not only from the Florentine abridgments of the *Trattato* but also from the Codex Urbinas itself; if they did indeed derive from Codex X, then that codex would not really be an abridgment of the *Trattato* at all but an otherwise undocumented parallel compendium of Leonardo's theory. It seems significant, finally, that Borghini did not exactly quote the Leonardo texts he knew. Rather, he incorporated his sources in a way that disguises their difference from the lines he was interpolating. What comes from Leonardo are abbreviated paraphrases rather than transcriptions, and Borghini's own turns of phrase assimilate the whole.[7]

In the end, then, Book Two of the *Riposo* looks less like plagiarism and more like commentary: the "Leonardo" passages tell us what certain lines from the *Trattato* meant to one well-connected critic of the 1580s. And with this new way of seeing Borghini's text in mind, it becomes significant that the paraphrase of Leonardo's comments on foreshortenings (*scorci*) appears two sentences after the following remark, which is among those with no identifiable source in Leonardo. "I say," asserts one of Borghini's speakers,

> that [poses] need to conform to the story and to the person that is
> represented. Thus, when painting sacred stories, it is necessary to make

the poses of the Patriarchs, the Prophets, the Saints, the Martyrs, and of the Savior, of the Queen of Heaven, and of Angels serious, modest, and devout, not fierce, and not forced. . . . When one has to paint wars and contests, [on the other hand] one can play with poses that are forced . . . just as, in depicting amorous things, the [painter's] job is to make the poses soft, delicate and gracious.[8]

Leonardo's original sentence on *scorci* had appeared with a reflection on what he called the *componimenti* of the *istoria*, an allusion to Alberti's theory of pictorial composition. The margin of Borghini's book, by contrast, labels the passage in question as a discussion "of poses" ("Sopra l'attitudini"). One could read it as a kind of reworking of Leonardo's thought, expanding the distinction the painter had already sought to draw between the portrait and the *istoria* so as to differentiate a larger set of possibilities: there are sacred paintings, violent paintings, and amorous paintings. Yet Borghini's main point is not that the subject of a work limited the kinds of actions it included, but rather that certain subjects required or allowed painters to invent in a different way. In depicting soldiers, Borghini writes, one can play with poses – "si può scherzare con attitudini." This is precisely the position taken in the *Trattato*: "in *istorie* and in battles, you should make *scorti* as you please."

Borghini's introduction of the "historia sacra" as a category aligns the *Riposo* with other Counter-Reformation texts and, here again, the fact that Borghini was working with an abridgment rather than with Leonardo's autograph writings may be relevant. If the Codex X from which the Florentine abridgments of the *Trattato* derived was produced after 1563, it would itself date to the era of Church reform. The *Trattato* and its abridgments already contained a nascent distinction between pictorial genres, and Borghini's interpolations may indicate that he and perhaps others, too, took those distinctions to stand in harmony with post-Tridentine principles. The "Leonardo" that Florentines read in that sense could have corrected Michelangelo's alluring model of license, and could have done so in the authoritative name of another key founder of the modern Tuscan school.

One detail of Borghini's variation on the *Trattato*'s advice invites particular attention. Whereas the *Trattato* specified that battles require "storciamenti e piegamenti," Borghini's paraphrase of Leonardo dropped those words, as though to distinguish the problem of bending the figure from that of foreshortening. Then, in the line that seems original rather than cited, Borghini reimbedded the very concept he had edited out, now however replacing the term *scorti* (foreshortenings) with what he calls "attitudini sforzate" (forced poses).

There are a number of reasons why he might have done this. To begin, the pages at issue show Borghini not simply adapting rules from Leonardo, but responding to recent Church writers, particularly Giovanni Andrea Gilio. Gilio had been concerned to distinguish the approaches that were permissible for history painters from those that artists could take to poetic subjects.[9] When Borghini proposes that battle scenes make room for forced figures, he follows Gilio's attempt to fit such figures into a system of genres. Gilio himself had held that the rules limiting the way artists paint history subjects do not apply to fictions: of the characters in the Hall of Psyche in the Farnesina, notably, Gilio approved of Raphael's inclusion of "those actions and *sforzi* that caprice brought to his mind."[10] In identifying an alternative to the sacred story and its restrictions, Borghini simply substituted the battle scene for Gilio's poetic subject. For Borghini, Leonardo's interest in contorted figures but also his remark about these being more appropriate for battle paintings than for other kinds of subjects seemed to reinforce a new set of values.

In Florence, those values would have run up against the goals of the Accademia del Disegno, the new state institution founded in 1563 with Michelangelo as its official (if unconsenting) leader. The return of Michelangelo's body to Florence after his death the following year and the elaborate obsequies held for him there would have made his example, and particularly the example of his Florentine works, all the more present to contemporary artists and theorists. Benedetto Varchi's funeral oration reminded listeners what there was to imitate in the now lost *Cascina* cartoon, with its figures in "extraordinary and imaginative poses."[11] And in these years, not surprisingly, battle paintings themselves began to change.

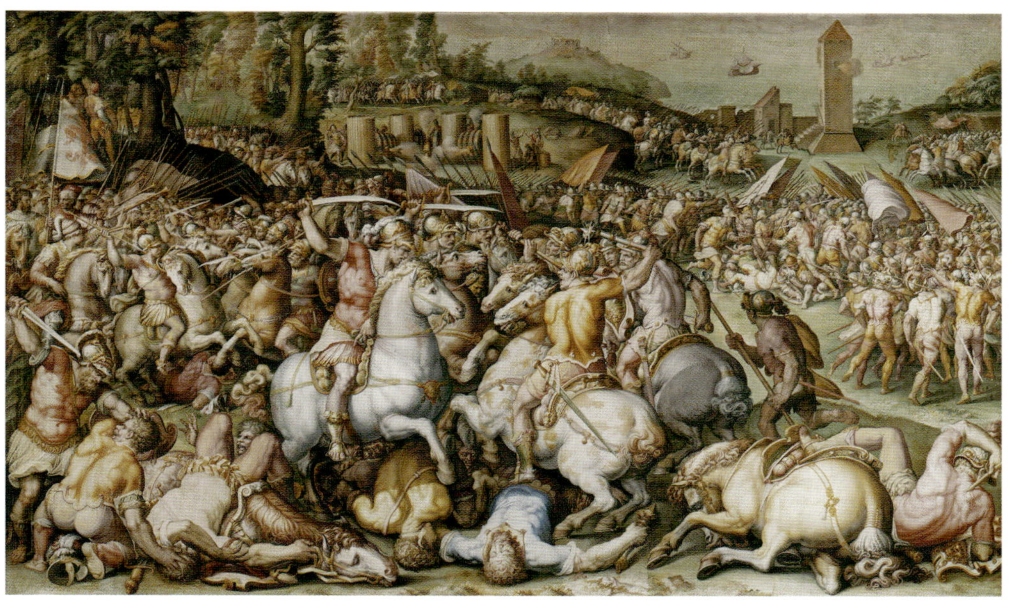

91   Giorgio Vasari, *Battle between Florence and Pisa at the Tower of San Vincenzo*, fresco, Great Council Hall, Florence

Borghini's *Riposo* is not primarily a prescription for a new way of artmaking; mostly, it is a description of recent developments in the city. The writer knew Florentine painting thoroughly, and the dialogue at times reads as a judgmental tourist guide. Florence's latest battle paintings may themselves help explain why he would have concluded that such scenes were spaces where artists could "play." Consider, for example, Vasari's fresco from the late 1560s of the battle between Florence and Pisa at the Tower of San Vincenzo (fig. 91). The idea of centering the scene on fighting horsemen, as well as details like the shouting faces and fantastical helmets, shows an obvious debt to the *Anghiari* – which the San Vincenzo painting essentially replaced.[12] Yet where Leonardo knotted bodies together, Vasari isolated poses. The substitution of leather for metal armor reveals the muscularity of the turned anatomy – the forced and forceful figure – while a series of gratuitously extreme poses line the painting's bottom edge. In Vasari's dialogue *I Ragionamenti*, the character of the prince makes

Borghini's very point, saying to Vasari, with regard to his painting: "this is a beautiful *storia*: you have had room to show your invention."[13] The battle scene, done following Leonardo's rules, suddenly cut against Gilio's alignment of history with truth.

I have been making much of the fact that Borghini draws on Leonardo's early theorization of genre but substitutes a principle of figural flexion for that of foreshortening. But in the end, were *scorti* and *sforzi* really so different from one another? There is, first of all, the orthographic proximity: the Venetian painter Paolo Pino writes of *figure sforciate* (with a c), Armenini of *scurzi* (with a z). Armenini also remarks that *scurzi* – foreshortenings – are demonstrations of "la forza dell'arte," a notion that the *figura sforzata* makes literal, as Gilio and Borghini both repeatedly observe. Already in Leonardo's *Trattato*, the concepts are metonyms: when justifying the employment of *scorci* (foreshortenings) in battle scenes, Leonardo invokes the necessity of showing *storciamenti e piegamenti* (flexions). Varchi's 1564 description of the *Cascina* singles out the figure who struggled (*si sforzava*) to pull on his stockings, but also counts this among the figures "who revealed all the muscles and nerves right down to the bone, with foreshortenings [*iscorci*] never before thought of or seen."

Finally, it is worth noting that when Borghini, reading Leonardo's *Trattato*, turned from part two to part three – from the discussion of composition to the analysis of human movement per se – he would have found individual figures, many of them fighters derived from Leonardo's *Anghiari* studies, floating in the margins of the page. In the late sixteenth-century Florentine apographs of the *Trattato*, these illustrations "drift": the figures align with different lessons from one apograph to the next (fig. 92; compare fig. 88). As a group, then – and Borghini encountered them as a group – the figures in the manuscripts come across not as illustrations, conceived to reinforce a particular textual point, but as a collection of pictorial inventions, loosely connected to the book's ideas, but also available as starting points for new works. The *Trattato* might have stated that the battle scene and the single figure were antithetical categories with different rules, but the illustrations did not bear that out. If anything, the frequent engagement of its figures in acts of violence would have encouraged the

92   "Man swinging a weapon," after Leonardo, as positioned in
the Codex Magliabechiano, 17,4, Biblioteca Nazionale Centrale, Florence

conclusion that soldiers were characters of a kind that did not have to conform closely to a specific narrative event.

We have already encountered one descendant of this sensibility, in Federico Borromeo's 1624 treatise *De pictura sacra*. Borromeo, who was as committed to decorum as any other church writer but also remarkably sympathetic to painterly ambition, recast Gilio's criticism of "modern painters" by focusing on their difference not from earlier Renaissance artists but from the ancients: "Whereas outstanding artists in times past concentrated on rendering the heads of human figures," more recent artists – who, Borromeo asserted, tend to avoid difficult things – "ignore the head and expend their efforts on the individual parts and members of the human body."[14]

Yet most important in the present context is the chapter "On Athletic Bodies," in which Borromeo writes of painters who devote themselves to "the bending of individual parts and limbs of the body," that "they add to those bodies of theirs such a violence in spirit and motion, and such a tension, that the body would not even be suited for a soldier."[15] The remark, which uses the very language of violence that Leonardo incorporated in his *Treatise*, also accords with Leonardo's ostensible attack on Michelangelo as an "anatomical painter" who became wooden through his overly strong indication of bones, sinews, and muscles.[16] In the next paragraph, Borromeo would refer specifically to Michelangelo's *Last Judgment*. Yet it is in the battle scene, Borromeo suggests, that one finds the most bespirited, tense bodies in painting: to say that a painter's athletic bodies "would not even be suited for a soldier" is to say they exceed the limits of the type that might seem most to permit them. It is perhaps not surprising to see a writer who begins his treatise with a chapter "On Decorum" concerning himself with pictorial genres. More striking, though, is the residual place of the battle painting in this scheme. Borromeo recalls the idea that runs from Leonardo to Borghini, that battle paintings provide space for artistic play, just in order to reject that very notion.

Possession

Why reject it?

To this question we can imagine various answers: paintings that gave up narrative for the sake of "play" sacrificed the didactic purposes that justified such paintings in the first place; artistic license came at the expense of the authority of the Church, something no longer tolerated in Borromeo's day. But, as a number of seventeenth-century writers make clear, the location of art in the figure rather than the composition also posed other dangers.

Consider Orfeo Boselli. Boselli's 1657 *Osservationi sulla scoltura antica* was intended to translate the lessons of ancient relief practices for modern artists. One of the topics it takes up is a basic problem that post-Albertian painters had to think through, the composition of groups. It does this by distinguishing between what Boselli calls the "attione," the action a depicted figure performs, and the "atto," the pose the painter gives the figure to convey that. The text encourages those rendering narratives to think at the level of the group, rather than the individual: in groups, "the action and the story are the soul, just as the tale is the soul of the poem." This metaphor of body and soul entails a concern with pictorial integrity far beyond that of Alberti's. And the same is true of Boselli's vision of *disunity*. The good "atto," he writes, must not only conform to the "attione" "but must also be made in a spirited [*spiritoso*], rather than cold way, all the while attending, however, that this movement is not possessed [*spiritato*]."[17]

The possibility Boselli introduces is that a painting in which a figure's actions appear motivated not by its place in the larger narrative but by something outside of it could seem *demonic*. And Boselli was not the only one to see things this way. In his 1649 *Sentimens sur la distinction des diverses manieres de peinture, dessein et graveure*, Abraham Bosse had already attacked an approach to figuration that, as he saw it, the likes of Bartholomeus Spranger, Hendrick Goltzius, and Jacques Bellange all exemplified:

> There have been some painters and draftsmen who affected such manners in the line, the contour, the action and the proportions of the human figures they represented, that one would say, seeing only a part of their works, either in painting or in engraving, that they took it as their task to compose novelties, and to do so with a most bizarre form, such that, in some of them, the actions seemed like those of persons who have been overtaken, in all of the members, by extraordinary cramps, distortions, and stiffenings.[18]

Bosse, whose vocabulary here indicates that he had an early conception of "Mannerism," regarded the stylistic hallmarks of one late sixteenth-century international school as an array of symptoms. While the passage begins with a reference to the products of painters and draftsmen, reminding the reader that actions, no less than contours and proportions, are merely properties of the artists' two-dimensional fictions, the last lines reconfigure both the subject being manipulated and the agency responsible for this, locating the distortions not in the renderings but in the bodies themselves. Figures that initially seemed merely affected and mannered ultimately appear to have been "overtaken," as if different from a shape they once had.

Boselli and Bosse were almost certainly unaware of one another; the fact that they arrived independently at such similar ideas shows the resonance of a line of criticism that goes back to the Counter-Reformation. In the 1570s or 1580s, Pirro Ligorio, writing in Ferrara, had responded to Gilio's condemnation of Michelangelo, reproving those who, rather than taking Raphael, Parmigianino, or Correggio as their model, preferred "the *cose sforzate* and displeasing things of the possessed." This was particularly evident, Ligorio went on, when painters showed bodies in empty, wrenched, compulsive acts, who made frenetic figures, with "mad and displeasing poses," figures that threatened the beholder. To such people, he concluded, "it appears that they have made beautiful and well-crafted things when in fact they have represented violence."[19]

Gilio himself had offered only a single example of a *figura sforzata* that suited the historical subject for which it was made: the possessed boy in Raphael's *Transfiguration*. That is, the motif that most bothered him in the painting of Michelangelo and his followers was a motif he identified with possession – the *possessed* figure had become the ultimate sign of artfulness.[20]

In another dialogue, published in 1564 under the same cover as the one on the errors of history painters, Gilio discussed the art of Michelangelo a single time, and came back to just this issue. In this text, entitled "On Customs Appertaining to Literati, Courtiers, and all other Gentlemen," the characters are discussing the condition of the modern Italian language when one named Gilio begins to express his misgivings about people "who want to be celebrated as the inventors of new things." In response, a character named Pandolfo Quirino comes to the defense of those who "find new things." Christopher Columbus and Ferdinand Magellan, he asserts, did not accept the limits of the worlds everyone knew, nor, he says, did Michelangelo. Had the artist contented himself with the manner of painting in his time, in fact, his field would not be as honored as it is today, and many would still believe, as they did previously, "that the ancient statues of bronze and marble were made with the art of necromancy."[21] This line of thought leads Quirino to consider the origins of the other practices, among them dance. The verses of Virgil, Ovid, and Horace, he maintains, were originally sung, the singers marking the meter with their feet, or with their entire bodies. "Behold, then," he concludes, "the origin of dances, of *moresche*, and of the *sforzi* invented by the devil . . ."[22] Quirino admires Michelangelo for his demystification: Michelangelo showed that humans can make things once attributed only to sorcerers. But even this character allows a twofold connection between Michelangelo's art and the demonic: the devil, like Michelangelo, *invents*, and the things both invent are *sforzi*.[23] As with Bosse after him, a particular kind of figure literally demonizes novelty.

If we were to track this idea back still further than Gilio, we would find roots in the *Cascina* and *Anghiari* projects. It was, as we have seen, a print by Marcantonio after the *Cascina* that first connected *sforzi* with invention. And among the earliest depictions of witchcraft in Italy is another engraving made in the late 1510s or early 1520s, conventionally entitled *Lo Stregozzo* (fig. 93). Lomazzo believed Michelangelo to be its designer, no doubt because its triumph of horrors includes a group of beautiful male nudes, one of them copied from the right side of the *Cascina* cartoon (see fig. 12).[24] It can be no coincidence that the two candidates today for the

93   Agostino Veneziano, *Lo Stregozzo*, engraving, British Museum, London

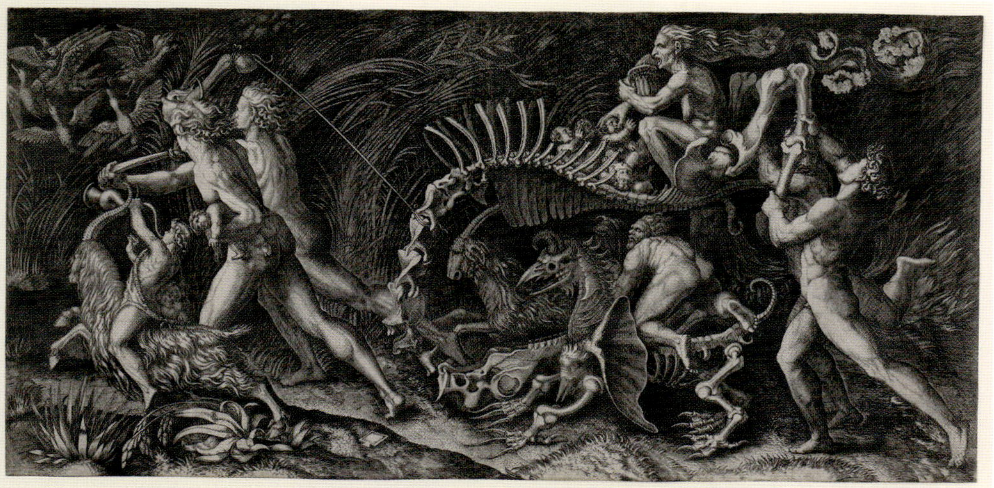

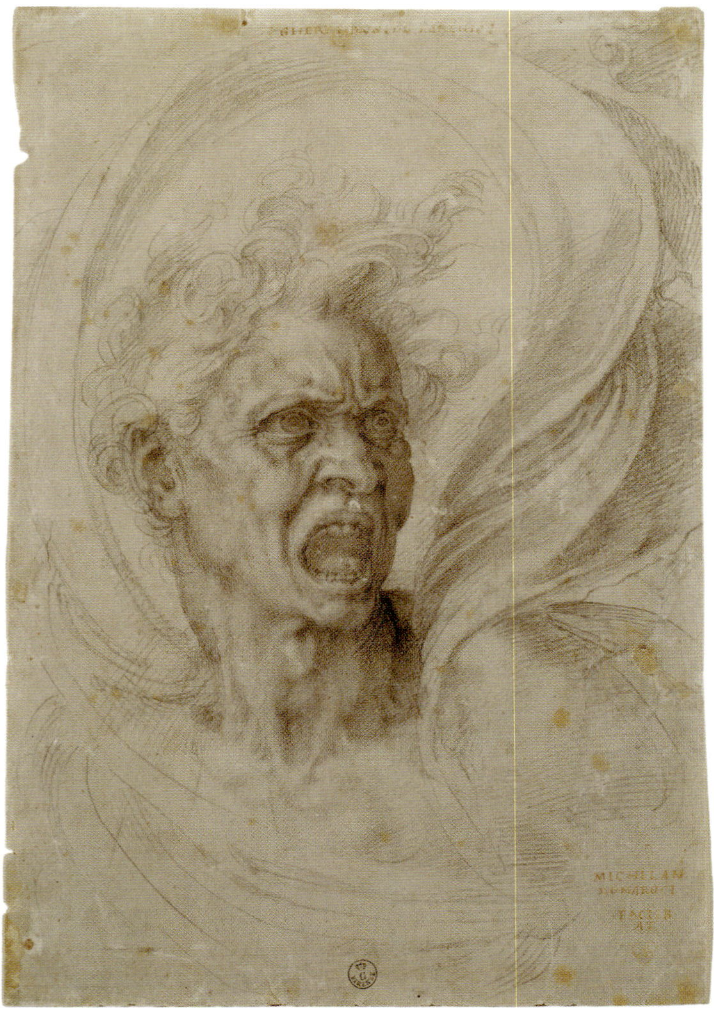

94   Michelangelo, *Furia*, red chalk on paper, Uffizi, Florence

authorship of the print, Agostino Veneziano and Marcantonio Raimondi, are also the two artists responsible for the other early prints made after the Cascina — all of which, as we have seen, also resituate Michelangelo's figures into new contexts. Michelangelo himself, in the period to which *Lo Stregozzo* dates, did a drawing later referred to as a representation of

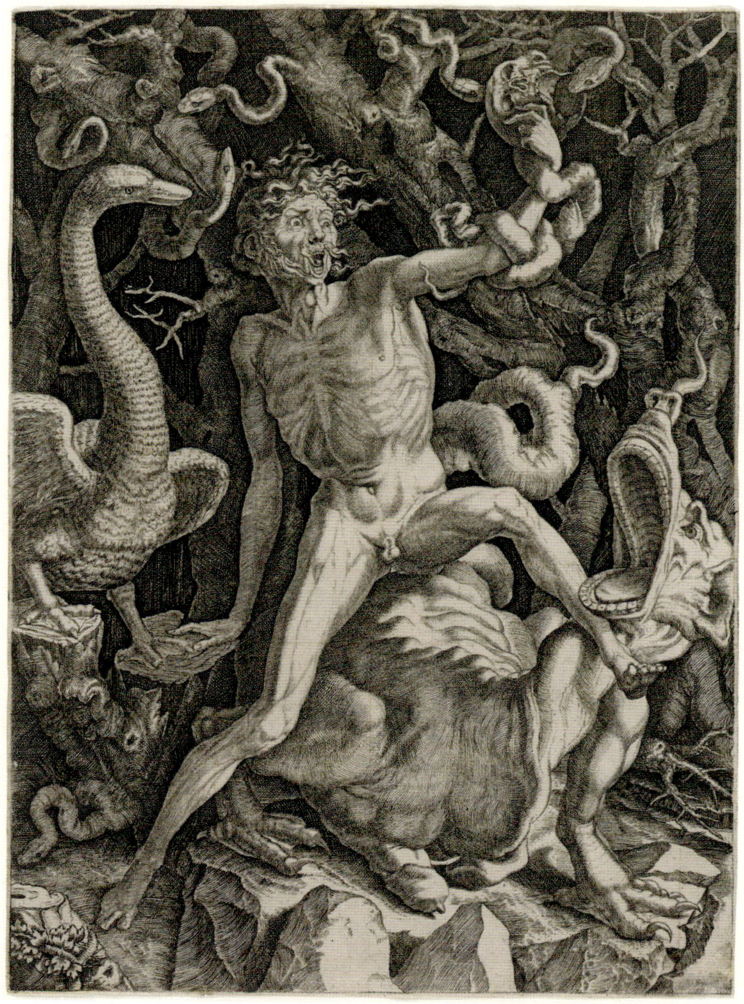

95   Jacopo Caraglio, after Rosso Fiorentino, after Michelangelo, *Furia*,
engraving, British Museum, London

furia (fig. 94); its features were then incorporated into a print designed by
Rosso Fiorentino and executed by Jacopo Caraglio, depicting a demonically possessed man in a field of serpentine monsters (fig. 95).[25] But just
as significant as what became of Michelangelo's drawing is where it came
from, for the face is Michelangelo's most direct response to the shouting

men Leonardo drew when preparing for his depiction of "bestial madness" (see fig. 10).[26]

As we have seen, what bothered Gilio most was his perception that Michelangelo neglected the story for the sake of the figure. But if the Counter-Reformation saw the beginning of a critical tradition that hinted that Michelangelo's figures might be demonically possessed, the subject matter Michelangelo did in fact favor is just to the point. Even beyond the prints that take licentious invention into the realm of the demonic, Michelangelo returned again and again to themes of bondage. Such motifs, as noted, could themselves enter the field of magic, but they also asserted that Michelangelo's work, however public, was also personal, that it could have come only from him, that it – unlike the shared repertories and practices of the past – belonged to him.

Occultation

Renaissance technicians who sought to convey what they understood had to choose whether to do so by open or secret means.[27] Patents like the ones granted to Brunelleschi for his inventions made for a kind of knowledge that was at once public and proprietary. One might say that this combination of qualities was necessary for the Renaissance notion of invention itself: to put out a treatise under one's own name was simultaneously to facilitate the spread of ideas beyond the walls of one's own workshop and to see that those ideas traveled with a declaration of origin.

Yet even as incipient notions of copyright transformed the relationship an engineer might have to a drawing, some artisans sought to preserve domains of secrecy. Giovanni Fontana wrote in cipher; Vasari remarked on the difficulty of reading Leonardo's backwards writing.[28] Antonio Manetti relates that when Brunelleschi set out to invent the machines he would need to build the dome of Florence cathedral, "through tests and experiments, with time and with great effort and careful thought, he became a complete master of these matters in secret, while pretending to be doing something else." Manetti goes on to say that while Brunelleschi was studying with Donatello in Rome, "Filippo told him nothing of his ideas." Francesco di Giorgio reports that that Brunelleschi advised him to keep his inventions secret, too.[29]

Such concerns pertain primarily to the categories of knowledge we now label "science." But if, around the *Cascina* mural, it became possible to think not just about a machine or a recipe or a procedure but also about a figure as an "invention," how did the question of openness and secrecy play out there? Vasari writes that while Michelangelo was making his cartoon at the Dyers Hospital of Sant'Onofrio, "he would never consent that anyone should see it."[30] When Vasari recounts how Bandinelli stole *segretamente* into the Medici palace to destroy Michelangelo's cartoon, he notes that no one quite knew Bandinelli's motives: "some said that he tore up [the cartoon] so that he could keep some pieces of the cartoon for himself; some judged that he wanted to take from other apprentices that advantage, so that they could not profit from Michelangelo and make themselves known in that art."[31] Secrets upon secrets: Bandinelli's act of destruction happened in the dark of night, when no one was looking. Why he did this was anyone's guess. And the best conjectures were that he wanted to make what was once public knowledge – the lessons Michelangelo taught – into his own secret, so that he but not others could use it to garner fame.

From 1505 onward, Michelangelo's work enabled these competing impulses. It revealed the way that the ancients had operated. It came from a man who worked alone, allowing no one to see what he was doing. It served first as a school and eventually as the foundation for an "academy." It required learned treatises to make its meaning clear. Its maker's own writings may have revealed his intentions, but those writings took the form of difficult, allusive poems.

Michelangelo's art has always been regarded as one that drew attention to its own making: Gilio's view, that Michelangelo had concerned himself with the figure at the expense of the story, is already a version of that. So is the remarkable fact that already in 1586, Armenini could come up with a description of how Michelangelo went about designing the *Last Judgment* that amounts to pure fantasy.

A primary thematic this book has followed is that of force; ultimately, this places Michelangelo's and Leonardo's activities within the history of magic. When we think about the conjunction between art and magic in pre-modern Europe, we tend to think in terms of what English speakers call the "power of images," Germans *Bildmagie*.[32] On this model, the magic at issue is something the picture itself effects. Magic has more to do with the viewing of things than with the making of them. What I have been after here is a notion of artistic force that goes first in the other direction, into the painting. At issue is the construction of the artist in terms of the kinds of actions he or she performs, and how pictures contribute to that.

The subject belongs to the history of craft more than to the history of cult practices. In his *General Theory of Magic*, Marcel Mauss wrote of the frequent affinity of the artist and the sorcerer:

> [H]uman skill can also be creative and the actions of craftsmen are known to be effective. From this point of view the greater part of the human race has always had difficulty in distinguishing techniques from rites. Moreover, there is probably not a single activity which artists and craftsmen perform which is not also believed to be within the capacity of the magician. It is because their ends are similar that they are found in natural association and constantly join forces.[33]

What we have been following is the near converse of Mauss's theory: it was not that Gilio and his ilk witnessed painters and magicians in action and found their ends to be the same; it was that these viewers saw the ends – the paintings themselves – and worried about their beginnings.

In part, the problem was simply one of audience; the conflict turned on the definition of the community for which art was made. Since the Middle Ages, the cliché that accompanied religious painting was that it was the Bible for the ignorant, that it was made for the unknowing. But then the abstruse courtly allegory, the puzzling painting that was meant to be deciphered by few or none, had challenged this paradigm. Artists in the age of Leonardo and Michelangelo recognized that if technicians could define a proprietary knowledge, a field of understanding that circulated in public but that only the adept could follow, artists could do the same. We might take Signorelli's Antichrist as an emblem of the new art: the depicted crowd, the public in the square, sees that he moves, perhaps even sees that he moves in odd ways, but does not know the reason. Only the prudent viewer in the chapel sees the force at work.

The marvel of the Quattrocento machine depended on an audience who did not quite understand how it produced its effect. And when Gilio suggests that an audience looking at an ancient statue might believe its dramatic gestures to be the work of a demon, he allows that secrecy, occultation, could be a matter not just of craft know-how, not just of poetic content, but of the depicted body itself. We tend to think of the Renaissance body in terms of anatomy, unveiling. The artist with anatomical interests was the one who exposed what was on the inside. But the counter-impulse, the visualization of the body's occultation, has its own history.

The earliest writer to identify the "forced figure" as a meaningful motif was Paolo Pino. In the dialogue on painting that Pino wrote in the 1540s, the speakers explicitly take up the matter of "invention" – which Pino classes with *disegno* and *colore* as one of the three parts of painting. And in this exchange, the Florentine character – "Fabio" – asserts that invention manifests itself especially in pictorial variety: "even if one has to make the same subject repeatedly, it will be reprehensible if one repeats in it the same figures and actions." This is a reformulation of Alberti's point and, as we saw, it opens the door to a fragmented form of painting, a painting of figures rather than compositions. More surprising, though, is Fabio's further recommendation: "in all of your works be sure to include at least one figure that is all *sforciata, misteriosa e difficile*, so that from it you may be seen to be a painter of worth by whoever understands the art's perfection."[34]

Twenty years before Gilio, we discover, it was possible to regard the forced figure as an attraction. The *mysteriousness* of the forced figure was its virtue. Those who accused Michelangelo of being "anatomical" had it wrong: he did not show what was inside his figures, he hid it.

NOTES

PREFACE

1   Francisco de Hollanda [sic], *Four Dialogues on Painting* (1548), trans. Aubrey F. G. Bell (London: Oxford University Press, 1928), 16. Vincenzo Danti described Michelangelo's complete preoccupation with the human form as a virtue: "E che ciò sia vero, da niuna altra cagione fu spinto il divino Michelagnolo a porre quasi tutto il suo studio e diligenza intorno al corpo umano, che dalla cognizione della perfetta et in tutte le parti compiuta et artifiziosa figura di quello; apertamente veggendo che ogni altra imitazione et ogni altro composto è a esso corpo umano per sì fatta guisa inferiore, che è poco da curarsi di qual si voglia altra cosa che ritrarre si possa od imitare." See Paola Barocchi, ed., *Trattati del arte del cinquecento: Fra manierismo e controriforma*, 3 vols. (Bari: Gius. Laterza, 1960), I, 212.

2   For an engaging study of non-figuration in one other fifteenth-century culture, see Carolyn Dean, *A Culture of Stone: Inka Perspectives on Rock* (Durham, N.C.: Duke University Press, 2010.) On the idea of the figure in sixteenth- and seventeenth-century Chinese art – and the higher prestige of subjects other than the human body – see Craig Clunas, *Pictures and Visuality in Early Modern China* (London: Reaktion Books, 1997), esp. 18 and 102–4. The topic is enormous in Islamic art; one frequently cited introduction is Terry Allen, "Aniconism and Figural Representation in Islamic Art," in *Five Essays on Islamic Art* (Sebastopol: Solipsist Press, 1988), 17–37.

3   Among Michelangelo's proponents, I think, for example, of Benvenuto Cellini's *Sopra i principi e 'l modo d'imparare l'arte del disegno*, probably from the mid-1560s, and Vincenzo Danti's 1567 *Primo libro del trattato delle perfette proportioni*. More generally, the Accademia del Disegno, which sought to rationalize Michelangelo's manner of making art, introduced anatomy lessons for its students. On the other side are texts like Carlo Borromeo's 1624 *De sacra pictura*, though Stephen Campbell, " 'Fare una Cosa Morta

Parer Viva': Michelangelo, Rosso, and the (Un)Divinity of Art," *Art Bulletin* 84 (2002), 596–620, shows that Michelangelo's detractors thought of his painting in relation to anatomy from early on.

4   See, e.g., Rose Marie San Juan, "Restoration and Translation in Juan de Valverde's *Historia de la composision del cuerpo humano*," in Rebecca Zorach, ed., *The Virtual Tourist in Renaissance Rome: Printing and Collecting the Speculum Romanae Magnificentiae* (University of Chicago Press, 2008), 53–61, with further references.

5   Georges Didi-Huberman, *Confronting Images: Questioning the Ends of a Certain History of Art*, trans. John Goodman (University Park: Pennsylvania State University Press, 2009) and idem, *Fra Angelico: Dissemblance and Figuration*, trans. Jane-Marie Todd (University of Chicago Press, 1995).

6   Aby Warburg, "Dürer and Italian Antiquity," in *The Renewal of Pagan Antiquity*, trans. David Britt (Los Angeles: Getty Research Institute, 1999), 553–8, here 558.

7   The first problem with the analogy is that a painted figure usually invites a kind of reflection on the relationship between its form and its meaning that a written word does not. This is true even in cases like those to which Georges Didi-Huberman drew attention, where meaning relies on dissemblance. At the same time, it was possible for Renaissance theorists to compare the formation of the human body to that of words. See the recent discussion of the ABCs of painting in Alexa Greist, "Learning to Draw, Drawing to Learn: Theory and Practice in Italian Printed Drawing Books, 1600–1700," PhD. diss., University of Pennsylvania, 2011.

8   Two notable exceptions are Alessandro Cecchi, "Niccolò Machiavelli o Marcello Virgilio Adriani? Sul programma e l'assetto compositivo delle 'battaglie' di Leonardo e di Michelangelo per la Sala del Consiglio Maggiore in Palazzo Vecchio," *Prospettiva* 83–4 (1997), 102–15, and Rona Goffen, *Renaissance Rivals: Michelangelo, Leonardo, Raphael, Titian* (New Haven and London: Yale University Press, 2002), esp. 143–70. Cecchi's essay is the most rigorous discussion of the artists' textual sources; Goffen treats the battle paintings within a more general survey of the two artists' relationship in the early years of the sixteenth century. Another recent study is Jonathan Jones, *The Lost Battles: Leonardo, Michelangelo and the Artistic Duel that Defined the Renaissance* (New York: Knopf, 2012). This book, written for a general audience rather than for specialists, is obviously also the product of long reflection, and the pages that follow will draw attention to some of Jones's many good observations. However, the book is really more about Leonardo and Michelangelo as personalities than about the Anghiari and Cascina paintings. From the bibliography at the end, it does not appear that Jones has read most of the basic historical literature on the two works (Köhler, Thode, Tolnay, Neufeld, Gould, Farago, Cecchi, and Fehrenbach are among the absent names.) As a consequence, his book has not been informed by the long-running debates about what historical personages and events the murals would have represented, which walls they were to decorate, and on which written sources the artists drew. Nor does Jones seem particularly interested in the planned or actual appearance of the two works: surprisingly, the book illustrates neither Aristotile da Sangallo's Holkham Hall painting nor any of the surviving sixteenth-century reproductions of Michelangelo's cartoon.

1 THE FORCE OF ART

1   Giorgio Vasari, *Lives of the Painters, Sculptors, and Architects*, trans. Gaston du C. de Vere, 2 vols. (New York: Everyman's Library, 1996; hereafter, Vasari, *Lives*), I, 620, 640; II, 669, 675, and 692; *Le Opere di Giorgio Vasari*, ed. Gaetano Milanesi, 9 vols. (Florence: G. C. Sansone, 1906; hereafter, Vasari-Milanese), IV, 11, 50; VII, 179, 185–6, 212. Although I am focusing here on Central Italy, there is a broader history to be written on force as an interest of Renaissance painters. A forthcoming monograph by Stephen Campbell will discuss the topic of force in Mantegna.

2   Giovanni Andrea Gilio da Fabriano, "De gli errori, e de gli abusi de' Pittori circa l'historie: con molte annotationi fatte sopra il Giuditio di Michelagnolo, & altre figure. . . ." in *Due dialogi* (Camerino: Antonio Gioioso, 1564 [facsimile Florence: SPES, 1986]), 70v: "E piu maravigliato mi sono, che questa bella, & eccellente arte non habbia ne libro, ne regola, che dia à pittori il modo e l'ordine di quanto in ogni maniera di figure à fare habbino: perche dunque à la scapestrata la maggior parte se ne vanno, ne l'historie infiniti errori commettono; come chiaramente in tutta Italia, e piu in Roma veder si puo. Onde mi pare c'hoggi i moderni pittori: quando à fare hanno qualche opera, il primo loro intento è di torcere à le loro figure il capo, le braccia, ò le gambe. acciò si dica che sono sforzate, e quei sforzi à le volte sono tali, che meglio sarebbe che non fussero, & al soggetto de l'historia che far pensano poco, ò nulla attendono." Gilio uses the term *historie* to refer to paintings of true subjects, whether or not these took place in the past. He considers Michelangelo's *Last Judgment* a *historia*, e.g., even though Judgment Day is still to come. In translating this passage, I have rendered his adjective *sforzata* with the cognate "forced," though it can mean labored or exerted or stressed or enervated. The *s* at the front can amplify or diminish. All translations mine unless otherwise noted.

3   Ibid., 89v–90r: "[disse M. Francesco] Per questo io non lodo gli sforzi che fanno gli Angeli nel giuditio di Michelangelo, dico di quelli che sostengono la croce, la colonna, e gli altri sacrati misteri; i quali piu tosto rappresentano mattacini, ò giocolieri, che Angeli: conciosia che l'Angelo sosterebbe senza fatica tutto 'l globo de la terra: non che una Croce, ò una colonna, ò simili. Disse M. Silvio quello fu fatto solo per mostrar il decoro, e la forza de l'arte."

4   Raffaello Borghini, *Il Riposo* (Florence: Marescotti, 1584 [Facsimile Hildesheim: Olms, 1969]), 82: "Ma perche di questo ne ha scritto largamente Giouanandrea Gilio da Fabriano in quel suo dialogo degli errori de' pittori sopra il Giudicio di Michelagnolo, voglio che mi basti l'hauerne detto questo poco per mostrare quanto longano dal vero habbia dipinto il Puntormo, il quale come sapete, ha fatto vn gran monte di corpacci, sporca cosa à vedere, doue alcuni mostrano di risuscitare, altri sono risuscitati, & altri morti in dishonesti attitudini si giacciano; e di sopra ha fatto alcuni bambocci con gesti molti sforzati, che suonano le trombe, e credo che egli voglia, che si conoscano per Agnoli."

5   In drawing attention to the representations of death that pervaded Pontormo's frescoes, Borghini at least nods to one significant way in which they departed from their Roman model. He may dwell on the angels because Gilio found Michelangelo's particularly objectionable or because they are the figures in the fresco that most readily allow a comment on "gesti sforzati."

6   Federico Borromeo, *Sacred Painting/ Museum*, ed. and trans. Kenneth S. Rothwell, Jr.,

with notes by Pamela M. Jones (Cambridge, Mass.: Harvard University Press, 2010), 52–3 (trans. modified): "Nonnulli rursus singulas corporis partes, articulosque, & flexus; & compages ita ostentant, quasi tabulas anatomicas sanandis vulneribus, non quasi incitamenta religionis exhibere vellent. Addunt vero corporibus istis eam in motu, spirituque violentiam, atque contentionem, quae militare etiam corpus dedeceret. Unde tanta spectantium oculis, animisque offensio oritur, ut simile quiddam patiantur, quod Theatri spectatores olim pati soliti erant, cum scilicet illo luctantium adspectu fatigati, & fracti, domum redirent."

7   Forty years later, in France, Gianlorenzo Bernini leveled a similar criticism, telling Paul Fréart de Chantelou that Michelangelo had more art than grace, that "for that reason he had never equaled the ancients, being principally attached to anatomy, as surgeons are." See Chantelou, *Journal de voyage du Cavalier Bernin en France*, ed. Milovan Stani (Paris: Macula, 2001), 132.

8   Pacheco writes about the Michelangelo Crucifix and its reception in Spain in *Arte de la pintura*, ed. F. J. Sanchez Canton, 2 vols. (Madrid: Instituto de Valencia de Don Juan, 1956), II, 103–4. He reprints Rioja's letter at the end of same vol., II, 377: "porque pinta la cruz con cuatro extremos y con el supedáneo en que están clavados los piés juntos. Vese plantada la figura sobre él como si estuviera en pie; el rostro con majestad y decoro, sin torcimiento feo, o descompuesto, así, como convenía a la soberana grandeza de Cristo nuestro Señor." See the fundamental discussion in Jonathan Brown, *Images and Ideas in Seventeenth-Century Spanish Painting* (Princeton University Press, 1978), 70.

9   Pacheco, *Arte*, II, 306–7: "Puso así Micael Angel una figura en la barca de Caron; cuya postura del medio cuerpo arriba yo seguí por honorar mi pintura con algo de tan valiente hombre, a quien es Gloria imitar en el arte (non tanto en el decoro, como veremos), como la han hecho otros mayors artifices . . . Últimamente se ven en todas estas figuras desnudas, buscada con arte y gracia la honestidad, porque los ojos castos y piós no se ofendiesen: y más en convent de monjas, y en altar donde se ha de celebrar el santo sacrificio de la Misa; no paresca de pequeña importancia lo dicho, ni pesada esta digresión. Cierto religioso, pío y grave, de la órden de San Agustín, me contó (siendo yo Obispo) que, celebrando un día ante un famoso cuadro desta historia, que está en su convent, en Sevilla (de mano de Martín de Vos), valiente pintor flamenco, acabado el año 1570, estando a la mitad de la Misa levantó los ojos y vió una figura frontera de mujer, con harta belleza, pero más descompostura, y fué tanta la fuerza que hizo a su imaginación, que se vió a punto de perderse; hallándose en el mayor aprieto y aflicción de espírtu que jamás tuvo. Y por haber navegado a las Indias, afirmaba, con encarecimiento, que tomara antes estar en el golfo de la Bermuda en una tempestad deshecha, que en tal paso. Y que cobró tanto miedo al cuadro, que no se atrevió jamás a ponerse en semejante occasion: y que tenía tan presente el caso, que habiendo pasado algunos años, aún le duraba el temor. Reirse han muy de espacio desto los pintores valientes o licenciosos; pero no valga para ellos esta advertencia."

10 Ibid., *Arte*, I, 23–4, 368.

11 Dagobert Frey, *Manierismus als europäische Stilerscheinung: Studien zur Kunst des 16. und 17. Jahrhunderts* (Stuttgart: W. Kohlhammer Verlag, 1964), 31: "Das zeigt sich deutlich in gewissen symptomatischen Erscheinungen wie der Anbringung, ja Überbetonung von Figuren, vielfach Aktfiguren, die zum dargestellten Inhalt beziehungslos sind und die vor allem eine rein ästetische Funktion zu erfüllen haben."

12 Arnold Hauser, *Der Manierismus: Die Krise der Renaissance und der Ursprung der modernen Kunst* (Munich: C. H. Beck, 1964), 13: "Oft ist es gerade dieses Pikante – ein übermütiges oder zwanghaftes Abweichen vom Normalen, etwas affektiert Tänzerisches oder gequält Grimassenhaftes –, das den manieristischen Charakter eines Werkes vor allem anderen verrät. Zur Pikanterie der manieristischen Kunst trägt vielfach auch das Virtuosentum bei, das sie stets zur Schau trägt. Ein manieristisches Kunstwerk ist immer auch ein Kunststück, ein Bravourstück, das Sichproduzieren eines Zauberers. . . . die Überspannung der Schönheit, die zu schön und darum irreal, der Kraft, die zu kräftig und darum akrobatisch, des Gehalts, der überfüllt und darum nichtssagend, der Form, die selbständig und damit entleert wird."

13 Georg Weise, *Il Manierismo: Bilancio critico del problema stilistico e culturale* (Florence: Leo S. Olschki, 1971), 31–58.

14 Pacheco, *Arte*, I, 465, purportedly quoting Karel van Mander: "Micael Angelo más atendió en el Juicio a cada figura de por sí, que a la disposición del historiado, y así usó pocas diminuciones y apartamientos." Presumably Pacheco is paraphrasing Van Mander's *Den grondt der edel vry schilder-const*: "Tis veel t'ghebruyck gheweest van Tinturetten/ T'ordineren soo met groeppen oft knoopen/ En Angelus oordeel is oock veel metten/ Hoopkens gheordineert maer doch besmetten/ Eenighe zijn eere niet om de hoopen/ Maer dat hy om de Beelden hem verloopen/ Heeft in t'gheen d'ordinanty mach belanghen/ Datter niet en zijn insichtighe ganghen./ Niet latende sien als eenighe souden/ Een insien van eenen hemel ontsloten/ En voor aen yet groots soo sy't wenschen wouden:/ Maer wie en sal dit niet ten besten houden/ Siende dit werck al vol Consten doorgoten/ Van de gheleerde handt des Bonarroten/ Soo veel acten verscheyden van satsoene/ Der naeckten daer het hem om was te doene." See the edition by Hessel Miedema (Utrecht: Haentjens Dekker & Gumbert, 1973), 132.

15 Michael Baxandall, *Giotto and the Orators: Humanist Observers of Painting in Italy and the Discovery of Pictorial Composition, 1350–1450* (Oxford University Press, 1991), 130.

16 This view, in essence Gilio's, is at the heart of Joost Keizer's "Michelangelo, Drawing, and the Subject of Art," *Art Bulletin* 93 (2011), 304–24; see especially the discussion of Alberti on p. 308.

17 Julius von Schlosser, *Lorenzo Ghibertis Denkwürdigkeiten (I commentarii): Zum ersten male nach der Handschrift der Biblioteca Nazionale in Florenz vollständig herausgegeben und erläutert*, 2 vols. (Berlin: Julius Bard, 1912), II, 41: "Comporre, bei Cennini einfach auf das technische Verfahren überhaupt gehend, wird bei Ghiberti schon auf die formale Gliederung des Kunstwerkes bezogen (compositore)."

18 Ibid., I, 22: "molte cose compuose, egli diede le misure et dette grande gentileza a questa arte, atteggiante le teste nascenti bene in sulle spalle. Ancora le figure con marauiglosi posari et colla saluega delli ignudi et con perfectissima arte."

19 Ibid., I, 47: "Fummi allogata l'altra porta cioe la terga porta di sancto Giouani la quale mi fu data licentia io la conducessi in quel modo ch'io credessi tornasse più perfettamente et più ornata et più riccha. Cominciai detto lauorio in quadri i quali erano di grandeza d'uno braccio et terzo, le quali istorie molto copiose di figure erano istorie del testamento uecchio: nelle quali mi ingegnai con ogni misura osseruare in esse cercare imitare la natura quanto a me fosse possibile, et con tutti i liniamenti che in essa potessi produrre et con egregij conponimenti et douitiosi con moltissime figure."

20 Antonio Manetti, *The Life of Brunelleschi*, trans. Catherine Enggass, ed. Howard Saalman (University Park: Pennsylvania State University Press, 1970), 48–9.

21 Anne Dunlop, for example, has recently used Alberti's *De pictura* to support the premise "that the male figure was the pre-eminent subject of Quattrocento Florentine art." See Dunlop, "Parading David," *Art History* 35 (2012), 682–701, esp. 684.

22 Megan Holmes, "Copying Practices and Marketing Strategies in a Fifteenth-Century Florentine Painter's Workshop," in *Italian Renaissance Cities: Artistic Exchange and Cultural Translation*, ed. Stephen J. Campbell and Stephen J. Milner (Cambridge University Press, 2004) 38–74, here 57.

23 Ibid., 58.

24 See Jean Cadogan, *Domenicho Ghirlandaio: Artist and Artisan* (New Haven and London: Yale University Press, 2000), 122–3.

25 See Rudolf Hiller von Gaertringen, *Raffaels Lernerfahrungen in der Werkstatt Peruginos* (Berlin: Deutscher Kunstverlag, 1999), and Alison Wright, "Dimensional Tension in the Work of Antonio Pollaiuolo," in Stuart Currie and Peta Motture, eds., *The Sculpted Object 1400–1700* (Aldershot: Ashgate, 1997), 65–79, esp. 70–71.

26 See Carmen Bambach, *Drawing and Painting in the Italian Renaissance Workshop: Theory and Practice, 1300–1600* (Cambridge University Press, 1998), 89.

27 Robert Vischer, *Luca Signorelli und die Italienische Renaissance* (Leipzig: von Veit, 1879), 352–2: "Item; che sia obligato dicto Maestro Luca ad pegnare le tre facciate de decta Cappella cioe quella da capo verso il Vescovato, et li dui che vengono per lo longo, figurate fine a dui fila sopra el piano della finestra murata, appresso li dicti corpi sancti, et più et manco che sia in arbitrio del Camerlengho et Soprastanti, et stuccarla secondo el disegno dato per lo maestro: se come più come parrà allui, ma non con mancho figure che ce habia dato nel disegno per ciascuna archata." Creighton Gilbert, *How Fra Angelico and Signorelli Saw the End of the World* (University Park: Pennsylvania State University Press, 2003), 117, refers to this contract as well, giving a slightly different translation of the passage.

28 Leon Battista Alberti, *On Painting and on Sculpture: The Latin Texts of "De pictura" and "De statua"*, ed. and trans. Cecil Grayson (London: Phaidon, 1972), *De pictura*, 3.53: "Atque ea quidem hanc habet vim, ut etiam sola inventio sine pictura delectet."

29 Leonardo da Vinci, *Il Codice atlantico della Biblioteca Ambrosiana di Milano*, transcr. Augusto Marinoni et al. (Florence: Giunti, 2006; hereafter, Codex Atlanticus), 534v, 11, 1041–2: "Dico che prima si debbe imparare le membra e sua travagliamenti e, finite tal notizia, si debbe seguitare li atti secondo li accidenti che accadano all'omo, e terzo comporre le storie, lo studio delle quali sarà fatto dalli atti naturali fatti a caso, mediante li loro accidenti, e porli mente per le strade, piazze e campagne, e notarli con brieve discrizione di liniamenti, cioè che per una testa si faccia uno *o*, e per uno braccio una linia retta o piegata e 'l simile si faccia delle gambe e busto, e poi tornando alla casa, fare tali ricordi in perfetta forma.

Dice l'avversario che per farsi pratico e fare opera assai, ch'elli è meglio che 'l tempo primo dello studio sia messo in ritrarre vari componimenti fatti per carte o muri per diversi maestri, e in quelli si fa pratica veloce e bono abito. Al quale si risponde che questo abito sarebbe bono essendo fatto sopra opera di boni componimenti e di studiosi maestri, e perché questi maestri son sì rari che pochi se ne trova, è più sicuro andare alle cose naturale, che a quelle d'esso naturale con gran peggioramento imitate e fare tristo abito, perché chi po andare alla fonte, non va al vaso."

30 Gian Paolo Lomazzo, *Scritti sulle arti*, ed. Roberto Paolo Ciardi, 2 vols. (Florence: Marchi & Bertolli, 1973–4), I, 101: "Sa tu che avrebbe detto il vulgo, e massime il prencipe, se

io avessi fatto la cena de modo che ti ho detto, che far, secondo il vero, si devrebbe? Avrebbe detto che cotesti apostoli, insieme con Cristo, paiono tanti forfanti fugiti di Gallea, sí come si dice ancora dil stupendo giudizio di Michel Angelo Buonarrotti."

31   Ibid., 101–2: "Dicesi che egli aveva pensato di fare in quella facciata una gabbia overo ciurma de fachini e de istrioni che andassero saltellando di là su, apponendo non star bene quei membri e coglioni sí aparenti, non solamente ne' diavoli e fantasmi ma ne' Santi. . . . Non sono molti mesi od anni che papa Paolo quarto, detto il Tiatino, la volse far trare a terra, dicendo non convenirsi in Santo Pietro quelle apparenze forfantesche de membri con quelli atti istrionici." Lomazzo's suggestion that Michelangelo's figures look like "porters" seems related to anecdotes that extend from the sixteenth to the eighteenth century of abusive artists placing porters in torturous poses for the sake of making life studies. I thank Adam Eaker for drawing my attention to this tradition and for referring me to David Young Kim, "The Horror of Mimesis," *Oxford Art Journal* 34 (2011), 335–53, which discusses one example on pp. 346–8.

32   Gilio, *Due dialogi*, 95v: "risplendenti, lucide, gloriose, in maestà sostenute con gran magnificenza da migliaia d'Angeli, non con quei groppi ne sforzi, ne moresche, ne bagattelle, che voi gli miriate che Michelagnolo gli ha fatti."

33   Giovan Battista Armenini, *De' veri precetti della pittura* (1586), ed. Marina Gorreri (Turin: Giulio Einaudi, 1988), 118–19: "Poiché ciò pure si vede, da chi punto considera nel Giudizio dipinto di Michelangelo, lui essersi servito nel termine ch'io dico. Né ci sono mancati c'hanno detto quivi ch'egli n'aveva alcune fatte di cera di man sua e che li torceva le membra a modo suo, immollandole prima le giunture nell'acqua calda, acciò quelle a rimorbidir si venisse; dalla qual via, come forse riuscibile, io ne lascio la prova all'arbitrio d'ognuno. Io so bene che Lionardo Vinci, vedendo quello e forse di ciò accorto, secondo ch'io intesi da un suo allievo in Milano, ebbe ardire di dire che questo solo li dispiaceva di quell'opera, che in troppo modi si era servito di poche figure e che perciò tanto li pareva veder muscoli nella figura d'uno giovane, quanto d'un vecchio et il simile esser de' contorni."

34   Carlo Pedretti, *Leonardo da Vinci on Painting: A Lost Book (Libro A)* (Berkeley: University of California Press, 1964), 137, was the first to note the anachronism. He writes "Obviously, Leonardo referred not to the figures of the 'Last Judgment' but to those of the Sistine Ceiling."

35   See the discussion in Fredrika H. Jacobs, "Aretino and Michelangelo, Dolce and Titian: Femmina, Masculo, Grazia," *Art Bulletin* 82 (2000), 51–67.

36   Giorgio Vasari, *La Vita di Michelangelo nelle redazioni del 1550 e del 1568*, ed. Paola Barocchi, 5 vols. (Milan: Ricciardi, 1962; hereafter, Barocchi, *Vita di Michelangelo*), II, 250. The insult Michelangelo delivered to Leonardo is a central event for Jonathan Jones, *The Lost Battles: Leonardo, Michelangelo and the Artistic Duel that Defined the Renaissance* (New York: Knopf, 2012), who imagines, 157, that Michelangelo took offense at Leonardo's lifestyle: "With his coiffed hair and his pink tights and his extravagant wardrobe, his equally finely got-up servants and followers, Leonardo simply repelled Michelangelo. There is real rage towards the older man's blurring of male and female beauty, his strange sensuality and 'family,' in the younger artist's responses to the Annunziata cartoon."

37   Jean-Paul Richter, *The Literary Works of Leonardo da Vinci*, 2 vols. (London: Low, 1883), II, 190: "O pictore anatomista guarda che la troppa notitia delli ossi, corde e muscoli non sia cavsa di farti vn pictore legnioso, col volere che li tua ignivdi mostrino tutti

li sentimenti loro." The original text comes from MS. E, 19b. The connection to Michelangelo was first made by Giovanni Gherardo de Rossi, *Trattato della pittura di Lionardo da Vinci* (Rome: De Romanis, 1817), 504. It is also discussed in Kenneth Clark, *Leonardo da Vinci* (New York: Penguin, 1989), 191, and in Pedretti, *Leonardo on Painting*, 137–8.

38   Charles de Tolnay, *Michelangelo*, 5 vols. (Princeton University Press, 1947), I, 209–10, assembles the evidence for the start date of Michelangelo's project: a 1524 letter from Michelangelo indicates that he had received the commission "in the second year of the pontificate of Julius II," that is, in 1504; the purchase of the paper for Michelangelo's cartoon happened on October 31, 1504; a December 31, 1504 document refers to the limning of "el cartone che fa Michelagnolo." For the implications of this and related documents, see Carmen C. Bambach, "The Purchases of Cartoon Paper for Leonardo's 'Battle of Anghiari' and Michelangelo's 'Battle of Cascina,' " *I Tatti Studies* 8 (1999), 105–33.

39   See Cecil Gould, "Leonardo's Great Battle-Piece: A Conjectural Reconstruction," *Art Bulletin* 36 (1954), 117–29, esp. 118–19 and n. 2.

40   Neri di Gino Capponi, quoted in Frank Fehrenbach, "Much Ado About Nothing: Leonardo's *Fight for the Standard*," in Philine Helas et al., eds., *Bild/Geschichte: Festschrift für Horst Bredekamp* (Berlin: Akademie Verlag, 2007), 397–412, here 400–01.

41   For these two drawings, see especially Carmen Bambach, ed., *Leonardo da Vinci: Master Draftsman* (New York: Metropolitan Museum of Art, 2003), 500–08, with extensive bibliography through 2003. Gould, "Leonardo's Great Battle," first advanced the idea that the Florentines are on the right, and a number of those who have followed him on this have tried to put names to faces. To survey just a few of the recent suggestions: Alessandro Cecchi, "Niccolò Machiavelli o Marcello Virgilio Adriani? Sul programma e l'assetto compositivo delle 'battaglie' di Leonardo e di Michelangelo per la Sala del Consiglio Maggiore in Palazzo Vecchio," *Prospettiva* 83–4 (1997), 104, proposed that Piergiampaolo Orsini was the mostly hidden older soldier ("presumably around fifty") in the background right. Frank Zöllner, "La *Battaglia di Anghiari* di Leonardo da Vinci, tra mitologia e politica," *Lettura Vinciana* 37 (Florence: Giunti, 1998), instead identified that figure as Ludovico Scarampo, taking Orsini to be the soldier in the right foreground, and further identifying the soldier at the far left as Francesco Piccinino (Niccolò Piccinino's son). Zöllner maintained these identifications in *Leonardo da Vinci: The Complete Paintings* (Cologne: Taschen, 2011), 169 and 173. Bambach, *Leonardo da Vinci*, similarly concludes that the "young Florentine" at right is Orsini; in addition, she takes the drawing for this figure to have been done from life, which would mean that Leonardo was more concerned to individualize the soldier and to capture a real expression than to preserve the features of a person from the past. Dati's *Trophaeum Anglaricum* was dedicated to Ludovico Trevisan and elevates him as the real hero of the battle; see the critical edition by Thomas Lindner (Vienna: Praesens, 2011).

42 Gunther Neufeld, "Leonardo da Vinci's *Battle of Anghiari*: A Genetic Reconstruction," *Art Bulletin* 31 (1949), 170–83, and Gould attempted reconstructions, which recent writers all reject. In 1994, Claire Farago could report that "the dominant view is that Leonardo painted the Battlepiece as an integrated narrative in three episodic scenes within a spatially unified landscape setting." See Farago, "Leonardo's *Battle of Anghiari*: A Study in the Exchange between Theory and Practice," *Art Bulletin* 76 (1994), 301–

30. By contrast, Alessandro Cecchi writes that "la porzione del cartone effettivamente disegnata e tradotta in pittura da Leonardo si limitò alla sola zona centrale, poichè l'artista sfruttò una clausola del contratto del 4 maggio 1504 che gli consentiva di prodursi inizialmente in un risultato parziale." See Cecchi, "Niccolò Machiavelli," 105.

43   See Cecchi, "Niccolo Machiavelli," esp. 107. For modern editions of the sources, see Matteo Villani, *Cronica: In continuazione di Filippo Villani*, ed. Giuseppe Porta (Parma: Fondazione Pietro Bembo, 1995), and Leonardo Bruni, *The History of the Florentine People*, ed. James Hankins (Cambridge: Harvard University Press, 2004).

44   Patricia Rubin, " 'Che è di questo culazzino!': Michelangelo and the Motif of the Male Buttocks in Italian Renaissance Art," *Oxford Art Journal* 32 (2009), 427–46, here 438, writes: "One soldier hurtles forward towards the beholder, possibly representing the fevered field commander, Galeotto Malatesta, risen suddenly from his bed, disoriented, and himself in danger of plunging into the river where one of his men has already drowned. Alternatively, it could be the Florentine captain, Manno Donati, rushing to arouse the soldiers with the false alarm and the terrifying cry 'noi siamo perduti.' " The Manno Donati identification goes back at least to Tolnay, *Michelangelo*, I, 107–8. Michael Hirst rejects it, on account of the figure's age, in Hirst, "I disegni di Michelangelo per la *Battaglia di Cascina* (ca. 1504)," in Eve Borsook and Fiorella Superbi Gioffredi, eds., *Tecnica e Stile: esempi di pittura murale del Rinascimento Italiano*, 2 vols. (Cinisello Balsamo: Silvana Ed., 1986), I, 43– 58, here 49. Zöllner, *Leonardo da Vinci*, I, 173, proposes that Malatesta is the man in the center of the composition, winding the cloth around his head, and that Donati is the man with helmet and shield at upper right. Robert Williams and Joost Keizer have a pointed exchange in the January 2014 *Art Bulletin*, 656–8, on the broader question of whether we should even be looking for historical individuals in Michelangelo's design. Williams returns to the possibility that "the gesturing figure at the center of the cartoon" is Donati; more fundamentally, he insists that Michelangelo's *istoria* would have required a serious treatment of subject matter. Keizer rejects even the inference that Michelangelo shows an alarm being given, let alone by Donati; as Keizer sees it, Michelangelo's entrancement with drawing led him away from any consideration of narrative. As will be evident from my other notes, Keizer and I have come to similar conclusions on a number of points; we agree that his approach to an assigned historical theme ultimately invited reflection on Michelangelo's artistic priorities. Yet I would not, as he does, explain this by arguing that the *Cascina* dismantles art's former dependence on text. Few great paintings from the previous century, it seems to me, could really be said to have been dependent on text. Conversely, distancing Michelangelo from his subject matter will lead us to miss what his making of art involved. The fact that Michelangelo's assignment was a battle painting seems highly relevant to his approach to drawing, as this book's emphasis on force and violence suggest. For an earlier and different perspective on the topic of art's new distance from storytelling in the sixteenth century, one in which Michelangelo also plays a prominent role, see Michael Cole, "Giambologna and the Sculpture with No Name," *Oxford Art Journal* 31 (2008), 337–60.

45   This was first noticed by Nicolai Rubinstein, "Machiavelli and the Mural Decoration of the Hall of the Great Council of Florence," in Ronald G. Kecks, ed., *Musagetes: Festschrift für Wolfgang Prinz* (Berlin: Gebr. Mann, 1991), 275–85. The best discussion is Fehrenbach, "Much Ado."

46   Vasari-Milanese, IV, 199, "nella quale sonotutti e'protettori del città di Fiorenza, e que'

Santi che nel giorno loro la città ha aute le sue vittorie." An excellent study of the commission and its related drawings is Chris Fischer, *Fra Bartolommeo: Master Draughtsman of the High Renaissance*, exh. cat., Museum Boymans-Van Beuningen Rotterdam, 1990, 219–33.

47 See Luke Syson, *Leonardo da Vinci: Painter at the Court of Milan*, exh. cat. (National Gallery, London), 2011, 289–91, for the argument that the cartoon which Vasari mentions is the drawing now in the National Gallery, London. On Michelangelo's drawing, now in Oxford, see esp. Paul Joannides, *The Drawings of Michelangelo and his Followers in the Ashmolean Museum* (Cambridge University Press, 2007), 59–64. The prominent place the cartoon gave to St. Anne would have been especially meaningful in Florence. It was on the feast of St. Anne that the Florentines, in 1343, had expelled the autocrat Walter of Brienne, linking her protection to the safeguarding of the Republic. For this reason, St. Anne also played a central role in Fra Bartolomeo's altarpiece in the Council Hall. See Roger Crum and David G. Wilkins, "In Defense of Florentine Republicanism: Saint Anne and Florentine Art, 1343–1575," in Kathleen Ashley and Pamela Sheinborn, eds., *Interpreting Cultural Symbols: Saint Anne in Late Medieval Society* (Athens: University of Georgia Press, 1990), 133–68, and Martin Kemp, *Leonardo da Vinci: The Marvellous Works of Nature and Man* (Oxford University Press, 2006), 217.

48 Leonardo made a drawing after the *David* that has come to be regarded as a criticism of the work. See the discussions in Joannides, *Michelangelo and his Influence*, 20; Carmen C. Bambach, "A Leonardo Drawing for the Metropolitan Museum of Art: Studies for a Statue of Hercules," *Apollo* 153 (2001), 16–23, and Rona Goffen, *Renaissance Rivals: Michelangelo, Leonardo, Raphael, Titian* (New Haven and London: Yale University Press, 2002), 129.

49 For Michelangelo's horse studies, see Goffen, *Renaissance Rivals*, 151.

50 Keizer, "Michelangelo, Drawing," e.g., writes that "it is difficult to imagine a representation of war further removed from tradition than Michelangelo's." Jones, *Lost Battles*, 243–4 and 268, finds that Leonardo's non-heroic portrayal of war ran so contrary to period expectations as to constitute a "heresy."

51 The foundational discussions are Wilhelm Köhler, "Michelangelos Schlachtkarton," *Kunstgeschichtliches Jahrbuch der K. K. Zentral-Kommission für Erforschung und Erhaltung der Kunst- und historische Denkmale* 1 (1907), 115–72, and Henry Thode, *Michelangelo: Kritische Untersuchungen über seine Werke*, 6 vols. (Berlin: G. Grote'sche Verlagsbuchhandlung, 1908), 1, 95. For Michelangelo's movements in these years, see the recent discussions in William Wallace, *Michelangelo: The Artist, the Man, and His Times* (Cambridge University Press, 2010), 62–71, and Michael Hirst, *Michelangelo: The Achievement of Fame* (New Haven and London: Yale University Press, 2011), 56–60.

52 Earlier scholars had maintained that both painters had been expected to work on the East wall of the room; see, for example, the still useful survey by Johannes Wilde, "Michelangelo and Leonardo," *Burlington Magazine* 95 (1953), 65–77, with a reconstruction on p. 73. A recent variation on this theory holds that Leonardo had been assigned the entire East wall of the room, and that Michelangelo was expected to paint opposite him, on the West wall. See the discussion in Rab Hatfield, *Finding Leonardo: The Case for Recovering the Battle of Anghiari* (Florence: Florentine Press, 2007). The most extensive version of the leading counter-proposal, that both Leonardo and Michelangelo were designing shorter murals to go beside one another on the West

wall, is H. Travers Newton and John R. Spencer, "On the Location of Leonardo's Battle of Anghiari," *Art Bulletin* 64 (1982), 45–62; it was sustained recently by Bambach, *Leonardo da Vinci*, 479 (with further references), and by Keizer, "Michelangelo, Drawing," 305 and n. 14. Just what Leonardo executed is also a matter of debate. Carlo Pedretti argued that Leonardo had nearly finished the central section of his mural, depicting the fight for the standard, when he broke off work; see *Leonardo da Vinci inedito: tre saggi* (Florence: G. Barbèra, 1968). Fehrenbach, by contrast, writes that "it is doubtful if Leonardo ever began to paint on the wall"; see "Much Ado," 398.

53 Köhler, "Michelangelos Schlachtkarton," 117; Thode, *Michelangelo*, I, 96.

54 Kenneth Clark, *Leonardo da Vinci* (New York: Penguin, 1989), 198; Barocchi, *Vita di Michelangelo*, II, 254. John Addington Symonds, *The Life of Michelangelo Buonarroti*, 2 vols. (London: John C. Nimmo, 1893), I, 171.

55 Vasari, ed. Barocchi, *Vita di Michelangelo*, II, 254: "Questa descrizione del Cartone di Cascina che risale tuta, salvo una breve variente, al 1550, è come testimonianza di un'ammirazione unanime per un'opera che aveva instaurato un nuovo gusto."

56 *Opere di Benvenuto Cellini*, ed. Giuseppe Guido Ferrero (Turin: UTET, 1980), 82.

57 Vasari, *Lives*, II, 658; cf. Vasari-Milanese, VII, 161.

58 Vasari, *Lives*, I, 712–13; Vasari-Milanesi, IV, 319–20.

2   CIRCUMSCRIPTION

1 In October 1503, Vespucci annotated an edition of Cicero with the remark that Leonardo, like the ancient painter Apelles, finished the heads and busts of his figures but left the rest of the bodies inchoate. He then pointed to the *Mona Lisa* and the *Virgin and Child with St. Anne* as examples of this practice before adding, "we shall see what he will do concerning the Hall of the Great Council." See Armin Schlechter's entry in Schlechter, ed., *Die edel kunst der truckerey: Ausgewählte Inkunabeln der Universitätsbibliothek Heidelberg* (Heidelberg: Winter, 2005), no. 20, and Luke Syson, *Leonardo da Vinci:Painter at the Court of Milan*, exh. cat. (National Gallery, London, 2011), 45. Vasari implies that it was the fame of the *Mona Lisa* that led to the *Anghiari* commission; see Jonathan Jones, *The Lost Battles: Leonardo, Michelangelo and the Artistic Duel that Defined the Renaissance* (New York: Alfred A. Knopf, 2012), 46.

2 On the connection between setting and medium, see esp. the discussion in Claire Farago, "Leonardo's *Battle of Anghiari*: A Study in the Exchange between Theory and Practice," *Art Bulletin* 76 (1994), 301–30. Leonardo Dati's *Trophaeum Anglaricum* and Macchiavelli's *Istorie fiorentine* both describe the river landscape in which the battle took place.

3 Jean-Paul Richter, *The Literary Works of Leonardo da Vinci*, 2 vols. (London: Low, 1883), I, 300–03.

4 Compare Johannes Wilde, *Michelangelo: Six Lectures* (Oxford: Clarendon Press, 1978), 45.

5 Early is William Page Smith, *Etude sur Michel Ange Buonarroti* (London: Trübner & Co., 1870), who wrote "Les anges sont des athlètes d'une anatomie exagérée." Howard Hibbard's classic *Michelangelo* (London: Penguin, 1975), 67, refers to "the athletic *Doni Madonna.*" Timothy Verdon, " 'Amor ab abspectu': Maria nel tondo Doni e l'umanesimo

cristiano," *Vivens Homo* 5 (1994), 534, writes of Michelangelo's "atleta femminile." See also the early descriptions collected in Barocchi, *Vita di Michelangelo,* II, 244.

6   See Hibbard, *Michelangelo,* 67.

7   John Addington Symonds, *The Life of Michelangelo Buonarroti,* 2 vols. (London: John C. Nimmo, 1893), I, 116. Verdon, more plausibly, sees in the *Doni Tondo's* manner an attempt on Michelangelo's part to differentiate himself from Leonardo: see "'Amor ab abspectu,'" 544–5.

8   See Fredrika H. Jacobs, "An Assessment of Contour Line: Vasari, Cellini and the 'Paragone,'" *Artibus et Historiae* 9 (1988), 139–50, and, for Allori's response to Michelangelo's *dintornare,* Marco Ruffini, *Art Without an Author: Vasari's Lives and Michelangelo's Death* (New York: Fordham University Press, 2011), 58–9.

9   Marcel Brion, *Michel-Ange* (Paris: Michel, 1939), 136, "Michelangelo déjà confondait les ressources de la peinture et de la sculpture"; Wilde, *Michelangelo,* 45, wrote: "it is like a free-standing sculptural group"; Charles de Tolnay, *Michelangelo,* 5 vols. (Princeton University Press, 1947), I, 167, "the painting of Michelangelo is made up of cool, clear colors, which give the impression of 'colored marble' "; Hibbard, *Michelangelo,* 68: "the figures in the painting are preternaturally clear and sculpturesque." More subtle is Rona Goffen's discussion, *Renaissance Rivals: Michelangelo, Leonardo, Raphael, Titian* (New Haven and London: Yale University Press, 2002), 165.

10 Agnolo Bronzino, in Paola Barocchi, ed., *Scritti d'arte del Cinquecento,* 3 vols. (Milan: Riccardi, 1971), I, 503: "dicono che, per questo, non imitano più la natura per far di rilievo che altrimenti, anzi tolgono la cosa che già era di rilievo fatta della natura, onde tutto quello che vi si truova di tondo e di largo o l'altro non è dell'arte, perché prima vi erano e larghezza et altezza e tutte le parti che si danno a corpi solidi, ma solo è dell'arte le linee che cercondano detto corpo, le quali sono in superficie; onde, com'è detto, non è dell'arte l'essere di rilievo, ma della natura." See also Jacobs, "Assessment of Contour Line," 148 n. 2.

11 Pliny, *Historia naturale,* trans. Christophoro Landino (Venice: 1481), book 35, ch. 10: "Et per confessione degli artefici acquisto la palma nelle externe linee. Questa e la soma subtilita nella pictura. Dipignere e corpi & el mezzo delle cose e grande difficulta: ma molti Vhanno acquistato Gloria. Ma fare le extremita de corpi & sapere concludere elfine dellarte e chosa che radeuolte nellarte si conduce a perfectione. Imperoche la extremita debba circundare se medesima & finire in modo che la prometta che possa altre chose & mostri etiandio quello che occulta. Questa Gloria hanno conceduto a Parrhasio." Alison Wright, "Dimensional Tension in the Work of Antonio Pollaiuolo," in Stuart Currie and Peta Motture, eds., *The Sculpted Object 1400–1700* (Aldershot: Ashgate, 1997), 72, notes that Ghiberti had already cited Pliny in his *Commentarii,* and brings the passage to bear on Pollaiuolo. See also the discussions of Parrhasius and contour in Sarah Blake McHam, *Pliny and the Artistic Culture of the Italian Renaissance: The Legacy of the* Natural History (New Haven and London: Yale University Press, 2013), esp. 47 and 105.

12 For elision as a pictorial device, see the discussion in Michael Fried, *The Moment of Caravaggio* (Princeton University Press, 2010), 180–81.

13 Leon Battista Alberti, *On Painting and On Sculpture: The Latin Texts of "De pictura" and "De statua,"* ed. and trans. Cecil Grayson (London: Phaidon, 1972), *De statua,* 139 (section 13): "There is the outline at which the surface we see from a particular viewpoint ends and is separated from the other we cannot see by virtue of the part that

stands between; and this outline, if it were drawn properly on a wall, would produce a figure exactly like the one a shadow would make by the interception of light, if the source of light were placed at the same point in space where the eye of the observer had been before." The connection was first noted by Jacobs, "An Assessment of Contour Line," 145; see also *De statua*, ed. Marco Collareta (Livorno: Sillabe, 1998), 47.

14 Alberti, *Della pittura*, 5: "Alcuni di questi razzi giugnendo all'orlo delle superficie misurano sue tutte quantità. Adunque perché così cozzano l'ultime ed estreme parti della superficie, nominialli estremi o vuoi estrinsici."

15 See Ubaldo Sedano Espín, "Reflectografía infrarroja," in *Ghirlandaio y el Renacimiento en Florencia*, exh. cat., Fundación Colección Thyssen-Bornemisza, Madrid, 2010, 234–7 and Susana Pérez, "Estudio radiográfico," in ibid., 240–45.

16 The best discussion of Alberti's geometric conception of contour is Roland Kanz, "Linien rahmen Körper: Albertis 'circonscrizione' und Donatellos Konturschatten im 'rilievo schiacciato,'" in Hans Körner and Karl Möseneder, eds. *Rahmen zwischen Innen und Außen: Beitrage zur Theorie und Geschichte* (Berlin: Reimer, 2010), 91–112. That artists at this moment associated contour and measure is demonstrated in a very practical way by drawings like Andrea del Verrocchio's horse study in the Metropolitan Museum, on which outlines are annotated with proportions.

17 Pliny, *Historia naturale*, book 35, ch. 11: "Questa arte trouo in corintho Dibutade sycionio maxime per opera della figluola laquale presa dallamore duno giouane uolendo lui ire in altri paesi con la lucerna fece lombra della sua persona apparire nel muro & poi con line la termino nellequali ponendo el padre suo la terra ne fece una forma & dipoi secca lamesse a chuocere coglaltri uasi." For the myth, see the engaging discussion in Victor Stoichita, *A Short History of the Shadow* (London: Reaktion, 1997), esp. 11–41.

18 For the availability of the myth in the Renaissance and its connection to other origin stories, see esp. Ulrich Pfisterer, "Künstlerliebe: Der Narcissus-Mythos bei Leon Battista Alberti und die Aristoteles Lektüre der Frührenaissance," *Zeitschrift für Kunstgeschichte* 64 (2001), 305–30. In making the connection to Lippi, I am following Alison Wright, "The Memory of Faces: Representational Choices in Fifteenth-Century Florentine Portraiture," in Giovanni Ciappelli and Patricia Lee Rubin, eds., *Art, Memory, and Family in Renaissance Florence* (Cambridge University Press, 2000), 86–113. I also borrow her resonant title phrase below.

19 See Marie-José Mondzain, *Image, icône, économie: les sources byzantines de l'imaginaire contemporain* (Paris: Éditions du Seuil, 1996), esp. 121–8 and 205, as well as the extract from the Horos that she includes in an appendix, 278: "Si quelqu'un s'efforce de circonscrire au moyen de couleurs matérielles dans des images anthropomorphiques la substance incirconscrite du Verbe divin et son hypostase en vertu de son incarnation, ne le considérant ni comme plus divin ni comme moins circonscrit après l'incarnation, qu'il soit anathème."

20 Nikephoros, cited and discussed in Charles Barber, *Figure and Likeness: On the Limits of Representation in Byzantine Iconoclasm* (Princeton University Press, 2002), 117–18.

21 Distinguished medievalists have certainly perceived these ideas still to be in play in later periods. Two important copies or repaintings of the face of Christ were those in Genoa and Rome and Herbert Kessler writes with regard to this broad category of objects that "[Copies] are to the Mandylion, what the Mandylion was to Christ; they entered the divine archetype into the physical order, leaving the true image uncircumscribed in matter, time, and place." See Kessler, "Configuring the Invisible: Facsimiles and

Copies of the Holy Face," in Kessler and Gerhard Wolf, eds., *The Holy Face and the Paradox of Representation* (Bologna: Nuova Alfa, 1998), 129–51, here 151. Similarly, Gerhard Wolf writes with regard to Claude Mellan's 1649 engraving of the face of Christ: "La linea oscillante di Mellan è una periferia che si sviluppa dal centro: il problema della rappresentabilità dell'Uomo-Dio vi è formulato in modo preciso, in quanto si è lavorato senza contorno. Dio non è circoscrivibile (*aperigraptos*), l'incarnazione permette sì l'immagine sensibile, ma la sua natura rimane paradossale." See Giovanni Morello and Gerhard Wolf, eds., *Il Volto di Cristo* (Milan: Electa, 200), 114. Ambrogio Catarino's important 1551 *Disputatio de cultu & adoratione Imaginum* – the earliest Renaissance treatise on sacred images – makes a point of specifying that God is "incircunscriptibilis," and meditates on the implications of this for painters. See Catarino (Rome: Antonius Bladus, 1552), 124.

22 Alberti, *Della pittura*, in Rocco Sinisgalli, ed., *Il nuovo* De pictura *di Leon Battista Alberti* (Rome: Edizioni Kappa, 2006), 172–3: "E dove la pittura studia ripresentare cose vedute, notiamo in che modo le cose si veggano. Principio, vedendo qual cosa, diciamo questo esser cosa quale occupa uno luogo. Qui il pittore, descrivendo questo spazio, dirà questo suo guidare uno orlo con linea essere circonscrizione." Compare also Leonardo da Vinci, Codex Atlanticus 437r, II, 814: "La cosa circumscripta sempre fia minore che quella che la circumscrive."

23 Vasari, *Lives*, I, 250; Vasari-Milanesi, II, 101: "in questa levato via il profilo che ricigneva per tutto le figure."

24 Karel van Mander, *The Lives of the Illustrious Netherlandisch and German Painters, from the first edition of the* Schilder-boeck *(1603–1604)*, ed. and trans. Hessel Miedema, 6 vols. (Doornspijk: Davaco, 1994), I, 212–15: "Nu sietmen de dinghen des grooten Buonarotti, vol binnewerck van Musculen begreyen ost omvangen met eenen Invighen schoonen omtreck een dinghen van groot verstandt gelyck sulcken uytuemenden Meester trachetende nae de hooghste schoonheyt door veel ervarens ondervonden hadde te behooren."

25 Francisco Pacheco, *Arte de la pintura*, ed. F. J. Sanchez Canton, 2 vols. (Madrid: Instituto de Valencia de Don Juan, 1956), I, 368–9: "De suerte que en la entereza de los perfiles, en la valentía de los músculos, en la verdad de los escorzos, en la gracia y variedad de los contornos, de las figuras desnudas, quien quisiere aprovechar ha de estudiar de las maravillosas obras del divino Micael Angel, y con aquella luz podrá ir a imitar las cosas naturales, y sin aquella manera se perderá. Porque de haber hecho la vista a los perfiles hermosos y enteros de Micael Angel, sabra elegir de lo natural lo major y desechar lo seco y desgraciado." Pacheco makes this comment in the course of explaining why Michelangelo was superior to Raphael, placing the contour in a competitive context.

26 Jean Cadogan, *Domenico Ghirlandaio: Artist and Artisan* (New Haven and London: Yale University Press, 2000), 134–5.

27 Ibid., 302.

28 Sara Nair James discusses one example of the former procedure, Signorelli's use of incisions to transfer designs at Orvieto. See *Signorelli and Fra Angelico at Orvieto: Liturgy, Poetry and a Vision of the End-Time* (Aldershot: Ashgate, 2003), 132, with a good photograph of the still visible lines that the process left in the wet plaster.

29 Cennino Cennini, *Il libro dell'arte*, ed. Fabio Frezzato (Vicenza: Neri Pozza, 2003), 77–8: "Bisogniati essere avisato:, ancora è una carta che si chiama carta lucida, la quale ti può essere molto utile per ritrarre una testa o una fighura o una meza figura, secondo

che ll'uomo truova di man di gran maestri. E per avere bene i contorni o dichiarata ogni tavola, o di muro o di carta, che proprio la vogli tor su, metti questa carta lucida in sulla fighura, over disegnio, attachata gientilmente in quattro canti con un pocho di ciera rossa o verde. Di subito, per lo lustro della carta lucida, trasparre la fighura over disegnio di sotto, in forma e in modo che 'l vedi chiaro. Allora togli o ppenna temperata ben sottile o ppennel sottile di varo sottile, e con inchiostro puoi andare ricercando i contorni e lle stremità del disegno di sotto; e cchosì gieneralmente tocchando alchune ombre, sì chome a tte è possibile potere vedere e fare; e levando poi la carta, puoi tocchare di alchuni bianchetti e relievi sì chome tu ài i piaceri su."

30 See the discussion in Alexander Perrig, *Michelangelo's Drawings: The Science of Attribution* (New Haven and London: Yale University Press, 1991), 31–4, esp. his remarks on tracing, 32.

31 All of this is proposed in the illuminating if controversial study by Francis Ames-Lewis, "Drapery 'Pattern'-drawings in Ghirlandaio's Workshop and Ghirlandaio's Early Apprenticeship," *Art Bulletin* 63 (1981), 49–62.

32 Cennini, *Libro*, 69: "se vuoi, poi chè ài collo stile disegnato, chiarire meglio il disegno, ferma con inchiostro ne' luoghi stremi e necessari."

33 Ibid., 149–50.

34 Cadogan, *Domenico Ghirlandaio*, 112–13.

35 For the category of "sculptural drawing" and its limitations, see Francis Ames-Lewis, *Drawing in Early Renaissance Italy* (New Haven and London: Yale University Press), 104–5. The most helpful recent discussions of the sheet are Alison Wright's entry in Patricia Lee Rubin and Alison Wright, *Renaissance Florence: The Art of the 1470s* (New Haven and London: Yale University Press, 2000), 244–7, and Alison Wright, *The Pollaiuolo Brothers: The Arts of Florence and Rome* (New Haven and London: Yale University Press, 2005), 158–62.

36 Vasari-Milanesi, I, 170–71: "perciocchè tutte queste cose, essendo immobili e senza sentimento, fanno grande agevolezza, stando ferme, a colui che disegna; il che non avviene nelle cose vive che si muovono."

37 See Cennini, 150 (ch. 123): "Sì cchome dei segniare i contorni delle fighure per mettere in campi d'oro." Note that the sketch that preceded the incisions would already have emphasized contours. In preparing their catalogue of Quattrocento paintings in the National Gallery of Art, Washington, D.C., Miklós Boskovits and David Alan Brown had the works examined using infrared reflectography. Their technical notes frequently draw attention to contour underdrawings, many then worked up with hatching or washes; *Italian Paintings of the Fifteenth Century* (New York and Oxford: Oxford University Press, 2003); p. 304 illustrates an infrared reflectogram of a painting that the catalogue attributes to Ghirlandaio.

38 Cennini, Libro, 161–2. The entries in Carl Brandon Strehlke's *Italian Paintings 1250–1450 in the John G. Johnson Collection and the Philadelphia Museum of Art* (University Park: Pennsylvania State University Press, 2002) include informative technical notes that offer many examples of the practice.

39 Most of the current gilding in the *Virgin and Child* is not original, and Cadogan raised questions about whether Ghirlandaio had gilded the painting at all. The subsequent technical examination carried out for the Gallery's catalogue, however, established that the present gilding covers remants of the original red bole and gold leaf. David Alan Brown remarked that the gold background was unusual in a work from the 1470s, but

he proposed that this would look less puzzling "if we assume that the picture was ordered by a patron with conservative taste"; Boskovits and Brown, *Italian Paintings*, 302. The Quattrocento painter's various uses of incisions might be compared with the practices of early engravers, who likewise established the contours of their figures before working up details. For a comparison of Mantegna and Dürer's approaches to the plate, see Peter Parshall, *The Unfinished Print* (Washington, D.C.: National Gallery of Art, 2001), 14–15.

40 See Jill Dunkerton et al., *Giotto to Dürer: Early Renaissance Painting in the National Gallery* (New Haven and London: Yale University Press, 1991), 188, on painters in tempera working color by color, not figure by figure.

41 This was, in fact, the very criticism that Galileo later leveled against Florentine academicians like Allori. See Erwin Panofsky, *Galileo as a Critic of the Arts* (The Hague: Nijhoff, 1954), 9.

42 Carmen Bambach, *Drawing and Painting in the Italian Renaissance Workshop: Theory and Practice, 1300–1600* (Cambridge University Press, 1998), 70, observes generally that "Fresco painters structured the sutures of *giornate* to coincide as much as possible with the main body outline of figures. And frequently in the case of monumental figures painted in multiple *giornate*, the first *giornata* would encompass the head down to its neck, shoulders or bust, the rest of the body being painted subsequently." Compare Gordon Hale, *The Technique of Fresco Painting* (New York: Dover Publications, 1956), 29: "In deciding on the contours of your day's piece, remember that curved line is less visible than a straight one . . . Joins are hard to find in the work of Renaissance painters, although they made no great effort to conceal them."

43 Alberti, *Della pittura*: "Io così dico in questa circonscrizione molto doversi osservare ch'ella sia di linee sottilissime fatta, quasi tali che fuggano essere vedute, in quali solea sé Appelles pittore essercitare e contendere con Protogene; però che la circonscrizione è non altro che disegnamento dell'orlo, quale ove sia fatto con linea troppo apparente, non dimostrerà ivi essere margine di superficie ma fessura."

44 Alison Wright emphasizes, for example, how Pollaiuolo's *St. Sebastian* "shows a deep engagement with tensions set up between space and contour." Wright, "Dimensional Tension," 70.

45 For the Pliny, see n. 11 above. For the identification of figure with contour, see Janis Bell, "Sfumato, Linien und Natur," in Frank Fehrenbach, ed., *Leonardo da Vinci: Natur im Übergang* (Munich: Fink, 2002), 229–56, esp. 232–5, who translates Leonardo's term *figura* not with the German cognate *Figur* but with *Umriss* ("contour"). Thus, she renders MS. A 92v (Richter *Literary Works*, I, 128), "Ogni forma corporea in quanto allo offizio dell'occhio si divide in 3 parti, cioè corpo, figura e colore" as "Jede körperliche Form teilt sich hinsichtlich der Aufgabe des Auges in drei Teile, nämlich Körper, Umriss (*figura*) und Farbe" and "se tu vederai uno omo da presso, tu conoscerai la qualità del corpo, la qualità della figura e similmente del colore" as "wenn du einen Mann aus der Nähe siehst, wirst du die Qualitäten des Körpers, des Umrisses (*figura*) und ebenso der Farbe erkennen." Cf. Trattato 59v in Leonardo da Vinci, *Treatise on Painting (Codex Urbinas Latinus 1270)*, trans. and annotated by A. Philip McMahon (Princeton University Press, 1956; hereafter, McMahon), 262: "Delle figure che compongono le istorie quella si dimostrara di magiore rilevo la quale sara finta essere piu vicina al'occichio [sic] . . . quel colore si dimostra di maggiore perfettione il quale ha men quantita d'aria interposta infra se e'l'occhio ch'el giudica."

46   Richter, *Literary Works*, I, 291: "Del comporre storie; del non riguardare le membra delle figure nelle storie come molti fanno che per fare le figure intere guastono i componimenti." Wright discusses the passage in a different context in "Dimensional Tension," 60.

47   Alexander Nagel, "Leonardo and Sfumato," *RES* 24 (1993), 7–20.

48   See Bell, "Sfumato," and Frank Fehrenbach, "Der Oszillierende Blick: 'Sfumato' und die Optik des späten Leonardo," *Zeitschrift für Kunstgeschichte* 65 (2002), 522–44.

49   Among the few Renaissance writers to understand *sfumato*, Nagel suggests, was Daniele Barbaro, who specifically responds to Pliny and his celebration of Parrhasius, "advertising how far the techniques of modern painting had surpassed those of the ancients: the clear outline had been superseded by new and more subtle effects, embodying a new understanding of the relation between the visible and the invisible." Nagel, "Leonardo and Sfumato," 17.

50   It is with this point that Kanz opens his important essay "Linien rahmen Körper."

51   This is clearly visible in the *Ginevra de' Benci* portrait, as David Alan Brown remarks in his technical note on the painting; Boskovits and Brown, *Italian Paintings*, 357.

52   It was also not the case that artists had to choose absolutely between one system or the other. Bell, "Sfumato," 255–6, emphasizes that while Leonardo eventually came to believe that contours did not exist in nature, he nevertheless continued to include such lines in his drawings and paintings. She concludes that he would have justified their presence as a kind of philosophical abstraction.

53   Nagel, "Leonardo and Sfumato," 7.

54   This would be an alternative reading of Barbaro's allusion to Parrhasius, discussed in Nagel, "Leonardo and Sfumato," 17.

55   Leonardo commonly made linear underdrawings for his paintings, as can be seen in infrared reflectograms and in incomplete paintings. The blurring of edges thus worked against a technique on which he himself depended. In my overview of contour, I have, where possible, been taking Ghirlandaio as my favored example, since it was in his shop that Michelangelo learned to paint. Megan Holmes has reminded me, however, that to underscore the agonistic dimension of Leonardo's *sfumato*, one might look equally to the Verrocchio shop. When Leonardo completed the *Baptism* that Verrocchio had left unfinished years before, he did not imitate his master's style or even use the same medium. Instead, he painted in oil, aiming to achieve softer effects. See Antonio Natali, *Lo Sguardo degli angeli: Verrocchio, Leonardo e il "Battesimo di Cristo"* (Milan: Silvana Editoriale, 1998), esp. 61–94.

56   This was one of the fundamental perceptions of John Shearman, "Leonardo's Colour and Chiaroscuro," *Zeitschrift für Kunstgeschichte* 25 (1962), 13–47.

57   McMahon 130 (translation slightly modified). The passage is similar to one of the most cited lines in the *Ashburton Codex*; see E. H. Gombrich, "Blurred Images and the Unvarnished Truth," *British Journal of Aesthetics* 2 (1962), 171; "Nagel, "Sfumato," 9–10 and Larry Keith, "In Pursuit of Perfection: Leonardo's Painting Technique," in Syson, *Leonardo*, 54–77, quotation 68–9.

58   For Michelangelo's technique in these drawings, see esp. Hugo Chapman, *Michelangelo Drawings: Closer to the Master* (London: British Museum Press, 2005), 81–6.

59   Michael Hirst, *Michelangelo and His Drawings* (New Haven and London: Yale University Press, 1988), 26–8.

60   For the complete poem, probably written between 1538 and 1544, see Christopher Ryan, ed. and trans., *Michelangelo: The Poems* (London: J. M. Dent, 1996), 138–41. Varchi's

commentary made this Michelangelo's most famous piece of writing. Pacheco, *Arte de la pintura*, I, 492, excerpted just the first stanza for his own discussion.

61   See Hirst, *Michelangelo and His Drawings*, 111–13, and Paul Joannides, *Michelangelo and his Influence: Drawings from Windsor Castle* (London: Lund Humphries, 1996), 64–71. The drawing dates to 1533.

62   Hirst, for example, illustrates Michelangelo's early and late style by comparing a drawing made for the Sistine ceiling and one made for the altar wall: "Put very crudely, the earlier drawing shows a more pronounced disjunction between contours and internal modeling"; *Michelangelo and His Drawings*, 30. James Elkins, by contrast, emphasizes continuity, using a late *Crucifixion* as an example of a drawing "where there are so many contours that they form a single dense braid on one side and slough off into thin air on the other," where "Michelangelo went back over his own contours, altering and correcting – but not erasing," placing this in a genealogy that goes back to the *Cascina* cartoon; Elkins, "Marks, Traces, 'Traits,' Contours, 'Orli,' and 'Splendores': Nonsemiotic Elements in Pictures," *Critical Inquiry* 21 (1995), 822–60, here 848. Keizer, "Michelangelo," 308–9, describes how "the contours of the [*Cascina*] figures, both in the preparatory drawings and in the cartoon, are thickened, as if to emphasize their self-containedness. The cartoon might best be characterized as an assembly of isolated figure drawings."

63   Ryan, *Michelangelo: The Poems*, 140.

64   Claire J. Farago, *Leonardo da Vinci's 'Paragone': A Critical Interpretation with a New Edition of the Text in the "Codex Urbinas"* (Leiden: E. J. Brill, 1992), 240–41: "La Musica non è da essere chiamata altro che sorella della pittura con ciò sia ch essa è subbietto dell'audito, secondo senso a l'occhio, e compone armonia con le congiontioni delle sue parti proportionali operate nel medessimo tempo. Constrette a nascere e morire in uno o più tempi armonici li quali tempi circondano la proportionalita de membri, di che tale armonia si compone non altrimente che si faccia la linea circonferentiale le membra di che si genera la bellezza humana."

65   For an overview of possibilities, see Michael Cole, "Harmonic Force in Cinquecento Painting," in Ulrich Pfisterer and Anja Zimmermann, eds., *Animationen/Transgressionen: Das Kunstwerk als Lebewesen* (Berlin: Akademie-Verlag, 2005), 73–94, with further references.

66   When Holanda later defined design as "a line or thin profile that surrounds the figure," he did so in a chapter entitled "What the Force of Painting Consists Of."

67   Pomponius Gauricus, *De Sculptura*, ed. André Chastel and Robert Klein (Geneva: Droz, 1969), 205: "Nos quoque hortamur, admonefacimusque identidem omnes quei Corynthii, non thuscanici esse cupiunt, ube corporis circumscriptionem fecerint, remque ad gestus Symmetriamque perduxerint, naturam ipsam diligenter inspiciant, habeantque et elegantissima et pulcherrima corpora."

68   Barocchi, *Vita di Michelangelo*, I, 27; II, 269–71.

69   Henry Thode, *Michelangelo Kritische Untersuchungen über seine Werke*, 6 vols. (Berlin: G. Grote'sche Verlagsbuchhandlung, 1908), I, 96.

70   Wilhelm Köhler, "Michelangelos Schlachtkarton," *Kunstgeschichtliches Jahr buch der K. K. Zentral-Kommission für Erforschung und Erhaltung der Kunst- und historische Denkmale* 1 (1907) 119–22; Thode, *Michelangelo*, I, 97–99; Ana Avila, "Repercusion de la 'Batalla de Cascina' en la pintura española del primer renascimiento," *Goya* 190 (1986), 184–201.

71   See Bernardine Barnes, *Michelangelo in Print: Reproductions as Response in the Sixteenth Century* (Farnham: Ashgate, 2010), esp. ch. 1, "Michelangelo in Fragments: Prints after *The Battle of Cascina* and Other Works"; see also Hirst, *Michelangelo and his Drawings*, 44, and Joost Keizer, "Michelangelo, Drawing, and the Subject of Art," *Art Bulletin* 93 (2011), 304–24, esp. 312. Wilde, "Michelangelo and Leonardo," 77, had already observed in 1953 that Michelangelo's followers characteristically studied the *Cascina* "in its components, single figures or groups of two or three figures. Vasari states this and adds that he knew no copy of the whole other than Aristotile da Sangallo's drawing."

72   The clearest survey is Thode, *Michelangelo*, I, 101–2, though fundamental also is Köhler, "Michelangelos Schlachtkarton."

73   Wilde, *Michelangelo*, 43. Michael Hirst argues that the isolation of the figures happened in the course of Michelangelo's compositional process, between the chalk drawing in the British Museum (fig. 22) and the lost cartoon. See Hirst, "I disegni di Michelangelo per la *Battaglia di Cascina* (ca. 1504)," in Eve Borsook and Fiorella Superbi Gioffredi, eds., *Tecnica e Stile: esempi di pittura murale del Rinascimento Italiano*, 2 vols. (Cinisello Balsamo: Silvana Ed., 1986), I, 43–58, esp. 45.

74   Vasari, *Lives*, II, 429; Vasari-Milanesi, VI, 434.

75   Keizer takes a different view, calling the Sangallo painting "a painted grisaille copy of the whole cartoon" and a "faithful copy of Michelangelo's cartoon"; "Michelangelo, Drawing," 305.

76   Thode, *Michelangelo*, I, 214.

77   Ibid., 215.

78   See Köhler, "Michelangelos Schlachtkarton," 148, and Thode, *Michelangelo*, I, 106.

79   "Soleva, dico, dal nascente sole sino all'imbrunita sera non levarsi mai il pennello di mano, ma scordatosi il mangiare ed il bere, di continovo dipingere. Se ne sarebbe poi state due, tre e quattro dì, che non v'avrebbe messa mano; e tuttavia dimorava talora una e due ore del giorno, e solamente contemplava, considerava, ed esaminando tra se, le sue figure giudicava. L'ho anco veduto . . . venirsene dritto alle Grazie, ed asceso sul ponte pigliar il pennello, ed una o due pennellate dar ad una di quelle figure, e di subito partirsi e andar altrove." Matteo Bandello, *Raccolta di novellieri italiani*, 2 vols. (Florence: Tipografia Borghi, 1833), I, 256, *Novelle* 58, dedication; Vasari-Milanesi, V, 584; Tolnay, *Michelangelo*, I, 215.

80   Vasari, *Lives*, I, 632; Vasari-Milanesi, IV, 30.

81   For Verino, see Edoardo Villata, *Leonardo da Vinci: i documenti e le testimonianze contemporanee* (Milan: Castello Sforzesco, 1999), 147, cited in Syson, *Leonardo*, 48.

82   For a broader perspective on Michelangelo's "arte da donna," see especially Philip Sohm, "Gendered Style in Italian Art Criticism from Michelangelo to Malvasia," *Renaissance Quarterly* 48 (1995), 759–808.

83   See Nicola Suthor, *Bravura: Virtuosität und Mutwilligkeit in der Malerei der Frühen Neuzeit* (Munich: Fink, 2010).

84   Benvenuto Cellini and Filippo Baldinucci, quoted in Michael Cole, "The *Figura Sforzata*: Modeling, Power, and the Mannerist Body," *Art History* 24 (2001): 520–51.

85   This is the argument in Matteo Burioni, "Grund und *campo*: die Metaphorik des Bildgrundes in der frühen Neuzeit oder: Paolo Uccellos *Schlacht von San Romano*," in Gottfried Boehm and Matteo Burioni, eds., *Der Grund: Das Feld des Sichtbaren* (Munich: Fink, 2012), 94–149.

86 Pomponius Gauricus, *De Sculptura*, 208–10. Here I am drawing on David Summers, "Michelangelo's 'Battle of Cascina,' Pomponius Gauricus, and the Invention of a 'Gran Maniera' in Italian Painting," *Artibus et Historiae* 28 (2007), 165–76. Summers understood Gauricus, with his notion of what Summers calls "despective," to be providing an optical rationale for the kind of space seen in Roman sarcophagi, which were themselves important precedents for Michelangelo's depiction of bathing soldiers. For Leonardo's *di sotto in sù* composition, see Bambach, *Drawing and Painting*, 50.

87 On this poetry fragment of Michelangelo's, see Julian Kliemann, "Kunst als Bogenschiessen: Domenichinos *Jagd der Diana* in der Galleria Borghese," *Römisches Jahrbuch der Bibliotheca Hertziana* 31 (1996): 273–311, esp. 303, with references to the earlier literature and to competing readings of the lines.

88 See the famous poem "I' ho già fatto un gozzo in questo stento," in Ryan, *Michelangelo*, 4–5. I refer to the stanzas four and five: "Dinanzi mi s'allunga la corteccia, / e per piegarsi adietro si regroppa, / e tendomi com'arco soriano. / Però fallace e strano surge il iudizio che la mente porta, / ché mal si tra' per cerbottana torta."

89 Vasari, *Lives*, II, 659; Vasari-Milanesi, VII, 164.

90 Ioan Couliano, *Eros and Magic in the Renaissance*, trans. Margaret Cook (University of Chicago Press, 1987), 88.

91 Vasari, *Lives*, II, 695. Cf. Vasari-Milanesi, VII, 215: "Questa opera mena prigioni legati quegli che di sapere l'arte si persuadono; e nel vedere i segni da lui tirati ne' contorni di che cosa essa si sia, trema e teme ogni terribile spirito, sia quanto si voglia carico di disegno; e mentre che si guardano le fatiche dell'opera sua, i sensi si stordiscono solo a pensare che cosa possono essere le alter pitture fatte e che si faranno, poste a tal paragone."

92 See, most recently, Maria Ruvoldt, "Michelangelo's *Slaves* and the Gift of Liberty," *Renaissance Quarterly* 65 (2012), 1029–59, with further references.

93 On this point, I see things differently from Rubin, who writes, 443, "The inward turn of the protagonists detaches them from the beholders. This history is contiguous, not continuous or contingent. The members of the Council could witness the action, but could not notionally participate in it or complete it in any way"; Patricia Rubin, "'Che è di questo culazzino!': Michelangelo and the Motif of the Male Buttocks in Italian Renaissance Art," *Oxford Art Journal* 32 (2009), 427–46. My thinking on the point was informed by Michael Fried's discussions of absorption, most recently *The Moment of Caravaggio* (Princeton University Press, 2010), which discusses Michelangelo on p. 70. See also Joseph Koerner, *Caspar David Friedrich and the Subject of Landscape* (New Haven and London: Yale University Press, 1990), esp. 162–6.

3   FLEXION

1 Recent discussions of the idea of invention in Italian printmaking include Silvia Gavuzzo-Stewart, "Sull'uso di *invenit* nelle stampe," *The Italianist* 10 (1990), 103–10; Evelyn Lincoln, *The Invention of the Italian Renaissance Printmaker* (New Haven and London: Yale University Press, 2000), and Lisa Pon, *Raphael, Dürer, and Marcantonio Raimondi: Copying and the Italian Renaissance Print* (New Haven and London: Yale University Press, 2004), all with further references.

2   See the discussion in David Landau and Peter Parshall, *The Renaissance Print, 1470–1550* (New Haven and London: Yale University Press, 1994), 143, who write that the print "dates almost certainly from 1509 when Marcantonio was in Florence," and in Bernardine Barnes, *Michelangelo in Print: Reproduction as Response in the Sixteenth Century* (Farnham: Ashgate, 2010), 13, which dates the work to around 1508.

3   Compare Pon, *Raphael, Dürer, and Marcantonio Raimondi*, 15, who writes that the MAF monogram is ambiguous: "though later usage of the letter F suggests a reading 'M[arc]a[ntonio] f[ecit],'Vasari tells us that the letters stand for *Marc' Antonio de' Franci*, in honor of Marcantonio's teacher, Francesco Francia." In fact, Vasari does not quite tell us this; he never mentions the MAF monogram at all, and of the related MF he simply states that "le carte furono da Marcatonio segnate con questi segni: per lo nome di Raffaello Sanzio da Urbino, RS., e per quello di Marcantonio, MF." The story of Marcantonio adopting his teacher's name appears elsewhere, and not in conjunction with inscriptions. It seems to me that this actually strengthens Pon's basic point about the openness of the monogram to competing interpretations. See Vasari, *Lives*, V, 404 and 412.

4   See esp. Lisa Pon, "Michelangelo's First Signature," *Source* 15 (1996), 16–21.

5   If Michelangelo had done all that he would on the cartoon before going to Rome in March 1505, then his work would all have fallen into what Florentines regarded as the 1504 calendar year, which rolled over in March, not January.

6   Landau and Parshall, *The Renaissance Print*, 143–4.

7   See Clifford M. Brown, with the collaboration of Anna Maria Lorenzoni, *Isabella d'Este and Lorenzo da Pavia: Documents for the History of Art and Culture in Renaissance Mantua* (Geneva: Droz, 1982), 160: "Se Zoanne Bellino fa tanto malvoluntieri quella historia, como ne haveti scripto, siamo contente remetterne al judicio suo, purché'l dipinga qualche historia o fabula antiqua aut de sua inventione ne finga una che representi cosa antiqua et de bello significate." Compare Isabella's remarks transcribed on p. 164: "Essendosi rissolto el Bellino de farne in loco del 'presepio,' uno quadro cum la Madonna et putto et san Zoan Baptista, ni piacerà et volemo se li pona ancora uno Santo Hieronimo cum le altre inventione che poi parerano a lui." Da Pavia also referred to Andrea Mantegna's "invencione," 83.

8   Ammanati's letter is published in Paola Barocchi, ed., *Trattati d'arte del cinquecento fra manierismo e controriforma*, 3 vols. (Bari: Laterza, 1962), III, 117–23: "E pur sappiamo, che il più degli uomini, che ci fa operare, non dà invenzione alcuna; ma si rimette al nostro giudizio, diecendone: qui vorrei un giardino, una fonte, un vivaio, e simili."

9   Philipp P. Fehl, "Veronese and the Inquisition: A Study of the Subject Matter of the So-Called 'Feast in the House of Levi,' " *Gazette des beaux-arts* 103 (1961), 325–54.

10   Alberti, *De pictura*, III, 94–5 (translation modified) "Atqui ea quidem hanc habet vim, ut etiam sola inventio sine pictura delectet." Cf. Alberti, *Della pittura*, 245–6: "Questi hanno molti ornamenti comuni col pittore; e copiosi di notizia di molte cose, molto gioveranno a bello componere l'istoria, di cui ogni laude consiste in la invenzione, quale suole avere questa forza, quanto vediamo, che sola senza pittura per sé la bella invenzione sta grata."

11   See Michael A. Jacobsen, "The Meaning of Mantegna's 'Battle of the Sea Gods,' " *Art Bulletin* 64 (1982), 623–9 and Ulrich Pfisterer, "Künstlerische *Potestas Audendi* und *Licentia* im Quattrocento," *Römisches Jahrbuch der Bibliotheca Hertziana* 31 (1996), 107–48, esp. 134–6.

12 Alberti, *Della pittura*: "lui adunque stieno alcuni ritti e mostrino tulta la faccia con le mani in alto e con le dita lieta fermi in su un piè. Alli altri sia il viso contrario e lo braccia rimesse, cò i piedi aggiunti. E così a ciascuno sia suo atto e flessione di membra."

13 Alison Wright aptly characterizes it as an example of the approach that Leonardo condemned in the passage from the Codex Atlanticus cited at Ch. 2 n. 45. See Wright, "Dimensional Tension in the Work of Antonio Pollaiuolo," in Stuart Currie and Peta Motture, eds., *The Sculpted Object 1400–1700* (Aldershot: Ashgate, 1997), 60.

14 This is the argument in Jill Burke, "Nakedness and Other Peoples: Rethinking the Italian Renaissance Nude," *Art History* 36 (2013), 714–39.

15 The most extensive overview of the evidence through 2002 concerning the dating of the print is Shelley R. Langdale, *Battle of the Nudes: Pollaiuolo's Renaissance Masterpiece* (Cleveland Museum of Art, 2002), 51–5; though Langdale's prose is cautious, the comments at the bottom of p. 53 seem to favor a dating as late as 1589. More recently, Gerardo de Simone has identified what he regards as "quotations" from Pollaiuolo's engraving in Lorenzo da Viterbo's Mazzatosta Chapel, which is datable to 1469. If this is correct, it suggests that the engraving may date as early as the mid-1460s; see Simone, "Per Lorenzo da Viterbo, dal Palazzo Orsini di Tagliacozzo alla Cappella Mazzatosta," *Predella* 11 (2011 [online only]).

16 On the manuscript and early printed editions, see Sergio Ricossa, ed., *Le macchine di Valturio nei documenti dell'archivio storico Amma* (Turin: Umberto Allemandi, 1988).

17 Francesco di Giorgio Martini, *Trattato di architettura* (Florence: Giunti Barbèra, 1979 [facsimile ed.]), 33v. See also the discussion in Pamela Long, "Picturing the Machine: Francesco di Giorgio and Leonardo da Vinci in the 1490s," in Wolfgang Lefèvre, ed., *Picturing Machines, 1400–1700* (Cambridge, Mass.: MIT Press, 2004), 117–42, esp. 122–5.

18 Archimede's writings seem generally to have been unknown in Italy before 1500. See the entry by Ivo Schneider in Anthony Grafton, Glenn Most, and Salvatore Settis, eds., *The Classical Tradition* (Cambridge, Mass.: Harvard University Press, 2010), 59–60.

19 Jonathan Jones, *The Lost Battles: Leonardo, Michelangelo and the Artistic Duel that Defined the Renaissance* (New York: Knopf, 2012), 155, poses the question "Michelangelo was doing something unprecedented in his personal odyssey of nude contortions – wasn't he?" He then answers "In reality, he was desperately competing with Leonardo." The argument here, by contrast, is that Michelangelo and Leonardo, in their fascination with figural flexions, were both responding to earlier practices but doing so in different ways.

20 Paolo Galluzzi, *Renaissance Engineers: From Brunelleschi to Leonardo da Vinci* (Florence: Giunti, 1997), 79, observes that Leonardo conceived the human body to have an armature and axles (*poli*) and to operate according to principles of anti-friction. He adds: "Leonardo frequently compared the action of the muscles to a wedge (*cuneo*). Moreover, he habitually rendered muscles as lines of force, calling them 'powers' (*potenze*). He also routinely used the terms 'lever' and 'counterlever' to explain the various motions of the upper and lower limbs."

21 See Paolo Galluzzi, "Il Rinnovamento dei saperi tecnici," in Giovanni Morello, ed., *Le macchine del Rinascimento* (Rome: Retablo, 2000), 19–67, here 41.

22 Francesco di Giorgio, cited in Frank D. Prager and Gustina Scaglia, *Brunelleschi: Studies of His Technology and Inventions* (Cambridge, Mass.: MIT Press, 1970), 150.

23 For the Baptistery project, see Bertrand Gille, *Les Ingénieurs de la Renaissance* (Paris: Hermann, 1964), 116; for the drawings after Brunelleschi's machines, Ladislao Reti, *Tracce dei progetti perduti di Filippo Brunelleschi nel codice Atlantico* (Florence: Barbèra, 1965).

24   For Brunelleschi's clocks, see Antonio Manetti, *The Life of Brunelleschi*, trans. Catherine Enggass, ed. Howard Saalman (University Park: Pennsylvania State University Press, 1970), 334; also Galuzzi, "Rinnovamento," 46.

25   David McGee, "The Origins of Early Modern Machine Design," in Lefèvre, *Picturing Machines*, 53–84, here 55: "none of the authors of early machine drawings were actually machine makers . . . the more fanciful drawings or impossible machines can be regarded as 'dreams,' or a form of play, composed by amateurs as entertainment."

26   Pfisterer, "Künstlerische *Potestas Audendi*."

27   Galluzzi, "Rinnovamento," 25.

28   See Francesco Paolo Fiore's illuminating book *Città e macchine del '400, nei disegni di Francesco di Giorgio Martini* (Florence: Olschki, 1978), 195r [facsimile], 92, 219v, and 119.

29   This is the proposal of Galluzzi, "Rinnovamento."

30   Galluzzi, "Rinnovamento"; idem, *Renaissance Engineers*, 76. Martin Kemp, *Leonardo da Vinci: The Marvellous Works of Nature and Man* (Oxford University Press, 2006), 72, refers to the "inner dynamos" of the figures Leonardo was already designing for his *Adoration of the Magi* in Florence. Similarly, Galluzzi, *Renaissance Engineers*, 78, cites Leonardo's notes for an anatomical treatise: "Arrange it so that the book on the elements of machines with its practice precedes the demonstration of the movement and force of man and other animals, and by means of these you will be able to prove all of your propositions."

31   An excellent introduction to the cycle is Marilyn Lavin, *Piero della Francesca: San Francesco, Arezzo* (New York: George Braziller, 1994).

32   Gille, *Ingénieurs*, 138.

33   For the history of this project, see Matthew Landrus, *Leonardo da Vinci's Giant Crossbow* (Berlin: Springer, 2010).

34   Leonardo, Codex Atlanticus, 683r (1338): "Il colpo dato da lieve pondo si fa potente, quanto era la potenzia della sua cagione. Cioè, una freccia pesa 3 once: una forza fatta da uno peso di 400 libbre tira la corda del balestro sino sulla noce e nel disfarsi che fa, detta forza si trasmuta e appiccasi alla freccia. Adunque, benché una freccia pesi 3 once, ella porta con seco nel suo corso la natura di tanto peso, quanto fu la sua cagione.

    Ogni pondo cacciato per violente moto aggiungne a sé durante la fuga tanto di potenzia, quanto fu quella della cagione del suo corso."

35   On the development of the concept of the "counter-natural" in the *Mechanical Problems* and other texts by Aristotle's followers, see esp. Gianni Micheli, *Le origini del concetto di macchina* (Florence: Olschki, 1995), 24–55, cited by William R. Newman in his own discussion, *Promethean Ambitions: Alchemy and the Quest to Perfect Nature* (University of Chicago Press, 2004), 20–21.

36   Leonardo, Codex Atlanticus, 842v (III, 1589): "Domandote: se questo balestro, ovvero corda del balestro, si tira da *a* a *c* con peso di 400 libbre, con quanto peso si moverà detta corda da *a* a *b*, cioè in mezzo fra *a b*?" I take the final "*b*" to be a mistake.

37   Ibid., 863v (III, 1613): "Domando: se uno balestro caccia una freccia 400 braccia, uno balestro che sia proprozionevolmente formato con quattro tanti forza e grandezza, caccerà elli quattro tanti più via la freccia?

    Domando: se uno balestro di pari peso e montata in queste varie grossezze sopra una medessima lunghezza, che effetto farà nelle distanzie sopra una medesima freccia?"

38   Ibid, 863v: "Forza. / La forza in ne' corpi non si può creare senza forza o peso insieme

col moto./ Forza. / Forza è causata da violente moto mediante il peso o altra forza. Se la cosa che si move, nella perseveranza del moto sarà di novo sospinta da maggior moto, essa cosa mossa raddoppia la velocità del moto."

39 Ibid, 576av (II, 1137): "Se l'omo fa forza colla spalla in loco che resista, il peso di tal forza tornerà ai sua piedi e se la cosa de' piedi acconsente, essa si moverà per la forza del distendersi dell'omo e per lo peso d'esso omo. Ma se nel medesimo tempo la cosa tocca dalla spalla ci acconsentissi e che tale acconsentimento tornassi col suo moto in favore del moto fatto per causa di detto omo, ciò che si fa poi colla spalla, non mancagli poi al piedi? Certo sì, e darò questo esempio. Uno balestro sta in piega per forza di 400 libbre 'n scambio di corda infra 2 pilastri e apre che ogni pilastro ne senta 200 libbre; onde se l'uno d'essi pilastri ha tanto di peso che resista a esse 200 libbre, il balestro doverebbe stare fermo in sua forza e non gittare, come fa, esso pilastro in terra."

40 I think, for example, of the series of drawings on 966r (1761), exploring the center of gravity, or of 724r (1408), a series of diagrams around the principle of cantilevering, which turns to an examination at the bottom of the sheet of how a man can extend his own body past an edge.

41 McMahon, I, 142, no. 373, and II, 106r–106v: "l'aparecchio della forza in ciasun mouimento uol essere con istorcimenti e piegamenti di gran uiolenza, et il ritorno sia con aggio e comodità, e così la operatione a buono efetto. perche il balestro, che non ha disposition uiolente, il moto del mobile da lui remosso sarà breue o' nulla. perche doue non è disfactione di uiolentia, non è moto, e doue non è uiolentia, ella no' po essere destrutta; e per questo l'arco, che non ha uiollentia, non può fare moto, se non acquista essa uiollentia e nell'acquistar' la non la caccia da se. / così l'huomo, che non si torce nè si piegha, non ha quistato potentia."

42 See Giovanni Fontana, *Bellicorum instrumentorum liber*, ed. Eugenio Battisti (Milan: Arcadia, 1984), 89 (52r–52v): "Supperator, quia sua violentia rappit et trahit omne resistens." Battisti dates the treatise to 1420/40.

43 Fabio de Chirico et al., eds., *Luca Signorelli*, exh. cat. (Milan: Silvana, 2012), 334–5, with further references. For a discussion of what Signorelli might have studied in Florence around 1487, see Tom Henry, *The Life and Art of Luca Signorelli* (New Haven and London: Yale University Press, 2012), 67–71.

44 Ibid., 324. A good part of the literature on the Hercules and Antaeus sheet has been devoted to underscoring or denying its formal connections to Pollaiuolo, who likewise treated the theme. On the "strong reinforcing of the figures' outlines," see Henry, *Luca Signorelli*, 204.

45 Ibid., 325.

46 I am not the first to see this scene in terms of "force." Compare Creighton Gilbert, *How Fra Angelico and Signorelli Saw the End of the World* (University Park: Pennsylvania State University Press, 2003), 86–7: "A diagonal push of forces, from upper right to lower left, starts from the three military angels in the sky who herd the goats the way they must go."

47 Sara Nair James, *Signorelli and Fra Angelico at Orvieto: Liturgy, Poetry and a Vision of the End-Time* (Aldershot: Ashgate, 2003), 61, writes "All of the figures – angels, damned, and devils alike – have human form. While armored archangels above impassively keep watchful guard, humans and devils below wage vicious hand-to-hand combat, evenly matched – same size and similarly vigorous."

48   The skeletons had long attracted attention, but Creighton Gilbert (*How Fra Angelico*, 122) was the first to realize that they are completely unprecedented.

49   On these *magistri sacre pagine*, see ibid., 119–20; James, *Signorelli and Fra Angelico*, 75, makes the connection to Ezekiel.

50   For a description of Signorelli's "wooden" style, see Gilbert, *How Fra Angelico*, 160.

51   Fontana, *Bellicorum instrumentorum*, 88 (51r), depicts a machine that involved skeletons of painted wood in an arca; a wheel below made their limbs move, "like the figures on clocks." On automata and resurrection themes, see Eugenio Battisti, *L'antirinascimento* (Milan: Feltrinelli, 1962), 233.

52   Jonathan B. Riess, *The Renaissance Antichrist: Luca Signorelli's Orvieto Frescoes* (Princeton University Press, 1995), 52: "The two figures seem nearly to merge, Antichrist apparently propped up in every sense by the infernal force that guides him, turning him into a kind of puppet manipulated by the demon thrust against him." James, *Signorelli and Fra Angelico*, 70: "Signorelli inseparably intertwined the two figures, who seem to share one pair of arms. A closer look reveals that the arms belong to the Devil, as he prepares to slip unseen into the body of the Antichrist as if he is donning a costume – the proverbial wolf in sheep's clothing – vividly demonstrating that the Antichrist and Satan are one and the same."

53   Riess, *Renaissance Antichrist*, 52.

54   Fontana, *Bellicorum instrumentorum*, illustrates two mechanical devils; the second (60v–61r) is operated with cords.

55   The phrase is Gilbert's, *How Fra Angelico*, 140–41. He takes the scene to be based on the events that follow the Deeds of the Antichrist in the *Golden Legend*.

56   Battisti, in Fontana, *Bellicorum instrumentorum*, 59, emphasizes Fontana's interest in transmitting force over distances, using cords.

57   The roundels presumably relate to the portrait, but this itself has been difficult to identify. Riess, *Renaissance Antichrist*, 128–9 gives the most recent and cogent defense of the traditional identification as Lucan. The case for Tibullus was first made by Donato Loscalzo, "Le fondamenta dei classici," in Giusi Testa, ed., *La Cappella Nova o di San Brizio nel Duomo di Orvieto* (Milan: Rizzoli, 1996), 191–213, esp. 194–6. Gilbert, *How Fra Angelico*, 143–4, tentatively favors "Silvius Aeneas."

58   The portrait was long referred to as "Homer" but all recent writers reject this. Riess, *Renaissance Antichrist*, 126–9, sees him as Cicero, Loscalzo, "Fondamenta," 192–3 and James, *Signorelli and Fra Angelico*, 89 and 128 as Sallust. Gilbert, *How Fra Angelico*, 147–50 considers various possibilities, but ultimately concludes that he should just be referred to as a "heretic." With regard to the roundel, there is not even agreement on what the depicted figures are doing. Riess, 122–3, writes "The frenzied figures look up, seemingly beyond the borders of the small scene, to the preaching Antichrist directly above, their outstretched arms suggesting veneration and acclamation of the Evil One. . . . The gestures of the upward-reaching figures consigned to the lower scheme of things are echoed in the *Resurrection*, where many figures extend their arms upward toward the true God as they prepare for the hoped-for ascent to heaven." Gilbert, 151, by contrast, describes how: "In the center, a woman is under violent stress, and in reaction four men surrounding her lift their arms, perhaps to keep her in bounds or calm her." Riess took the tondo to be inspired by an episode from Cicero's *Philippics*, Loscalzo and James thought the scene might come from Sallust's *Conspiracy of Catiline*.

59   Vasari, *Lives*, I, 612; Vasari-Milanesi, III, 690.

60   William Wallace (private communication) drew my attention to the letter Michelangelo wrote in 1518, telling of having spent some days with Signorelli in Rome five years earlier. Hugo Chapman and Patricia Rubin both propose that Michelangelo stopped in Orvieto on his way to Florence in 1501, and that Signorelli's drawings and paintings shaped Michelangelo's approach to the *Cascina*. See *Il Carteggio di Michelangelo*, ed. Giovanni Poggi et al., 5 vols. (Florence: Sansoni, 1965), II, 7–8; Michael Hirst, *Michelangelo: The Achievement of Fame, 1475–1534* (New Haven and London: Yale University Press, 2011), 119, Hugo Chapman, *Michelangelo Drawings: Closer to the Master* (London: British Museum Press, 2005), 91, and Patricia Rubin, " 'Che è di questo culazzino!': Michelangelo and the Motif of the Male Buttocks in Italian Renaissance Art," *Oxford Art Journal* 32 (2009), 427–46, here 440.

61   McMahon, I, 110, no. 266 (translation modified), and II, 59v: "Ricordati, fintore, quando fai una sola figura, di fugire li scorti di quella, si delle parti, come del tutto, perche tu avesti da combattere con la ignorantia delli indotti di tale arte, ma nelle istorie fanne in tutti li modi che ti accade, et massime nelle bataglie, doue per nescessita accade infiniti storciamenti e piegamenti delli componitori di tale discordia, o' uo' dire pazzia bestiallissima."

62   Carlo Vecce emphasized this in a talk at the University of Virginia in April 2012, "Leonardo and the War."

63   Goffen, *Renaissance Rivals*, 152, notes that Michelangelo's cartoon showed most of his figures from the back, and Rubin explores the significance of this at length in " 'Che è di questo culazzino!' "

64   Influential discussions of the topic include Erwin Panofsky, " 'Imago Pietatis': Ein Beitrag zur Typengeschichte des 'Schmerzensmanns' und er 'Maria Mediatrix'," *Festschrift für Max J. Friedländer zum 60. Geburtstage* (Leipzig, Seemann, 1927), 261–308; Sixten Ringbom, *Icon to Narrative: The Rise of the Dramatic Close-up in Fifteenth-century Devotional Painting* (Åbo: Åbo Akademi, 1965); Hans Belting, *Likeness and Presence: A History of the Image before the Era of Art*, trans. Edmund Jephcott (University of Chicago Press, 1994); and, with regard to Michelangelo in particular, Alexander Nagel, *Michelangelo and the Reform of Art* (Cambridge University Press, 2000).

65   The classic study is Patricia Simons, "Women in Frames: The Gaze, the Eye, the Profile in Renaissance Portraiture," in Norma Broude and Mary D. Garrard, eds., *The Expanding Discourse: Feminism and Art History* (New York: Icon Editions, 1992), 38–57.

66   Bernardine Barnes's illuminating chapter "Michelangelo in Fragments" in *Michelangelo in Print*, 10, remarks: "Since most of the artists who copied the cartoon were young and still learning their craft, it should not be surprising, in light of contemporary workshop practice, that they copied only single figures or small groups." This does not mean, as Joost Keizer paraphrases her, that "young artists were incapable of copying whole compositions"; rather, it allows that an emphasis on the figure, still central to early sixteenth-century artistic training, bears on the cartoon's function as a "school." Keizer does also point to the example of Raphael, who copied the single figure from Michelangelo but the *group* of horsemen from Leonardo. But this may tell us as much about the different lessons the Michelangelo and Leonardo designs were thought to hold as it does about the competencies of young draftsmen generally. See Keizer, "Michelangelo, Drawing, and the Subject of Art," *Art Bulletin* 93 (2011), 304–24, here 312 and n. 76. The contrast between Leonardo's pursuit of "unity" and Michelangelo's "composition of individual bodies," was already observed by Goffen, *Renaissance Rivals*, 152.

67 Vasari, *Lives*, I, 637; Vasari-Milanesi, IV: 41–2: "dove appiccato le mani un soldato, con la forza delle spalle, mentre mette il cavallo in fuga, rivolto egli con la persona, aggrappato l'aste dello stendardo per sgusciarlo per forza delle mani di quattro … v'è dua figure in iscorto che combattendo insieme, mentre uno in terra ha sopra uno soldato, che alzato il braccio quanto può, con quella forza maggiore gli mette alla gola il pugnale per finirgli la vita."

68 *Opere di Benvenuto Cellini*, ed. Giuseppe Guido Ferrero (Turin: UTET, 1980), 82: "Se bene il divino Michelagnolo fece la gran cappella di papa Iulio da poi, non arrivò mai a questo sego alla metà; la sua virtù non aggiunse mai da poi alla forza di quei primi studii." Compare Vasari, *Lives*, II, 429, writing of a copy made of the cartoon – probably the one in Holkham Hall – who observed that "since [Bastiano] applied himself to it with all the earnestness that was in him, it proved that he was afterwards able on any occasion to render an account of the attitudes, muscles, and movements of those figures, and of the reasons that had caused Buonarroti to depict certain difficult postures." Cf. Vasari-Milanesi, VI, 434: "E perché vi attese con quanto studio gli fu mai possibile, ne seguì che poi ad ogni proposito seppe render conto delle forze, attitudini e muscoli di quelle figure, e quali erano state le cagioni che avevano mosso il Buonarroto a fare alcune positure difficili."

 MOTIVATION

1 See Elena Avanzini's pathbreaking but now outdated book *Il Riposo di Raffaello Borghini e la critica d'arte nel '500* (Milan: Gastaldi, 1960), 49: "Il Borghini prese quindi da Leonardo senza mutare neanche la frase, come fece per il Cennini, perchè lo stile di Leonardo era già per conto suo perfetto." Although the editor of the major recent edition of Borghini's book dismissed Avanzini as a dilettante, her observation about the appeal to Borghini not just of the content but also of the style of Leonardo's *Trattato* may be significant, suggesting that the *Trattato* was compiled rather late in the century, close to Borghini's own time. The mean-spirited remark appears in Raffaello Borghini, *Il Riposo*, ed. Mario Rosci (Milan: Edizioni Labor, 1967), xv and xx, where Rosci incorrectly gives Avanzini's first name as "Emilia."

2 See Marco Rosci, "Leonardo 'filosofo,' Lomazzo e Borghini 1584: due line di tradizione dei pensieri e precetti di Leonardo sull'arte," in Pietro C. Marani, ed., *Fra Rinascimento, manierismo e realtà* (Florence: Giunti Barbèra, 1984), 53–77, here 74, quoting from *Il Riposo*, 180: "Consiglierei etiandio il pittore che doendo fare una figura sola fuggisse gli scorti si delle parti come del tutto, ma nelle historie, e nelle battaglie ne potebbe fare a suo piacimento."

3 Rosci, "Leonardo 'filosofo,' " 70–71. For the history of the abridged *Trattato*, see the recent volume edited by Claire Farago, *Re-Reading Leonardo: The "Treatise on Painting" across Europe* (Farnham: Ashgate, 2009). The abridgments themselves can now be consulted on the enormously useful website launched by Francesca Fiorani, http://www.treatiseonpainting.org/.

4 See Carlo Pedretti, *The Literary Works of Leonardo da Vinci, Compiled and Edited from the Original Manuscripts by Jean Paul Richter: Commentary by Carlo Pedretti*, 2 vols. (Oxford: Phaidon, 1977), I, 12–47, with a chart summing up Pedretti's arguments (28).

5 This is the hypothesis of Rosci, "Leonardo 'filosofo,' " 72: "si potrebbe avanzare con ogni cautela l'ipotesi che il Borghini si bassasse su una redazione 'ridotta' del Trattato diversa da quelle pervenuteci, e comprendente brani leonardeschi oggi perduti."

6 See Claire Farago, "Who Abridged Leonardo da Vinci's *Treatise on Painting?*" in Farago, *Re-Reading Leonardo*, 77–106, and Robert Williams, "Leonardo and the Florentine Academy," in ibid., 61–76.

7 Cf. Rosci, "Leonardo 'filosofo,' " 61, who refers to passages like this as "plagi letterali." I also read Borghini differently from Williams, "Leonardo and the Florentine Academy," 64, who describes Borghini's derivations from Leonardo as "quotations" that "follow one another in quick succession."

8 Borghini, *Il Riposo*, 179–80: "Ma passando all'attitudini dico, che quelle deon essere in tutto conformi all'historia, & alla persona, che dimostrano; perciò che dipignendosi historie sacre si deon fare l'attitudini de' Patriarchi, de' Profeti, de' Santi, de' Martiri, del Saluador del mondo, della Reina de' Cieli, e degli Agnoli graui, modeste, e diuote, non fiere, e non isforzate; ma quelle de' Tiranni, e de' ministri loro sarà molto conueneuole far le fiere, e crudeli; ma non dishoneste, e lasciue, per non iscemare la diuotione, che s'ha nel rimirare i Santi che à quelli sono appresso. Quando si dipingono guerre, e contese all'hora si può scherzare con attitudini sforzate, gagliarde, e terribili, si come figurando cose amorose fa di mestiero far l'attitudini molli, dilicate, e gratiose."

9 See Charles Dempsey, "Mythic Inventions in Counter-Reformation Painting," in P. A. Ramsey, ed., *Rome in the Renaissance: The City and the Myth* (Binghamton, N.Y: Medieval and Renaissance Texts and Studies, 1982), 55–75.

10 Giovanni Andrea Gilio da Fabriano, *Due dialogi* (Camerino: Antonio Gioioso, 1564 [facsimile Florence: SPES, 1986]), 75r: "Quando è puro poeta, penso che lecito gli sia dipingere tutto quello, che il capriccio gli detta; con quei gesti, con quei sforzi sieno però convenevoli a la figura, che egli fa: del che habbiamo l'esempio ne le loggie del Chisi dove Raffaello dipinse la cena de gli Dij con quegli atti e sforzi che il capriccio gli mise in capo."

11 *Orazione funerale di M. Benedetto Varchi* (Florence: Giunti, 1564), 18, cited in Giorgio Vasari, *La Vita di Michelangelo nelle redazioni del 1550 e del 1568*, ed. Paola Barocchi, 5 vols. (Milan: Ricciardi, 1962), II, 256: "Chi si sforzava di mettersi le calze in gamba, chi si gittava i panni a bardosso, chi correva con essi o in capo o sotto 'l braccio in quel verso dove s'udiva il romore . . . erano le figure di questo grandissimo cartone in diverse, stravaganti e bizzarrissime attitudini, chi vivo, chi morto, chi disteso in terra, chi ginocchinoi, chi ritto in varie maniere. . . . e tutti scoprivano tutti i muscoli e tutti i nerbi infino all'ossa con iscorci mai non più pensati, non che veduti."

12 This is the argument Patricia Reilly made in an unpublished paper, "Leonardo in Vasari's Palazzo Vecchio," at the 2011 Renaissance Society of America conference, Montreal.

13 Vasari-Milanese, VIII, 215: "questa è una bella storia: avete avuto luogo di mostrare la vostra invenzione."

14 Federico Borromeo, *Sacred Painting/ Museum*, ed. and trans. Kenneth S. Rothwell, Jr., with notes by Pamela M. Jones (Cambridge, Mass.: Harvard University Press, 2010), 37.

15 See Ch. 1 n. 6.

16 See Kenneth Clark, *Leonardo da Vinci* (New York: Penguin, 1989), 191.

17 Orfeo Boselli, *Osservationi della scoltura antica, dai Manoscritti Corsini e Doria* (1657), ed. Phoebe Dent Weil (Florence: SPES, 1978), 37r: "di piu statue insieme che uolgarmente

si chiamano Gruppi, l'attione e l'Historia anima loro; si come la fauola è Anima de Poemi"; 39v: "L'Atto per esser bono, oltre l'esser proprio dell'attione, come si e detto, si deue fare più tosto spiritoso, che freddo: ma con reguardo che non sia spiritato, ne che balli la ciachona ne che imiti la marainata."

18   Abraham Bosse, *Sentimens sur la distinction des diverses manieres de peinture, dessein et graveure* (Paris: Bosse, 1649), 28–9: "Il y a eu des Peintres & Desseignateurs qui ont affecté de telles manieres au trait, Contour, action & proportion des figures humaines qu'il representoient, qu'on diroit à voir une partie de leurs Ouvrages, soit en Peinture, soit en Taille-Douce, qu'ils avoient pris à tasche d'en composer de Nouvelles, & d'une forme tres-bizarre & dont de quelqu'unes les actions paroissent comme des personnes entreprises de tous leurs membres, par Crampes, Detorces, & Roidissements extraordinaires; Et pour en voir quelques exemples, cela se peut, en diuerses oeuures de *Spranger, Goltius, Bellange*, & de plusieurs autres . . ."

19   See Ligorio's "Trattato di alcune cose appartenente alla nobiltà dell'antiche arti, et massimamente de la pittura, de la scoltura et dell'architettura …," 12v–13r, edited in Anna Schreuers, *Antikenbild und Kunstanschauungen des neapolitanischen Malers, Architekten und Antiquars Pirro Ligorio (1513–1583)* (Cologne: Verlag der Buchhandlung Walther König, 2000), here 412–13: "gli pare sia cosa ordinaria imitare il stile di quelli che sono stati i migliori. Vorrebbono essi che si seguitassero le cose sforzate et dispiacevoli da spiritati. / Cosi dungque perlo amore di costoro cosi bravi *entriamo a parlare di quel che chiamano snocciolamento, o vogliamo dire delli sforzamenti degli atti del corpo delle mani et dale braccia et coscie dell'huomo, tutte fatte senza proposito, et con ogni sorte di storcitura poste in opera, che per fignere le figure pronte nell'atto l'hanno fatte furiose, con attitudine pazzesche et dispiacev-ole più tosto menaccianti, che suadenti o demostrante quell que la natura porge nell'occasioni delle historie. . . . A questi dunque quando hanno rappresentate le violenze le pareno haver fatte cose vaghe et artificiose.*" Schreuers connects Ligorio's position to Gilio's condemnation of Michelangelo (whom Ligorio makes a point of not naming), 185–9. I owe thanks to Ginette Vagenheim for this reference.

20   In his great book on the Renaissance grotto, Philippe Morel drew attention to a distinction articulated in the late sixteenth-century by the Urbinate priest, poet, and doctor Bernardino Baldi, between an *intrinsic* principle of movement, a soul that moves a body, and an *extrinsic* principle, a force that moves the body from the outside: "Ne fa mentione parimente il medesimo Filosofo nel suo Libretto del moto de gli Animali, dove dice, che l'anima, laquale ha la sua sede nel cuore, dà il moto a i membri, come apunto aviene alle Machine Semoventi, il principio interno del moto dà il moto alle parti organiche essendo in queste il ferro, il legno, e le corde, in un certo modo, come ne gli animali sono l'ossa, & i nervi." Art, Baldi wrote, is one such extrinsic principle. Philippe Morel, *Les Grottes maniéristes en Italie au XVIe siècle: théâtre et alchimie de la nature* (Paris: Macula, 1998), 110.

21   Gilio, *Due dialogi*, 31r: "Se il gran Michelagnolo Buonaroti, se ne fusse stato contento de la maniera del pingere de' pittori del suo tempo; non sarebbe al mondo con tanto honore hoggi la pittura, ne si saperebbe la forza, ne la vaghezza de l'arte, che molti di quel tempo credettero fermamente, che le antiche statue di bronzo, e di marmo fussero state fatte per arte di negromantia?"

22   Ibid., 31v: "Eccoui dunque l'origine di balli, de le moresche, e de gli sforzi ritrouati dal Demonio ne giuochi, e prima ne sacrifitii da i Coribanti."

23   The other term Gilio uses here, "moresche," is interchangeable with *sforzi* in his attack

on the *Last Judgment* as well. With regard to Michelangelo, he has a character lament (ibid., 95v) that Christ should be "resplendent, shining, glorious, held in majesty with great magnificence by thousands of Angels, not with those tangles, nor with *sforzi*, moresques, or bagatelles, which you admire just because Michelangelo did them" ("risplendenti, lucide, gloriose, in maestà sostenute con gran magnificenza da migliaia d'Angeli, non con quei groppi ne sforzi, ne moresche, ne bagattelle, che voi gli miriate che Michelagnolo gli ha fatti").

24 See Stephen J. Campbell, "'Fare una Cosa Morta Parer Viva': Michelangelo, Rosso, and the (Un)Divinity of Art," *Art Bulletin* 84 (2002), 596–620, whose discussion was particularly important for my thinking; also Patricia Emison, "Truth and Bizzarria in an Engraving of Lo Stregozzo," *Art Bulletin* 81 (1999), 623–36, which first drew attention to the print's citations of earlier art and connection to Michelangelo; Christopher S. Wood, "Countermagical Combinations by Dosso Dossi," *RES* 49/50 (2006), 151–70; and Charles Zika, *The Appearance of Witchcraft: Print and Visual Culture in Sixteenth-century Europe* (New York: Routledge, 2007), 125–7.

25 See esp. Campbell, "Fare una Cosa Morta," and Eike Schmidt, "'Furor' und 'Imitatio': visuelle Topoi in den Laokoon-Parodien Rosso Fiorentinos und Tizians," in Ulrich Pfisterer and Max Seidel, eds., *Visuelle Topoi: Erfindung und tradiertes Wissen in den Künsten der italienischen Renaissance* (Munich: Deutscher Kunstverlag, 2003), 351–83, both with further references. I accept the traditional view that the Rosso design followed the Michelangelo rather than the other way around, though Campbell observes, n. 38, that this cannot be proven.

26 Jonathan Jones, *The Lost Battles: Leonardo, Michelangelo and the Artistic Duel that Defined the Renaissance* (New York: Knopf, 2012), 165, draws attention to Leonardo's fascination with *furia* in preparing the *Anghiari*.

27 See Pamela O. Long, *Openness, Secrecy, Authorship: Technical Arts and the Culture of Knowledge from Antiquity to the Renaissance* (Baltimore and London: Johns Hopkins University Press, 2001).

28 Vasari, *Lives*, I, 634; Vasari-Milanesi, IV, 35.

29 Antonio Manetti, *The Life of Brunelleschi*, trans. Catherine Enggass, ed. Howard Saalman (University Park: Pennsylvania State University Press, 1970), 52.

30 Vasari, *Lives*, II, 657; Vasari-Milanesi, VII, 160, "nè però voles mai che altri lo vedesse." See esp. the discussion in Rona Goffen, *Renaissance Rivals: Michelangelo, Leonardo, Raphael, Titian* (New Haven and London: Yale University Press, 2002), 147.

31 Vasari, *Lives*, II, 267; Vasari-Milanesi, VI, 138: "di che non si sapendo la causa, alcuni dicevano che Baccio l'aveva stracciato per avere appresso di sé qualche pezzo cel cartone a suo modo; alcuni giudicarono che egli volesse torre a' giovani quella commodità, perché non avessino a profittare a farsi noti nell'arte . . ."

32 Touchstones in the large literature are David Freedberg's classic *The Power of Images: Studies in the History and Theory of Response* (Chicago and London: University of Chicago Press, 1989) and Horst Bredekamp's recent *Theorie des Bildakts* (Berlin: Suhrkamp, 2010). See also Gerhard Wolf's illuminating entry for "Bildmagie" in Ulrich Pfisterer, ed., *Metzler Lexikon Kunstwissenschaft* (Stuttgart: J. B. Metzler, 2003).

33 Marcel Mauss, *A General Theory of Magic*, trans. Robert Brain (London and New York: Routledge, 2001), 24.

34 Mary Pardo, "Paolo Pino's 'Dialogo di Pittura': A Translation with Commentary," PhD. diss., University of Pittsburgh, 1984, 335.

ACKNOWLEDGMENTS

My idea of writing a book around the battle paintings of Leonardo and Michelangelo initially developed as I was planning an international symposium on the two works at the University of Pennsylvania in 2004–5. I am grateful to Penny Marcus and Nicola Gentile for their support and collaboration on that memorable event. I presented various sections from the book at the Clark Art Institute and at the University of Colorado at Boulder in 2009; at the Renaissance Society of America meeting in Venice in 2010; at the Huntington Library in 2011; at the Institut National d'Histoire de l'Art in Paris and at the University of Virginia in 2012; and at the Kunsthistorisches Institut in Florence, at Columbia University, at McGill University, and at Harvard University in 2013. I owe thanks to Marc Gotlieb, Claire Farago, Christy Anderson, Alexander Marr, Philippe Morel, Francesca Fiorani, Alessandro Nova, Fabio Frosini, Matthew Hunter, and Harvard's Graduate Student Lecture Committee for those opportunities. Comments by Diane Bodart, Matteo Burioni, Thierry de Duve, Eva Lajer-Burchart and Jonathan Unglaub in particular impelled me to rethink several arguments. I completed a draft of the book while a visiting scholar at the Center for Advanced Studies at the Ludwig-Maximilians-Universität in Munich in 2012; I wish to offer particular thanks to Ulrich Pfisterer, who initiated this invitation, and *ein Prosit* to the welcoming and always helpful Center staff. Stephen Campbell, Megan Holmes, Patricia Rubin, Madeleine Viljoen, Alison Wright, and two anonymous referees for Yale University Press all took the time to read the complete manuscript; they offered valuable observations, corrections, and references, and they generously answered further questions. Katharine Ridler was a terrific copyeditor. Sarah Ortega and Asha Banerjee served as research assistants in the final months of work, helping me to collect photographs and check sources. The book would not have the form it does had I not had the great fortune to work with Gillian Malpass, who provided well-timed encouragement and much sage advice along the way.

INDEX

PHOTOGRAPH CREDITS

Illustrations have been provided by the owners or guardians of works unless otherwise indicated below. Additional credit lines required are likewise listed below.